VILLAGE VOICES

VILLAGE VOICES

Forty Years of Rural Transformation in South India

T. Scarlett Epstein
A.P. Suryanarayana
T. Thimmegowda

SAGE Publications
New Delhi/Thousand Oaks/London

First published in 1998 by

Sage Publications India Pvt Ltd
M-32 Market, Greater Kailash - I
New Delhi-110 048

Sage Publications Inc.
2455 Teller Road
Thousand Oaks, California 91320

Sage Publications Ltd
6 Bonhill Street
London EC2A 4PU

Published by Tejeshwar Singh for Sage Publications India Pvt Ltd, typeset by Siva Math Setters, Chennai and printed at Chaman Enterprises, Delhi.

Third printing 1998

Library of Congress Cataloging-in-Publication Data

Epstein, T. Scarlett
    Village voices: forty years of rural transformation in South India/
    T. Scarlett Epstein, A.P. Suryanarayana, T. Thimmegowda.
        p. cm. (cloth: alk. paper). (pbk.: alk. paper).
    Includes bibliographical references.
    1. Rural development—India. 2. Social change—India. 3. Villages—India.
    4. India—Rural conditions. I. Epstein, T. Scarlett (Trude Scarlett) II. Suryanarayana,
    A.P., 1931- . III. Thimmegowda, T., 1945- .
    HN690. Z9C685376 1998   303.4'0954—dc21   98-24646

ISBN: 0-7619-9265-0 (US–HB)   81-7036-723-9 (India–HB)
        0-7619-9266-9 (US–PB)   81-7036-724-7 (India–PB)

Sage Production Team: Vandana Madan, M.S.V. Namboodiri and Santosh Rawat

We dedicate this book to our many friends in Dalena and Wangala whose ingenuity in coping with difficult rural development problems we greatly admire

Contents

1. Introduction: Village Studies with a Difference   9
    T. Scarlett Epstein

PART I: EXPERIENCES OF A RESEARCH ASSISTANT   19
    A.P. Suryanarayana

2. My First Experience of Village Life   21

PART II: AN INSIDER'S VIEWS   35
    T. Thimmegowda

3. Wangala's Traditional Social System   37
4. How Wangala's Economy has Changed since 1954   46
5. How Wangala's Political and Cultural Practices have Changed   56
6. The Pros and Cons of Wangala's Socio-economic Development   76

PART III: A RESEARCHER'S VIEWS   87
    T. Scarlett Epstein

7. The Preliminaries of a Field Study   89
8. The Impact of Canal Irrigation on Wangala and Dalena, 1954–56   101
9. Re-exposure to Mysore Villages in 1970   110
10. Predictions Based on Micro-society Studies   125
11. Another Re-study in the 1990s   133
12. How the Two Villages have Changed   143
13. Economic Change Factors   160
14. Political Change Factors   172
15. New Lives and Old Traditions   183
16. Predictions: Wrong and Right   199

PART IV: THE WAY AHEAD   207
    T. Scarlett Epstein and T. Thimmegowda

17. What the Future Holds   209

Appendix 1: Note on Documentary Film   233
Appendix 2: Poems   235
Appendix 3: Questionnaire   237
Glossary   239
About the Authors   241

ONE

Introduction: Village Studies with a Difference

T. SCARLETT EPSTEIN

*D*ear Reader,

Before you begin to read this book I want to make you aware that it differs from most other literature on village studies and may not be what you expect. I believe this to be so simply because most available village studies are either academic or journalistic publications. Academic studies make for heavy reading and journalistic accounts usually lack academic rigour. On the other hand, this book deviates from the usual treatment of rural development in general, and village studies in particular. Not simply for the sake of being different but as an attempt to meet what my two co-authors and I consider are real, felt needs among a large proportion of the reading public. We have found that there are many people—both in developing and developed countries—who have no connection with academia but are keen to get an insight into whether, and how, rural societies are changing. Available publications so far have rarely satisfied these needs. This realisation induced us to produce here not a learned thesis but a more popular, informative and stimulating account, yet with a scientific basis. With this book we hope to take you into a magic journey to South India over a period of more than forty years.

We describe and analyse the changes that have taken place since 1955 in Wangala and Dalena, two South Indian villages. The names of these villages are pseudonyms to conceal the identity of our informants, but the two villages are very real and so are the villagers. Here, we set out in detail the thrills as well as the difficulties involved in living in and at the same time studying rural societies. We also outline and explain our fascination with grassroots rural development.

We trust that this book will not only whet your appetite for more information on village life, but more importantly hope that it will encourage you to help promote smoother rural changes by involving yourself in one way or another in rural development issues. If this happens it will create a more informed public discussion, and lead to more enlightened rural development policies.

If you happen to be familiar with my two earlier books published in 1962 and 1973, which recount my first studies of Wangala and Dalena as already mentioned, you will find that this book differs. We target here a wider audience outside the narrow circle of specialists which academic village studies usually reach. They fail to have wider public appeal usually because they invariably have many pages interspersed with academic jargon, contain lots of dry, theoretical arguments supported by numerical data, critically review other relevant materials and conclude with long bibliographies. My own first book represented the revised version of my doctoral thesis and therefore had to follow similar academic norms. Such publications are of course important, but they fail to meet the requirements of the wider public interested in developmental issues. We therefore decided to write in a 'user-friendly' style, which we believe will complement rather than substitute similar but largely academic publications.

Stemming from our endeavour to present a user-friendly study, this book differs from others in five major ways:

- It recounts forty years of change observed by the same researcher;
- it is a collaborative effort;
- it re-humanises village studies;
- it encourages a continuing dialogue; and
- it provides the basis for a documentary film.

FORTY YEARS OF CHANGE IN TWO SOUTH INDIAN VILLAGES

Micro-studies of the same societies over a period as long as four decades offer a rare insight into the process of rural development. This is one of the aspects that distinguishes our presentation. As far as I could establish, the studies of Wangala and Dalena are the only ones in India where the same researcher observed the changing scene over so many years. Together with A.P. Suryanarayana, my research assistant, I first moved into Wangala in 1954 and the following year into Dalena. In both villages we collected relevant primary and secondary data for my doctoral thesis titled 'The Impact of Irrigation on the Socio-economic System of two South Indian Villages'. It was my first visit to India, my first field study and altogether my first personal involvement with Third World societies.

To collect primary socio-economic data as part of a one-off village study in a strange culture is not easy. It takes a lot of time, effort and personal adjustment to unaccustomed living conditions before the researcher can establish rapport and gain the trust of informants. A re-study by the same researcher is much easier, which I discovered on my return to Wangala and Dalena in 1970. Almost immediately after my arrival I managed to re-activate the close relationships that had evolved between these villagers and myself during my earlier stay with them. I was overjoyed when I saw how ready they were to spend time answering my many searching questions. This enabled me to gather in only a few weeks enough material to write a book and a number of articles. Whereas the data collection was a lot easier during my re-study, than it had been during my first stay in the villages, I found the analysis of changes over time more trying. It posed a challenge I was eager to meet. When preparing the manuscript of my re-study I became fascinated with the phenomenon of socio-economic change. I not only related and analysed the changes that I perceived had occurred since 1955, but also predicted how these villages will change in future.

Predictions at the macro-level abound, although they often rely on highly suspect statistics. By contrast, there is still a dearth of prognostication based on micro-studies. For the sake of scientific advance I ventured to predict in my 1973 publication how these two villages would develop in the subsequent thirty years, extrapolating from trends observed since 1955.

When I made those predictions in the early 1970s I was already almost fifty years old. I did not expect then that I would still be alive at the end of the century. Yet I hoped that some young researcher would be interested when the time came to check how far my predictions turned out to be correct, and if I had gone wrong, why?.

In the 1990s I began to realise how wrong I had been about how long I would live: far from having passed away I was still fit and energetic enough to return to Wangala and Dalena. I thus saw a chance for myself to test the accuracy of my 1970s predictions and welcomed the idea of getting involved in updating my earlier studies, only this time I wanted it to be a joint effort.

A *Collaborative Effort*

I did not want to publish only my own narration of what and why changes occurred since my first study, which is the genre of most longitudinal village studies. Instead I sought to provide a more varied account. Besides my own description and evaluation seen from the vantage point of the seasoned expatriate researcher, I tried to get South Indian co-authors, to show how they perceive and judge the changing societies of Wangala and Dalena. As each of us comes from a different background, we therefore view rural changes from a different angle. It was not easy to synchronise the writing of three co-authors separated by long distances, just as getting different perceptions of the same phenomenon to gel into a coherent presentation without too much repetition was also not easy. After numerous discussions and exchanges of faxes and letters we managed to reach a consensus. We agreed that whenever feasible we would let our village informants speak for themselves. We want our book to reflect 'Village Voices'.

A. P. Suryanarayana (called Suri for short) originates from Mysore city. After he got his B.Sc. he joined me in 1954 as a research assistant. Two years later when I left South India he became a public servant and worked for the Bureau of Statistics in Karnataka's capital. Whenever I revisited South India he was always ready at short notice to accompany me to the villages; we worked together again in 1970 and 1996. Our village friends have come to regard us as an inseparable team.

In Part I he begins by relating the difficult adjustments working together with me in villages meant for him. As a young Brahmin graduate who grew up in a large city he had to leave his familiar urban environment and move to a strange village, where he had to share the same house with a foreign female researcher. Moreover, he had to tackle the difficult task of collecting socio-economic data from villagers. All this was obviously entirely new to him. He sets out in detail how we divided our responsibilities in collecting the various data we needed. Though I have known Suri for a long time and over the years we have become close friends, I never realised until now what a taxing proposition his first job with me had been for him.

T. Thimmegowda was a bright, young Peasant[1] boy when I first moved into his native Wangala. By 1970 he had succeeded in getting a first class master's degree in economics. Today he is a well-respected high-ranking IAS officer and resides in the capital of Karnataka. Yet he still identifies himself with his native village and does everything in his power to assist his fellow villagers, irrespective of their caste. From this book it clearly emerges that his influence has played a large part in the improvements that have taken place in Wangala during the last few decades. I cannot help but feel proud of the way he has developed. As far as I can judge he makes a 'model' IAS officer: as a public servant he appreciates the need to involve the people under his control in administrative measures that concern them and ensures that his subordinates also act accordingly; as an educated villager he has a laudable image in mind of how he would like his native Wangala to change and tries his best to see this implemented. We do not always agree on matters concerning rural development, but I carefully listen to his views, which I always find well-considered. His extensive administrative experience complements my own research skills and we understand and respect each other.

Over the years there have developed close links between T. Thimmegowda and myself. He and his family look upon me as a mother figure. I very much enjoy this relationship and try my best—not always successfully—to live up to their expectations.

I, **T. Scarlett Epstein**, as a student of development economics and anthropology, pursue an interdisciplinary approach to societal studies. Such hybrid study is widely accepted today but in 1954 it was still the exception. I began my fieldwork by drawing up an ambitious and complex plan of action that set out the various data I would gather. It included the collection not only of a lot of quantitative economic data but also qualitative socio-political materials. Mine was a novel research venture. Therefore, there were no established methods for me to follow. In many instances I had to create my own new methods of research and data processing.

My interdisciplinarity has meant that I have never been fully accepted either as economist or social anthropologist by my academic colleagues. This obviously had its serious disadvantages. On the other hand, it also had considerable advantages: it offered me a wider scope and relieved me from the constraints of disciplinary boundaries. It allowed me freedom as a researcher to follow my intuition and venture into new fields as I saw fit. This I much enjoyed.

In Part III, I present a researcher's view of India's changing rural scene. I begin by familiarising readers with my personal background and the academic influences that led me to study South Indian societies. I also relate the logistics of the studies I conducted in Wangala and Dalena over the past forty years. Moreover, I try to explain to readers why I have become so attached to my South Indian village friends. They welcomed me with open arms, and made me enjoy the warmth of belonging. In all my extensive travels throughout different parts of the world I have never encountered the same thrilling experience anywhere else.

Having set out the personal and emotional background of my South Indian field studies I turn to a summary of my 1962 and 1973 publications. Then I go on to describe what changes I found most striking in Wangala and Dalena when I walked through the villages on my return in 1996. There follows an account of the main factors responsible for these readily observable changes. I also discuss their deeper impact on village life and check the validity of the predictions I made in 1970.

It clearly emerges that the two villages continued over the years to pursue different paths of development. Wangala, with its wet lands remains village-introverted with a strengthened village identity. Dalena, with its dry lands continues its village-extroversion; it is well on the way to becoming an urban suburb. These are some of the features I predicted correctly in 1970. As was to be expected, I was not right in every respect; for instance, I had not attached sufficient weight to the impact of education and liberal legislation on rural societies. My contribution concludes with a discussion of the advantages of change and its social costs.

I hope that Part III will engage you, the reader, in the excitement of village studies and make you keen to learn more about rural life. By voicing your informed views you may then affect the shaping of more enlightened rural development policies and programmes in the future.

In the concluding part, T. Thimmegowda and I join forces in writing 'The way ahead'. On the basis of our studies of Wangala and Dalena we discuss what we perceive as the major problem areas in the context of rural development. We are aware that it is difficult to generalise from a sample of two societal studies, but we maintain that the issues we raise have wider significance.

Even if Part IV does no more than lead to arguments and discussion about what we see as the way ahead, we shall consider our efforts have been worthwhile. We do not pretend we know the solutions to the various problems we discuss; we therefore put a number of searching questions rather than offer easy answers. We hope our book will challenge the reader to explore solutions and play an active and positive part in furthering rural development in tune with villagers' own aspirations, whenever appropriate.

Re-humanising Village Studies

We try here to re-humanise village studies by re-introducing the human element that has been disengaged in many such publications, thereby making them less entertaining and more remote from the complex social reality. By re-humanising village studies we hope to involve you in the lives of villagers and give you a flavour of fieldwork.

In our appraisal of changes in Wangala and Dalena we describe the different personalities and experiences of both researchers and informants involved and the way they interact. We consider it important to make readers aware of the subjective influences of socio-economic changes on our perceptions, to facilitate evaluation of bias.

Many social scientists still regard the attempt to re-humanise village studies an unscientific exercise. Statements by researchers on their personal involvement in the societies they studied are at best considered irrelevant and at worst damned for putting data and analysis into doubt. Our own experience makes us question the validity of this view.

Each of us has in a different way developed close and emotionally charged links with many of our major informants. These close ties have undoubtedly influenced our views. At the same time they also enabled us to establish good rapport and relationships of trust. These have helped us collect information we believe we would otherwise have failed to get. We always cross-check our data and even our analyses with different informants and revise them in line with their comments. We are convinced that personal involvement in field studies promotes rather than reduces the reliability of researchers' data and analyses, but at the same time we realise its subjectivity. Since it seems impossible to disengage the human factor from primary data collection we stress the ethical importance of re-humanising the analysis of village studies. We aim to encourage a continuing dialogue between those who organise or study rural development and the large number of people who seek information about it. We shall be pleased if readers will meet the challenge this book poses and will share their views with us by completing the questionnaire at the end of this book and contacting us via our publishers.

A *Documentary Film*

In support of our endeavour to make village studies reach a wider public we pursued the possibilities of using the film media. It was not easy to make the necessary arrangements. Many attempts failed, because we encountered serious funding problems which we found terribly frustrating. Fortunately, our perseverance was rewarded. We succeeded in getting a positive response from the German Institute for Scientific Films at Göttingen. Two of their staff members, Dr Beate Engelbrecht, a qualified anthropologist and experienced documentary film producer, and Manfred Krüger, an outstanding camera operator, enthusiastically agreed to film our villages.

Together with them we spent May 1997 in Wangala and Dalena. Filming village life was a thrilling experience for all of us. When we arrived we explained to large audiences in the two villages the object of the exercise. They got very excited when they heard they would star in a film. It is generally known that villagers like to pose for photographs. Many of them failed to grasp that filming differed from photography. Whenever they saw the camera operator approach they stood rigid expecting to be photographed. This was the last thing the film makers wanted. They wanted to film villagers moving around in the pursuit of their daily activities. It took some time to make villagers realise this. Yet in the end it all worked out to everybody's satisfaction.

We expect the film to reinforce our attempt to inform large audiences about the realities of rural development. We hope it will engage a wider public including relevant policymakers and administrators in the many problems facing the different strata of villagers.

Only Time Can Tell Whether We Succeed.

Note

1. We give names of castes in English and print them with capital initials. For example, a Peasant denotes a person belonging to that caste, while a peasant is a farmer. Similarly, a Blacksmith is a man of that caste, whereas in his occupation he is referred to as blacksmith. We use the collective term Functionary castes to denote all servicing castes. We provide an English–Kannada glossary in an appendix.

PART ONE

Experiences of a Research Assistant

A.P. SURYANARAYANA

TWO

My First Experience of Village Life

INTRODUCTION

*I*n 1954, I obtained a B.Sc. degree from Mysore University with physics, mathematics and statistics as my optional subjects. I then began to search for a job, registering my name with the local employment exchange. I also applied for the post of investigator with the Programme Evaluation Organisation, Government of India, located in Mandya.

One day, my elder brother, Professor A.P. Srinivasamurthy, received a letter from Mr H.P. Narasimhamurthy, Project Evaluation Officer, Mandya, intimating that a research scholar from Manchester University had arrived in the state of Karnataka intending to stay in Mandya district to conduct socio-economic studies in selected villages. The letter also mentioned that this research scholar needed an assistant to help her conduct her studies and indicated the address where she was staying in Mysore at the time.

On 9 November 1954, my brother, sister-in-law and I met Scarlett and introduced ourselves. She explained that she planned to study the impact of irrigation on multi-caste rural communities. For this purpose she wanted to select two multi-caste villages in Mandya *taluk:* one village with irrigated or wet lands, and the other with only dry lands. As I listened to her, I was spellbound. It was the first time in my life that I was hearing a European woman speak, sitting so close to her. It was a strange experience which after all these years is still fresh in my memory.

After that first encounter, I met Scarlett several times and discussed with her the duties I would be expected to perform in the villages. She also lent me some books to read pertaining to rural studies, which I did. I frankly confessed to her my doubts about living in a village. She tried to reassure me and after a few meetings, appointed me as her assistant. She explained that she would provide board and lodging for me in the villages along with a salary. Since this was the first job offered to me, I accepted. Some of my Mysore friends encouraged me to join Scarlett since this presented a rare opportunity to work closely with a foreigner.

In Malavalli

In order to acquaint ourselves with rural life and the methods of extracting information from villagers, I accompanied Scarlett to Malavalli (a *taluk* headquarters in Mandya district) to visit a Pilot Community Development Project. In Malavalli, we stayed in the Traveller's Bungalow for four days from 15 December 1954. I benefited a lot from visits to many villages with the investigators of the Programme Evaluation Organisation, closely watching how they collected data from villagers. Scarlett and I also had many discussions with the investigators, project evaluation officer and project executive officer.

In Wangala

On 20 December 1954, I left Mysore and reached Mandya by train. From the station I went to Wangala by *jatka*, a horse-drawn cart, taking along my luggage. As soon as I got down from the *jatka*, I saw two bullocks, tied with a rope, standing in front of the PWD (Public Works Department) quarters I was to share with Scarlett. I still remember that this made me feel that the two bullocks were there to welcome me. As the quarters were lying vacant, the PWD had allowed us to use them.

As I walked to the PWD bungalow the Wangala *patel* (village headman) Choude Gowda, approached me and asked me why a British lady and I had come to stay in their village. Very soon, some more people assembled. They were also anxious to know why we wanted to stay in the village and what we would do there. We first explained the purpose of our stay in Wangala. Scarlett then wrote an article in English indicating the purpose of our stay in the selected villages and I translated it into Kannada. This was published in the *Mysore Sakkare*, a quarterly journal of the Mysore Sugar Company Ltd, Mandya. Since this journal had a wide circulation it helped us in our studies.

This was the first time I was staying in a village. It was something new to me, and besides Wangala had no electricity. Gradually, as I enumerated each household, I began to get to know the villagers and was soon able to identify all the men in Wangala. When I collected household budgets and property data from the families I interviewed, the information given by men was supplemented by the women. Thus, I was also able to identify some of the local women. As a sincere student of statistics, I wanted to collect reliable information. Hence, I visited each and every household irrespective of caste. Sometimes I sat on the floor in front of the house, sometimes on the borders of paddy fields and sometimes in the *hotelu* (village coffee shop) and collected the information. Some people offered us mats to sit on while interviewing them. Others offered us milk or coffee. In order to continue our conversation while collecting data, I too offered *beedis* (country cigarette) to our informants. While staying in Mysore, Scarlett had learnt Kannada and was able to follow the conversations I had with villagers while collecting data. Because we stayed in the village with them, the Wangala people came to trust us and patiently answered our many questions. Living in the village made it easy for us to cross-check the data we collected. Scarlett focused on gathering genealogies and other sociological data while I gathered the statistical information. Sometimes we went around together, sometimes separately. In the beginning Scarlett guided my data collection, always encouraging me in my work.

The Wangala *shanbhogue* (village accountant), Nanjundaiya, let us have the basic village statistics, such as the area under different crops, number of houses, population, agricultural implements, etc. Being a student of statistics, I had no problem in dealing with these figures and enjoyed my work. The collection of input–output data on the four major crops, namely paddy, ragi, jowar and sugarcane, also required me to study the various agricultural operations of these crops.

We usually spent the days collecting the data we required. After dark we wrote up our notes by the light of a pressure kerosene lamp. Often Scarlett typed at night the information collected during the day. I never found her going to sleep without having recorded the field notes she had collected during the day. In the evenings when we sat together I often asked Scarlett about life in England. She explained at great length the different lifestyle, habits and employment situation that existed in her country. I learnt a great deal in the course of these long talks.

As mentioned, Wangala had no electricity. It was thus pitch dark at night, even though small lamps lit up some of the village homes. During the full moon nights, the open fields were calm and cool and very different from the new moon days. I never felt this difference in cities and towns.

It was a rare opportunity and a unique experience to stay with Scarlett and a cook in Wangala's PWD quarters. There was a well in front of our quarters and Masanamma, a Wangala lady who belonged to the Fisherman caste, fetched water for us. We got milk from one of the houses in Wangala and the cook went to Mandya once a week to bring provisions like vegetables and fruit.

I often wondered how a foreigner who came from a background of plenty could adjust to living in a South Indian village without electricity and most of the amenities to which she must have been accustomed. Scarlett obviously sacrificed many comforts. I assume that this was mainly due to her strong determination to study the impact of irrigation on rural communities and submit her Ph.D. thesis to Manchester University. I admired her perseverance, which encouraged me also to adjust to village life. Since this was my first job I too was determined to complete the data collection conscientiously.

Unlike the city where there are recreation facilities, there were none in the village. We had no set working hours and sometimes I felt so fed up with the work that I wanted to leave. But then I would wonder: if a foreigner like Scarlett could adjust to the village environment why not me? These thoughts helped me continue the survey work till its very end. Besides, whenever I went to Mandya I visited my sister's house, which always helped. Scarlett's continued interest in studying the changes taking place in the villages made me visit the villages even after Scarlett had left for England.

Since we lived in the village, some people came to our quarters to spend time after sunset. While gossiping with them, we also collected data. We enjoyed some jokes with them. I often wondered how these villagers managed to be happy with their few facilities and never seemed worried about the future.

Scarlett and I attended most feasts and other functions that took place during our stay in the village. We recorded the proceedings in detail. Scarlett also took photographs. Of all the feasts I attended in Wangala the *Marihabba* impressed me the most. The *konda* (fire-walking) and *bandi* (cart parade) were the two important components of the *Marihabba*, which I still remember vividly. Selected carts were decorated and paraded along the village roads. Wangala's Peasant caste was divided into two groups of lineages, namely *Gandahalli Palu* (male group) and *Hennahalli Palu* (female group). In the morning, in front of the *Marichowdi* temple, some persons walked over fire. It was a thrilling scene. As part of the *Marihabba,* a male Peasant carries on his head the deity's idol decorated with flowers, dancing rhythmically as Scheduled Caste villagers beat the drums. This was a very attractive and memorable scene.

Apart from my routine work of collecting data, I also had some amusing experiences in the village. In 1955 Wangala had developed only to the east of the bus route. On the west side of the road there was only one Mangalore tiled house and a small thatched hut. In the Mangalore tiled house lived Veerachari, a Blacksmith. Veerachari was an enterprising man who experimented with the conventional iron plough. His improved plough was tested on the field near his house. I liked to watch these experiments. In the hut, a Muslim operated a shop. On some evenings, I sat in front of this shop eating groundnuts and gossiping with villagers. Sometimes we competed in the eating of groundnuts, which was great fun and attracted the villagers who would buy *beedis* from the shop. The owner of the shop was thus pleased to have us there since it meant business for him.

I had a bicycle while I was in Wangala. Whenever I had work in Mandya, I used to cycle the 8 kilometres along the road to the town. It was then still a mud road; now it is sealed. Except when it was raining I enjoyed the ride; I liked to watch the green fields on either side and the flowing water in the canal. Sometimes I joined villagers and traveled by bullock cart. I found this too an enjoyable experience.

Many Wangala villagers went to Mandya on Thursdays to purchase things or sell their goods since it was the *sandy* (fair) day. This has now lost its significance. These days there are so many shops and bazaars in Mandya that villagers do not depend on the *sandy* any more. Villagers now visit Mandya according to their needs and convenience; many have their own conveyance and there are also many more buses.

While I stayed in Wangala, a number of memorable incidents took place; one in particular I still remember clearly. On the evening of 15 August 1955, Scarlett and I, accompanied by the adult education organiser, went to Bevenahally village to participate in the Independence day function. Scarlett drove us in her car. After the inauguration and speeches there were cultural programmes. The entertainment was so interesting that we did not want to leave. When the function was over, it was well into the night. On our return the adult education organiser got off at Mandya. Scarlett and I proceeded towards Wangala. It was dark and raining heavily, making the mudroad treacherous. There were no street lights so Scarlett drove very slowly. About midnight when we were near Haniyambadi, a village about 4 kilometres from Wangala, both left wheels of the car went into a ditch and the car got stuck. We could not get it to move despite all our efforts. We decided that the only thing to do was for me to walk to Wangala to get help.

The night was calm; everybody was asleep. It was pitch dark and pouring. Holding an umbrella, I walked all the way to Wangala with the help of a small torch. On both sides of the road there were paddy fields; I heard the sound of water flowing in the irrigation channels. It was all a bit frightening. On reaching Wangala, I sent sheets and a big torch with the cook to be handed over to Scarlett. That night Scarlett slept in the car. The next morning when she arrived back at Wangala in her car she told me that the villagers, with the help of bullocks, had lifted the car back onto the road. When I wrote the incident up in my diary I noticed that the day was a new moon day. It certainly was a thrilling experience.

In Wangala, Scarlett and I also watched Peasant marriages and she took many photographs. A Peasant wedding ceremony is like a community exercise where many other castes also participate. Peasants, other castes such as Washermen, Barbers, Fishermen, and Scheduled Castes each contribute work during marriages in line with their traditional caste occupation. I could not help but wonder how the entire village manages during a marriage to act as if it were one large family.

While staying in Wangala, many important people such as ministers of the federal and state government, the chairman and general manager, Mysore Sugar Co. Ltd, the Mandya district deputy commissioner, the *tahsildar*, the project evaluation officer, renowned sociologists as well as many other officials visited us in the village. They came to see for themselves how Scarlett, a foreigner, managed to live in a small village with hardly any of the facilities to which she must have been accustomed. Some westerners also visited us in the village. I learnt a great deal by talking to these various individuals coming from different backgrounds. It was a rare opportunity for me, which I enjoyed very much.

In Dalena

Dalena is a roadside village situated on the highway at a distance of about 9 kilometres from Mandya, the district headquarters. Village lands are above the canal level and therefore remain dry. Some farmers possessed wet lands in neighbouring irrigated villages.

Dalena is smaller than Wangala, but in terms of caste composition and mode of living the villages were similar. In both villages, Peasants were the dominant caste.

My life in Dalena differed slightly from what it had been in Wangala. In Dalena, Scarlett, our cook and I lived in a recently built house that belonged to a farmer. Unlike Wangala, Dalena had access to electricity. Scarlett arranged to have electric light in the house in which we stayed. This was an exciting change for us. Dalena had power connections so that the *patel's* younger brother could operate a flour mill and power cane-crusher. Wangala then had none of these facilities.

In Dalena too, many people asked us why a foreigner should want to stay in their village. I explained the purpose of our investigation and what we intended to do. Many villagers in the area already knew about our stay in Wangala. This made it easier for us to convince Dalena people that there were no hidden reasons for our stay.

We could remain in Dalena only for a shorter period than in Wangala. Therefore, Scarlett appointed one more research assistant. Sharma joined us and stayed with us till the completion of our field studies. Hence, we divided the work between him and myself. We made the approach road to the village the dividing line. I collected data from the households residing on the right side of the approach road while Sharma collected data from the households residing on the left side of the road.

In the evenings villagers often came to our house; while we gossiped we collected more information. As in Wangala, there was a well in front of our house from which we got water. The cook continued to go to Mandya once every week to buy what was needed and prepared our meals. Since Sharma and I are vegetarians and Scarlett agreed to abide by our dietary constraints, our household was vegetarian.

As in Wangala we also attended a number of marriages and feasts in Dalena. We observed the religious customs and Scarlett took many photographs. I remember best the *Sankranti* feast which takes place annually on 14 or 15 January. On that day villagers decorate their bullocks lavishly and colourfully paint their horns. In the evening, villagers prepared a fire in an open field and made bullocks, sheep and other animals jump over the fire. This was a memorable sight. To make sure the animals would not come to any harm the veterinarian also attended this function.

Once during our stay in Dalena, on 16 February 1956, a circus came to the village and gave a performance in the open yard. This was a welcome recreation for the villagers and for us.

I also still remember the *Heriyamma* feast celebrated in Indavalu, another roadside village near Dalena on the Bangalore–Mysore high-way. Usually this feast is celebrated at night. On 6 April 1956, Sharma and I left Dalena in the evening and went to Indavalu. The two major components of the *Heriyamma* feast resembled those I had observed in Wangala at the *Marihabba* feast. There was also *konda* (fire-walking) and *bandi* (cart parade). One person carried the nicely decorated idol on his head and danced in tune with the beating of drums. He danced like this right through the night covering almost all the streets of the village. This was a beautiful scene which after all these years is still fresh in my memory. Early in the morning, the *bandi* function was over. Afterwards many people gathered in the village square, where an open fire was blazing. We all watched a man running over the fire. This was an unforgettable experience. Early the next morning Sharma and I returned to Dalena.

Nanje Gowda, the Dalena *patel*, was a reserved and withdrawn man. He hardly mixed with us; he preferred to concentrate on farm improvements. Yet whenever we wanted any information, he was ready to answer our questions. The ex-chairman, Hanume Gowda, was a more outgoing person. He frequently came to our quarters and while talking he revealed a lot of interesting information which we carefully recorded.

Altogether, I found my stay in the villages interesting rather than boring. When we came to the end of Scarlett's field study I felt sorry that it was all over.

COLLECTION OF RESEARCH DATA IN VILLAGES

As I have already outlined, I helped Scarlett in data collection ever since she first came to South India in 1954. Since then every time she returned to South India I accompanied her to Dalena and Wangala. This gave us a chance to observe the changes that have been taking place in these villages. I myself became interested in watching and recording village development, not only to meet Scarlett's data requirements, but also for my own enlightenment. Often T. Thimmegowda joined us on our village visits. As a native of Wangala he had a lot of insight into the changes that had occurred there. Because of this I have left it to him to focus on Wangala. As we have no contribution from a Dalena villager I decided to concentrate here on my observation of socio-economic changes in that village.

FOUR DECADES OF SOCIO-ECONOMIC CHANGE IN DALENA

In 1956, Dalena was a village slightly smaller than Wangala; it consisted of 707 individuals (366 males and 341 females) living in 153 households. During the subsequent fifteen years the population increased by 52 per cent to 1,072 living in 235 households. According to the 1991 Census the population increased to 1,566. The panchayat accountant estimates that by 1996 it had further grown to about 2,600 individuals, i.e., by another 140 per cent. Thus during a span of forty years, Dalena's population, like Wangala's, more than trebled.

Amenities

Electricity Unlike Wangala where we had to depend for light on a pressure lamp, Dalena already had electricity in 1956. Its main road had street lights and a few of the wealthy families had electricity in their homes.

In Dalena, where we rented a local villager's house, we installed electricity and it was a pleasant change for us to switch on lights after dark. The younger brother of the *patel* (village headman) had been instrumental in Dalena's electrification in 1952. As an enterprising villager he wanted to establish a power-driven flour mill and cane crusher. These processing facilities were in place by the time we moved to Dalena in 1955. In 1996 most houses had electric light and six had television sets; there were also fifteen power-driven sugarcane crushers and thirtyfive irrigation pump sets, most of which drew water from the canal. Access to electricity thus proved a great asset for Dalena.

Water Supply   In 1956, there were six wells in Dalena but there was no tank or pond. Women drew water from these wells and/or carried it from a tank situated about 2 miles outside the village. In the subsequent fifteen years the number of wells increased to ten. By 1995, two mini water supply works were in operation. An overhead water tank constructed near the approach road supplied water to many taps in the village.

Transport   Since Dalena is situated by the side of a highway, in 1956 villagers already had access to frequent bus services. This made it easy for them to go to Mandya, Mysore and Bangalore. Some of them cycled to Mandya and most visited Mandya on the weekly fair day to make their purchases. By 1996, Dalena villagers already possessed four lorries and fifteen scooters.

Education   In 1956 a primary school functioned in the village temple. In 1960 a *pucca* school building situated near the approach road which offered grades I–IV was inaugurated. By 1996 it was upgraded to higher primary school up to VII standard. It had two hundred students altogether (one hundred and two girls and ninetyeight boys) with three teachers teaching in three rooms. The shortage of rooms and teachers necessitated teaching of a mixed standard nature. Some Dalena boys and girls have taken advantage of the educational facilities offered in Mandya where they acquire degrees and diplomas. In 1996, there were three M.B.B.S. graduates (Bachelor of Medicine and Bachelor of Surgery), one B.E. (Bachelor of Engineering) and four lecturers.

There were then also two full day nurseries for Dalena's children: one operated by the council located in the dairy quarters and another private one.

Medical Services   A Keralite Christian organisation acquired some Dalena land on the west of the Bangalore–Mysore highway and opened a health centre in 1980. Its staff includes two nurses and four field workers. It offers first aid and distributes medicines. The centre covers twenty villages. Field workers regularly visit the villages and advise people on health problems. In two villages they also run tailoring training courses for altogether twentythree trainees. This missionary complex includes a church, residential quarters and a borewell; so far no attempt seems to have been made to convert villagers to Christianity.

Miscellaneous Facilities In 1956, Dalena had one cafe and one shop. Forty years later there are eight cafes and five shops. Villagers have access to the fair price depot located in Mayanna Koppal (a kilometre from Dalena).

Economic Activities

Agriculture and Animal Husbandry Since yields derived from dry lands are low compared to wet lands, many Dalena villagers sought income from sources outside their village borders. They bought wet lands in nearby villages and diversified their economic activities. Between 1956 and 1970 Dalena farmers increased their wet land holdings by 80 per cent. Others became cattle traders or reared cattle to sell milk. By 1996 they had acquired even more wet land and their milk sales showed a marked improvement. In 1986 a milk producers' co-operative society opened in the village. In 1996 this had two hundred and forty shareholders of whom about fifty supplied milk to the society.

Employment In 1956, twentysix persons went daily for work outside Dalena. By 1970, the figure increased to fortyone, of whom thirtytwo commuted and nine had moved away; twentysix years later as many as seventytwo were employed outside Dalena, many of whom had moved to the place of their employment. Some of them have either taken their families with them or they return periodically to their village homes. Among those working outside the village there are some lawyers, doctors, lecturers, teachers, engineers, electricians; a number work in the nearby sugar factories of Mandya and Pandavapura. Seven of the seventytwo individuals working outside Dalena belong to the Scheduled Castes, who have taken advantage of the public service positions reserved for them.

Industrial Development In 1956, there was not a single manufacturing venture on Dalena lands. By 1996, an industrial estate had been established to the west of the highway that runs through Dalena (see sketch maps). On both sides of the Bangalore–Mysore highway there are now several commercial establishments. These include the not yet operational Emm Gee Steel Wires Manufacturing Company and a cement pole manufacturing factory owned by people from Mandya; a cycle repair shop owned by a man from Mayanna Kopal, a nearby village; Shankar traders, dealers in cement and other such enterprises.

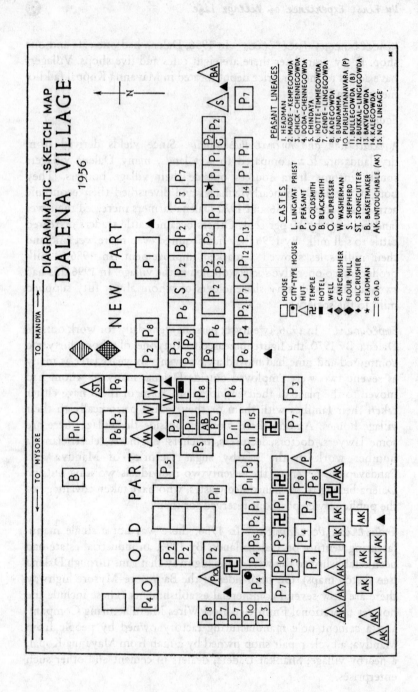

DIAGRAMMATIC SKETCH MAP
DALENA VILLAGE
1956

N

OLD PART

NEW PART

TO MYSORE

TO MANDYA

CASTES

L. LINGAYAT PRIEST
P. PEASANT
G. GOLDSMITH
B. BLACKSMITH
O. OILPRESSER
W. WASHERMAN
S. SHEPHERD
ST. STONECUTTER
B. BASKETMAKER
AK. UNTOUCHABLE (AK)

HOUSE
CITY-TYPE HOUSE
HUT
TEMPLE
HOTEL
WELL
CANECRUSHER
FLOUR MILL
OILCRUSHER
HEADMAN
ROAD

PEASANT LINEAGES

1. HEADMAN
2. MADDE – KEMPEGOWDA
3. CHICK – CHENNEGOWDA
4. DODA – CHENNEGOWDA
5. CHINDAYA
6. HOTTE – TIMMEGOWDA
7. CENDE – LINGEGOWDA
8. KADEGOWDA
9. BUNDAMMA
10. PURUSHIYANAVARA (P)
11. BULLEGOWDA (B)
12. BUKKAL – LINGEGOWDA
13. BAKVEGOWDA
14. KALEGOWDA
15. NO LINEAGE

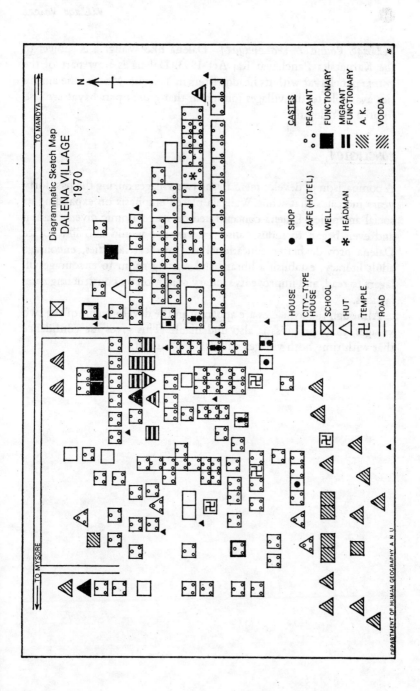

Diagrammatic Sketch Map
DALENA VILLAGE
1970

N

TO MANDYA

TO MYSORE

CASTES

○ ○ PEASANT
○ ○

■ FUNCTIONARY

▥ MIGRANT
    FUNCTIONARY

▨ A. K.

▨ VODDA

□ HOUSE

□ CITY-TYPE
   HOUSE

⊠ SCHOOL

△ HUT

卍 TEMPLE

＝ ROAD

● SHOP

■ CAFE (HOTEL)

▲ WELL

✳ HEADMAN

DEPARTMENT OF HUMAN GEOGRAPHY A.N.U.

Village Council (Panchayat) Dalena like Wangala is subject to the Karnataka Panchayat Raj Act 1993. Dalena is now part of the *grama* panchayat with its headquarters in Yeleyur. Most of the amenities available to the villages joining in that *grama* panchayat are also located in Yeleyur.

CONCLUSION

A comparison of development in the two villages during the past forty years indicates that while Wangala placed emphasis on expanding its social amenities, Dalena concentrated on its economic diversification and even began to industrialise. However, I would also like to see Dalena provide better educational and medical facilities, encourage adult literacy, establish a library and reading room to encourage villagers to read, and improve its sanitary condition by constructing rural latrines.

Although inadequacies are apparent in the development of the two villages, their progress is also undeniable. This gives me confidence that with time both villages will develop further.

PART TWO

An Insider's Views

T. THIMMEGOWDA

THREE

Wangala's Traditional Social System

EARLY REFLECTIONS

*W*angala, a fascinating village, lies in the lush green plains of Mysore's Deccan Plateau, 6 kilometres from Mandya town, the district headquarters. It is surrounded by beautiful streams, canals, coconut gardens, and fields of sugarcane and paddy. The name Wangala signifies the *auspicious* in the vernacular.

I consider myself fortunate to have been born in this beautiful village. Wangala's centuries' old magnificent temples, lithographs and inscriptions herald the glory of its rich historical and cultural heritage; for instance the Malleswara temple near the village tank displays the Chola style architecture. The reign of the Cholas from AD 999 to 1100, the Hoysalas from AD 1100 to 1343, and the Vijayanagara Emperors from AD 1343 to 1600 left an indelible imprint on Wangala's sociocultural life. One of the inscriptions in the village describes that Wangala was gifted by the Vijayanagara emperor, Sadashivaraya, to his local chief, Jnana Wodeyar, in the sixteenth century. The Wodeyars as the Maharajas of Mysore were known for their benevolent rule and progressive welfare measures. First as feudatories of the Vijayanagara kingdom and later as feudatories of the British, they nurtured the traditions and culture of Wangala. A major dam across the river Cauvery and canal irrigation scheme was built during the reign of Krishnaraja Wodeyar IV. Named after the ruling Maharaja, the Wangala peasants benefited greatly from the scheme.

Prior to canal irrigation, Wangala was mainly a dry village often facing drought conditions. Epidemics such as cholera, plague and small-pox had devastating effects on the lives of the villagers. The introduction of canal irrigation in the 1930s had an important impact on the economic development of Wangala. But the tradition-bound village society with its rigid caste structure at first inhibited the process of development. The pace of change began to accelerate only in the 1950s after the introduction in Mandya district of the Community Development Programme; the Intensive Agricultural District Programme; the advent of electricity accompanied by the establishment of cane crushers and the jaggery price boom. The introduction of an elected panchayat, and a host of other social reforms improved public facilities. All this led to the emergence of enlightened political leadership in Wangala and brought profound changes in the village's traditional socio-economic and political system.

Some Childhood Memories

I was born in 1945 in Wangala as the first male child in a middle-class Peasant family that already had two daughters. At the time of my birth most Indian couples desired to have a male child to continue their family heritage and occupation. My mother too was anxious to have a son and hence she prayed to God that her next issue be a son. She believed that her prayers were answered when I was born. My father Doddi Thimme Gowda had studied up to class IV. He was respected for his helpful nature and judicious counselling in the settlement of intra-familial and village disputes. Although he did not belong to any of the powerful Peasant caste lineages of Wangala, he was regularly invited to attend the meetings of the traditional *nyaya* panchayat, the hereditary Peasant caste council. In 1964 he was elected member of Wangala's panchayat. My mother, Ningamma, was respected for her courage and uprightness. As my father devoted much of his time to village problems and sorting out family land disputes, she had to take on the responsibility of managing day-to-day agricultural operations and household affairs. She was a guiding spirit in our street and was instrumental in organising a number of social and cultural functions to maintain harmony among village women. When I was young my mother carefully nurtured and protected me. When I was a little older I joined other village boys to play marble games and indulged in chatting. Like them I wore a loose shirt with knee-level shorts and walked around barefoot. My parents gave me the nickname 'big son' and even today my elder sisters call me by that name. My mother often took me with her to the fields to teach me cultivation practices. I grew up in a rustic environment surrounded by lush green fields of paddy, ragi (millet) and sugarcane crops.

My parents wanted me to study up to primary school and then to take up the responsibility of cultivating the family lands. But I had altogether different ideas. My ambition was to pursue further studies. The challenge was big and hurdles many. Wangala had only a primary school up to class IV, conducted in the *Marichowdi* (the village deity) temple. Classes were held in the open inner courtyard around the *sanctum sanctorum*. One headmaster and two assistant teachers looked after all the classes on a rotation basis. Though more than a hundred children were enrolled, only about fifty—mostly boys—attended school. I went to school regularly, and after school hours and during holidays I helped my mother with her household chores and in agricultural operations.

As a small boy in Wangala in the early 1950s, I remember peasants taking their bullock-carts to the fields in the morning and women cleaning their houses and bringing fresh water from nearby wells and ponds. They cooked food and took it to the fields to serve their menfolk and the labourers. While the men ploughed and prepared the lands for sowing and transplanting, women assisted them in weeding, manuring, transplanting and other supportive activities. Small children played in the streets. The old and infirm squatted on the verandas of their houses. Older children and some of the elderly villagers were sent to graze the cattle. Bullock-carts were used to transport agricultural implements, grain, manure and sugarcane. Traditional village Functionaries helped Peasants by providing tools, implements and services. The Blacksmiths used their age-old lathes to sharpen the sickles and axes and repaired agricultural tools and implements. Goldsmiths made nose and ear rings, bangles and necklaces. Washermen collected dirty clothes from the Peasants' households and took them to nearby streams for cleaning. Potters churned and crushed the clay and turned the wooden wheel to make clay pots and hand-made tiles. Barbers cut men's hair and shaved their beards. Peasants and Functionaries supported each other in their activities and existence. Scheduled Caste (*Adi Karnataka*) men and women provided the agricultural labour required by Peasant families.

Village Lifestyle

Wangala had a large area of wet and a small area of dry lands; paddy and sugarcane were the major wet land crops; and ragi, jowar and pulses were grown on dry lands. The traditional varieties of paddy, viz., *Rathnachudi* and *Bangarasanna* were widely used; they are known for their tall growth and delicious taste which met the needs of both food grains and fodder. Sugarcane was supplied to the sugar refinery situated at Mandya. Paddy and ragi were the staple food grains produced mainly for domestic consumption; the marginal surplus, if any, was either sold or retained for marriages and other purposes. A small quantity of pulses, greens and vegetables was also grown for domestic consumption. Cows and buffaloes were reared for milk, butter and buttermilk. Cattle-dung was the main farmyard manure supplemented by alluvial silt taken from the village tank. Chemical fertilisers were then used only rarely and cultivation methods were altogether primitive. Traditional tools and implements were used for agricultural operations. Wooden ploughs were common and iron ploughs were few. Sickles were used for harvesting paddy, ragi and sugarcane, and axes for cutting firewood. Weeding was done by hand and sometimes with small sickle-like iron instruments. Cattle were fed with paddy and ragi hay and sometimes with green fodder. Thrashing was done manually in the fields with the help of cattle and small stone rollers. Grain was stored in barns attached to the houses. In these hutments grain was kept in big bamboo baskets and jars. Hulling was done manually with a wooden pole that had a metal cap used for pounding. Ragi was ground into flour by using a round crushing stone installed permanently in each house. Jungle-wood and farm waste were used as fuel for cooking and heating water. Cooking was done in earthen pots; later wealthy peasants switched over to brass, aluminium and copper vessels. Drinking water was brought in pots and stored in clay and brass jars from village wells and the pond situated half a kilometre away from the village. Cattle were tied up during the night inside the house on a separate platform opposite the living arena. There were no latrines in the houses. Men and children attended to nature's calls in the fields outside the village in the morning and women during the night. There was no electricity and there were no street lights. Glass-covered kerosene lanterns were used for lighting purposes during the night.

The village had three main streets, viz., Headman, Muslim and

Shepherd streets. Most of the leading Peasant houses were constructed in a well-planned manner. Several other houses and hutments were on the periphery. Major temples were located in the eastern part of the village near the *Marichowdi*, the village temple. These temples have large open areas in front of them reserved for people to congregate during festivals and village council meetings. Some temples are also located in the Headman Street. The houses had mud walls and hand-made tiled roofs. Most of these houses belonged to Peasants; a few houses of Priests and Functionaries were interposed. The *Adi Karnatakas* lived in thatched-roof huts in a separate settlement on the south-western periphery of the village.

Wangala is considered auspicious, as it is said that its foundation was based on auspicious architectural designs. Its founding fathers had the vision and forethought in the way they located the streets, temples, wells, etc., to suit both convenience and tradition. The ancient temples were built on the eastern side of the old village and the *Malleswara* temple is situated towards the north-east which is considered to be 'The God's abode'. Many old drinking water wells are situated in the open areas in front of temples. Tradition, socio-cultural practices and rituals have a significant influence on villagers' lives.

Wangala's annual festivals invigorated the villagers and formed a vital part of their social life. The village deity festival was always celebrated with pomp and grandeur with the collective concern and involvement of all sections of the village. The roles of each individual, family and caste—including Scheduled Castes and Functionary castes—were clearly defined by tradition. Each caste also had its own role in the celebrations: Priests, Peasants, Functionaries, and Scheduled Castes, each received *veelya* (betel leaves and areca nuts) in return as the customary recognition of privileges. The village women actively participated in the celebrations along with the men, carrying the holy *Arathi Tatti*, the decorated plates, singing devotional songs praising the gods and goddesses. Colourful decorations, folk dances, singing and processions accompanied by the beating of drums were all part of the festival celebrations. It was always a great occasion to watch these events and rituals.

Marriages were other happy occasions for a social get-together in Wangala. Preparations for a marriage started about a month in advance. Villagers freely helped the families of the bride and groom as a matter of collective concern. Houses in which marriages were to be held were white-washed and often decorated with colourful paintings and a temporary canopy was erected covered with green leaves and flowers. Each marriage was celebrated for three days during which meals were offered to a large gathering of friends, relatives and villagers. Though it was quite expensive, the villagers always offered *Muyyi*, a voluntary reciprocal goodwill gift or contribution to help families meet part of their marriage expenditure. A record was kept of the individual donations to ensure an appropriate subsequent return at the time of their family's marriage celebrations. Most marriages were between blood relations; for example, a man married his elder sister's daughter. There was no dowry system prevailing at that time.

The girls were married at an early age either before or immediately after attaining puberty. Family planning consciousness was then totally lacking among villagers and the birth of a child was seen as God's blessing. A female child was however not welcomed and daughters were not given a share in the family property. Most households were composed of joint families with moral and social values imposed by the head of the Hindu undivided family. Women were confined to menial tasks in the homes and also on the land.

However, women did play a key role in the village, ensuring continuity and harmony. They were the guiding spirit behind men in the observance of rituals at festivals and marriages. They were always keen to continue traditional social and moral values, cultural heritage and customary religious practices. Though their prime responsibility was the upbringing of children, many Wangala women formed informal groups and periodically conducted socio-cultural activities in the village.

Caste System

Aradhyas were a caste of lay priests respected for their skills and knowledge of rituals. They performed religious rites solemnising the observance of festivals, marriages and other ceremonies. They made holy *karaga* (pots) during the festival of *Mariamma* and *Huchamma*. These *karaga* were taken in procession by peasants and Scheduled Castes along the streets of Wangala. People took blessings from the *karaga* carriers by touching their feet. They offered small payments as a token of gratitude for their services. Priests had small areas of lands which they themselves cultivated.

Peasant Caste Peasants dominate Wangala numerically as well as in the socio-economic and political fields. They composed more than two-thirds of the village population and owned about 90 per cent of village lands. The peasant caste is made up of several hereditary *vataras* (lineages), which settled in blocks of houses on the main streets and peripheral roads of Wangala. Each lineage occupied a certain social status and enjoyed privileges in the village festivals and marriage ceremonies. In recognition of their rights and privileges, they were offered *veelya* during marriage ceremonies. This practice is still in vogue. Lineage tradition ensures unity among its members. Whenever there was a dispute between families of different lineages, the members of the whole lineage rallied round and supported their lineage families. This unity and solidarity has helped the dominant Peasant lineages to assume higher social status and political authority in the village. Chowdegowda, the then *patel*, enjoyed political power on a hereditary basis. Yet his younger brother, the then Chairman, Kempegowda, who had a more forceful personality established sociopolitical supremacy in Wangala. Similarly, a few other Peasant lineages—e.g., Mallegowda, Kalasegowda, Chowdegowda and Bevuregowda—were traditionally recognised as major Peasant lineages.

Scheduled Castes (Adi Karnatakas), the Hale Makkalu System and Untouchability

Adi Karnatakas were the second largest caste in Wangala, but they were poor and mostly landless. They depended on Peasants for their livelihood and worked mainly as agricultural labourers.

A traditional system of *Hale Makkalu* (old children) has existed for a long time between Peasants and *Adi Karnataka* families. This involved a continued hereditary allegiance, a patron-client relationship between Peasants and *Adi Karnatakas*. Peasant patrons provide their *Adi Karnataka* clients with certain amenities like food, clothing, utensils, cattle and some cash for marriage and other expenses. In turn, the *Adi Karnataka Hale Makkalu* offered their services to their Peasant patrons by providing them preferential manual labour in the households and on the lands, apart from performing some rituals in Peasant ceremonies. For a long time Wangala *Adi Karnatakas* have accepted this customary practice, probably because breaking away from their peasant masters would have meant even greater hardship in terms of lack of social and economic security. In her 1973 book, Professor Epstein observed that the 'Wangala *Adi Karnatakas* (Scheduled Castes) seem to accept their social inferiority as the price they have to pay for the assured minimum subsistence which they enjoy and which is part of their traditional hereditary relationship with local Peasants' (p. 213).

Untouchability   Scheduled Castes were considered untouchable due to certain social and ritual practices over generations. This discrimination against Scheduled Castes was strictly observed by the upper caste households in public places such as cafes, restaurants and temples, and also in social and religious rituals. Nevertheless, they had certain functions and duties to perform during Wangala's religious and social ceremonies. Traditionally, they were drum-beaters in the village and in return they customarily received payments in kind or cash. The practice of drum-beating was hereditary. The Scheduled Castes were also a major source of agricultural labour for Peasant families. Even to this day, Wangala Peasants depend mainly on them for their agricultural operations. Many Scheduled Castes also worked as contract labourers on fixed emoluments and perks. They used to live in thatched-roof huts to the south-west of the village so that the north-east monsoon wind should not pass through their huts towards Peasant houses. Thus the stigma of untouchability had its tentacles spread even in the wind's way. They were not allowed inside the living rooms of Peasant houses or the inner courtyards of temples. They were not permitted to draw water from the wells situated in the Peasant colony and had their own temples and source of drinking water.

Functionary Castes   Goldsmiths, Blacksmiths, Carpenters, Potters, Washermen and Barbers were the hereditary Wangala craftsmen castes known for their specialised skills in their respective crafts. Their number was small and they were largely dependent on Peasants for their livelihood. Functionaries also owned small areas of agricultural lands which they cultivated themselves. They were respected for their skills and craftsmanship and enjoyed higher status and some privileges when compared to the Scheduled Castes. Functionaries provided Peasants with goods and services, in return for which they received annual payments mostly in kind in the form of food grains during harvest times. They lived side by side with the Peasants in the main streets of Wangala. Among the Functionaries, Veerachari, a Blacksmith, was known and respected for his literary talent and innovative skills. He directed several mythological and folk plays in the village in which Peasants participated.

Muslims   In earlier years, Muslims also lived in Wangala. They owned lands in the village which they sold to Peasants after partition, when they migrated to towns and cities fearing insecurity in the villages.

Voddas   were poor and landless agricultural labourers who came from Tamil Nadu, a neighbouring state. Increased demand for labour due to the onset of irrigation and attractive wages encouraged Voddas to migrate to the irrigated villages of Mandya district. Initially, Vodda families, such as Kannan and his brothers, came and settled in small thatched-roof huts on the outskirts of Wangala, followed by many others. Wangala Peasants were pleased to have their additional labour requirements met, no longer being dependent on Wangala's Scheduled Caste. Gradually, the Vodda settlement grew and became an independent colony. Their economic conditions were deplorable as they were dependent solely on wages and they lived under congested and unhygienic conditions. They were considered socially inferior and also untouchable by Peasants and other upper castes. Since they were migrants, they had no social status and established privileges in Wangala. Even Wangala's Scheduled Castes considered them socially inferior and therefore Voddas were not allowed to take water from their well or to participate in their socio-religious ceremonies.

As a young boy in Wangala, I had the opportunity to visit some Voddas to call them for work on our lands. Eera, a tall, well-built Vodda, became our family contract labourer with whom I worked in our fields during my school days. He was basically a hardworking and warmhearted person who often shared his feelings freely with me. Economic development and change had not improved their living conditions as they had no lands and other means of production at their command. In later years, the government granted them some lands and sites.

These different castes were economically interdependent while at the same time they gave the village a hierarchical social structure. The place each caste occupied in this structure could be easily identified by prevailing inter-dining rules: all those from whom cooked food could be accepted were considered of higher rank, those households that inter-dined freely were equals, and those from whom no cooked food was accepted occupied a lower rank. It needed the passage of generations before such a deeply engrained cultural practice would begin to change.

FOUR

How Wangala's Economy has Changed since 1954

FROM SUBSISTENCE TO CASH FARMING

*C*anal irrigation reached Wangala in 1932–33. It enlarged the scope and potential of agricultural yields and generated employment opportunities in Wangala. Although it helped farmers grow paddy and sugarcane on a large scale, prevailing socio-economic conditions limited the effects of the phenomenal increase in farm output. For nearly two decades after the advent of canal irrigation, Wangala remained predominantly a subsistence economy. Population growth and the larger number of surviving children per family increased the pressure on land, which is the basic and central means of Wangala's livelihood. Laws of inheritance and succession accompanied by a growing awareness of the advantage of nuclear families accelerated the break-up of joint families. This led to family partitions and division of land holdings. As a result, a large number of small and uneconomical fragments of holdings were created. Wangala's land holdings had a pyramidal structure, consisting of a few magnates owning more than 10 acres of wet land, followed by several upper class peasants with holdings ranging from 5 to 10 acres and a large number of middle level farmers owning between 2 and 5 acres of wet land. Small farmers including Functionaries and Scheduled Castes occupied the bottom rank, owning less than 2 acres of wet land. Many rich and upper class peasants managed to increase their crop yields and income by adopting improved methods of cultivation. They also employed more Scheduled Caste and Vodda labourers and paid them in cash or in food grains. Middle class peasants depended mostly on their family members for the conduct of agricultural operations, with only occasional employment of casual labourers for transplanting, weeding and harvesting. They largely continued their traditional methods of cultivation and applied customary inputs. With assured irrigation, they could generate a small marginal surplus in agricultural production which was utilised mainly for their own subsistence consumption, marriages and festivals. The poorer small holders, Scheduled Castes and Functionaries, and even more so the landless, were unable to produce sufficiently to meet their requirements. Only peasants with large wet land agricultural holdings produced a surplus. The majority of Wangala's small holders remained subsistence farmers during the earlier decades of canal irrigation.

CHANGE FACTORS

Government Programmes and their Impact on Agriculture

The introduction of the Community Development Programme in 1956 and the Intensive Agricultural District Programme in 1962 in Mandya district had a considerable impact in transforming traditional into modern agriculture. Both these government programmes aimed at maximising agricultural production by advising and helping farmers to adopt scientific methods of cultivation, application of improved variety of seeds, fertilisers, implements and pesticides.

The *gram sevak*, a trained village level worker attached to community development blocks, visited villages regularly and encouraged farmers to adopt modern methods of farming. For instance, the Japanese method of paddy cultivation, such as line transplanting, was introduced. Improved iron ploughs and weeding implements were used in both paddy and sugarcane cultivation. High yielding varieties of paddy, ragi and sugarcane were propagated. Improved inputs and implements were given free of cost to many farmers as an incentive to encourage them to adopt the new methods. Intensive cultivation and crop rotation practices were encouraged. Supplies of inputs, implements, fertilisers and farm credit as part of a package programme under the Intensive Agricultural District Programme were channelled through village co-operative societies, and demonstration plots on the land of selected farmers were arranged to show and explain to other farmers the effects of the new methods and the application of inputs.

A few progressive Wangala peasants eagerly adopted these improved methods, others gradually. Agricultural yields of these peasants increased substantially and consequently, their income and economic status also improved. The average yield of paddy and sugarcane increased by more than 50 per cent during the 1960s and 1970s, creating a considerable marketable surplus in Wangala's economy.

The Rise and Fall of Wangala's Service Co-operative Society

The Wangala Service Co-operative Society was established in 1960 as a government initiative to promote rural credit and the use of improved inputs. The society had the jurisdiction over the Wangala group panchayat area comprising four neighbouring villages, viz., Hebbakavadi, Lokasara, Marasinganahalli and Thimmana Hosur. A few rich and progressive farmers of these five villages contributed the initial share amount necessary to promote the society on a co-operative basis.

The society gave short-term crop loans and medium-term land improvement loans to farmers at a low rate of 6 per cent interest. Earlier, Wangala farmers had borrowed from local money lenders and paid exorbitantly high interest rates of more than 12 per cent. Apart from credit, the society also supplied improved seeds, fertiliser, agricultural implements, pesticides, and even helped farmers in marketing their produce. Wangala Peasants benefited from the society by the timely credit and the supply of inputs it offered. The rich Peasants with better credit worthiness borrowed more and utilised the facilities for further improvement of their economic status. The amount of money a member could borrow was limited by the number of shares he possessed and the size of his land holding. Most poorer and many middle class farmers borrowed only small amounts which they often misutilised by spending the money for purposes other than agriculture. They could not repay their loans and became defaulters, thereby rendering themselves ineligible for further loans. These farmers had to revert to the local money lenders for their credit needs and increased their debt burden. Gradually, the co-operative society became defunct with large amounts of outstanding debts which prevented the advance of fresh loans. Thus, the co-operative movement, which started in Mandya district as a successful experiment to improve agriculture and rural credit, lost its importance.

The Advent of Electricity

The advent of electricity in 1960 ushered in a new era of economic development. Hindus celebrate Divali, the festival of lights, in the month of October every year. It signifies the dawn of enlightenment in one's life by driving away the darkness of ignorance and evil. By analogy, Wangala was infested with age-old customary values, beliefs and superstitions, fuelled by illiteracy, a conservative socio-economic outlook and ignorance. The advent of electricity marked a breakthrough by initiating a process of change in the outlook and attitudes of Wangala's population.

Bevegowda, an enterprising Wangala Peasant, was instrumental in getting electricity to energise his first power-driven cane crusher in 1960 in the outskirts of the village. He also pioneered the installation of a huller and a flour mill. Taking advantage of the availability of power in the outskirts of Wangala, some panchayat members, including my own father Doddi Thimme Gowda, took the initiative and persuaded the authorities to sanction village electrification and street lighting. The proposal also contained a minimum number of house connections. After completion of the necessary formalities, it was sanctioned by the government in 1962 and commissioned in 1963.

Wangala's residential area turned bright with electric lights in the streets and in houses. The village wore a festive look nicely decorated with flowers and buntings. Men, women and children happily celebrated Wangala's electrification as their Divali, the festival of light, and it signified the dawn of a new era of prosperity and change. The new light activated men and women to extend their household chores in the night and helped school children study longer everyday to complete their homework. Many villagers bought radios and listened to music and weather forecasts; they were also keen to listen to farm broadcasts to learn about improved methods of cultivation. Electrification also energised the entrepreneurial ambitions of some progressive farmers who now used power for irrigating their dry lands. Thus, the advent of electricity had an overwhelming impact in initiating socio-economic changes in Wangala.

The Presence of an Outsider

The presence of an outsider living amidst villagers was another change factor. Scarlett Epstein's arrival in Wangala in 1954 introduced a process of awareness as well as understanding of a new culture and lifestyle. As a British national in her early 30s, she obviously reflected western culture and lifestyle. Since Wangala was a highly traditional and conservative society, her visit evoked interest and curiosity among men, women and children. Her dress, complexion, hairstyle and mannerisms became the talk of the village, just as her sincere, hardworking and well-disciplined life had a great impact on the villagers. The deserted Wangala PWD bungalow, where she stayed, became a centre of attraction.

As a small boy, I was amused to see a foreigner at our doorstep and felt immensely proud to be with her. I joined other boys and girls to visit her bungalow regularly to say 'Hello' and to exchange greetings. Scarlett always responded warmheartedly. She ate vegetarian food during her stay in Wangala and led a simple life. When she first came to Wangala, the village had no electricity. After dark Scarlett worked by the light of a kerosene lamp. She was an early bird, discussed her day's programme with A.P. Suryanarayana, her Indian assistant, and went from house to house on the streets of Wangala. She always greeted people with a smile of affection and learnt Kannada and spoke the vernacular with an English accent to the delight of villagers. This helped her quickly establish a rapport with men, women and children. Borgowda, a lower middle class Wangala Peasant, became her main informant. Karegowda, the small boy who lost his mother in childhood, became her affectionate child. She generously gave fruit, *beedis* and cigarettes to men, betel nuts to women and mints and chocolates to children. She always attracted crowds of men, women and children, who followed her during her walk through the village. The villagers liked her smile, good manners and friendly greetings, and soon developed a strong affection for her. She won the hearts of the Wangala people and was affectionately called 'Wangala Kempamma' (Wangala's Red-Woman). Men, women and children thronged the streets of Wangala waiting to see their Kempamma. While many shook hands, saluted her and greeted her with folded hands, women touched her hands and feet to express their goodwill and affection. She became a role model among the children and progressive thinking young men and women of Wangala. Her close association with Wangala villagers, brought a change in their attitudes, illustrating their openness and desire for change. Dogmatic ideas and the imposition of unrestricted customary social values had resulted in their conservative outlook and had perpetuated social discrimination. The mindset of socio-economic superiority and inferiority among villagers had promoted bias and discrimination in the existing social system. In this context, Scarlett

Epstein's presence as a social anthropologist had a tremendous impact on the thoughts, ideas and attitudes of the Wangala people. If they could adapt to a foreigner, it was possible for them to adapt to their own Scheduled Castes and Voddas, provided appropriate socio-economic conditions and adequate opportunities were created. Her stay in Wangala came to be generally regarded as an important event that was cherished in the hearts of local people. When she left Wangala in 1955, many villagers shed tears and pleaded with her to visit Wangala again and again. She was always remembered as a member of the village community who settled abroad and reciprocated the affection by developing a deep attachment to 'her' South Indian village.

THE DYNAMICS OF DEVELOPMENT

Wangala's economic development, which was triggered off by the introduction of canal irrigation, increased at a rapid pace only after the introduction of the Community Development Programme and the Intensive Agricultural District Programme. The advent of electricity in the early 1960s initiated the process of change in the villagers' outlook and attitudes. The adoption of the various aspects of modern methods of farming and the establishment of sugarcane crushers and irrigation pump sets greatly increased agricultural yields. Self-sufficiency in food production enabled farmers to concentrate more on cash cropping by extending their area of sugarcane cultivation. The surplus sugarcane after meeting the contractual obligations of the Mandya Sugar Refinery was converted into jaggery. Soaring prices of jaggery increased the profitability of converting sugarcane into jaggery. Consequently, the number of sugarcane crushers increased. All this unleashed the dynamic forces of development with the multiplier effect on production, income and employment, resulting in greater expansion of the village economy. The extension of canal irrigation, the package programme and the jaggery price boom in Mandya district injected further growth into an already expanding economy.

Many local farmers extended their holdings by purchasing lands when the Mysore Sugar Refinery auctioned their Wangala plantation. Irrigated land became more and more productive and remunerative. It attracted outside investors to purchase lands in Wangala and cultivate it by using the more profitable way of adopting scientific methods. This further strengthened the modernising of Wangala's agriculture.

The increased demand for the limited lands caused inflation in land prices. Wangala's agricultural lands became a potential resource for development and profitable use. Many farmers owning cane crushers now sell their jaggery at Mandya's public auction. They thereby avoid middlemen and consequently increase their earnings. Some of them purchase standing sugarcane crops from other farmers on the basis of an approximate estimate of the quantity and a calculation of the cost of the cane at the rate offered by the sugar refinery, less cutting and harvesting charges. Later, at the opportune time it is processed into jaggery in their cane crushers. Such transactions yield large profits for these entrepreneurs. Sugarcane cultivation and processing of cane into jaggery created more employment opportunities and increased the income and economic status of many Wangala farmers. The rising incomes are reflected in a changing outlook and lifestyle of many Wangala rich Peasants. They started adopting improved standards of living and comfort. Rich Peasants, like Chairman Kempegowda, and many others built new two-storeyed RCC (Reinforced Concrete Cement) houses. A large number of farmers bought improved implements and replaced wooden carts with tyre-wheeled carts. Many have purchased tractors, power tillers, motor cycles and scooters, television sets, household equipment, telephones, fans, radios, kitchen aids etc. Wangala's rapidly growing economy led to the establishment of many flourishing business ventures, mainly processing and service facilities. Wangala now has a touring cinema house, four hullers and four flour mills, nine provision stores, seven small shops, nine vegetarian and three non-vegetarian hotels, two cloth shops, three tailoring shops, a bakery, a mutton stall, two cycle shops, a dry cleaning shop, two fertiliser shops, several engineering workshops, etc. All these developments over a period of time have gradually turned Wangala into a fast growing society.

Increasing Economic Disparity

Population growth and economic prosperity have brought changes in the distribution of income and wealth within Wangala. A few progressive and enterprising peasants exploited the benefits offered by the new economic opportunities and the black market. A large number of small and marginal farmers, *Adi Karnatakas* and Vodda Tamilian migrants remained poor, facing difficulties in making ends meet. Even among Peasants the traditionally rich, who did not venture to become progressive and enterprising, became comparatively poorer due to the division of their holdings and increase in their family size coupled with soaring prices of agricultural inputs and a high cost of living. The new-rich have further improved their income and economic status by investing in profitable ventures such as money lending and altogether diversifying their activities.

Entrepreneurship and Economic Success

A few enterprising Peasants such as Kalegowda and Ujjanigowda, whose family had earlier owned more than 10 acres of wet land, continued to retain and improve their economic status among the richest Wangala magnates. They anticipated the trends of changes in jaggery prices and converted their large area of sugarcane crops into jaggery at the most profitable time. In contrast, the two sons of Chairman Kempegowda, who built the first two-storeyed house in Wangala and who had earlier established traditional socio-economic and political supremacy in the village, have become poorer due to their complacency and lack of entrepreneurship. Having partitioned their father's 12 acres of wet land and established separate homes, they recently had to sell some of their ancestral lands.

Likewise, the sons of the *patel* and Devaraguddana Kempegowda also lost their wealthy elite status because of the partition of their ancestral property. The younger generation only just managed to retain their upper class status. It remains to be seen what socio-economic status their descendants will occupy in Wangala. Mallegowda's case similarly illustrates how lack of entrepreneurship can downgrade the economic status of even the richest landowners over one or two generations. The old man Mallegowda owned the largest acreage in Wangala, but it was dissipated over two successive generations. Karegowda, Mallegowda's grandson, who as a little boy was favoured by Scarlett Epstein, now ranks among the lower middle farmers. His father, who was an only son, and Karegowda together with his brother have sold large parts of their ancestral landed property and thereby have become poorer.

In contrast, Srinivas, a Class IV employee at the Mandya Engineering College who a few years ago inherited from his father no more than about 1.5 acres of wet land, has now become one of the wealthiest Wangala magnates. Initially, he cultivated land on a lease basis and paid a fixed rent to the land owners. His entrepreneurship and ability and the adoption of scientific methods quickly improved his economic status. Being a salaried employee he was able to invest his increased agricultural income in money lending and in the purchase of new lands. He has now constructed several shops in front of the new panchayat building, a prime area in Wangala. He leases these properties out on high rent and takes heavy advance deposits. Srinivas has thus set an example for many young and enterpising Wangala Peasants. The benefits of new economic opportunities have largely helped a select few enterprising rich and upper middle class Wangala peasants to improve their economic position.

The Slippery Slope of Land Sales

A large number of middle and small farmers who were unable to manage their meagre resources became poorer due to the increase in their family size and consequent increase in consumption expenditure. Even if the overall income of a household increased, it often failed to provide enough to keep the increased number of members— the rate of population growth had outstripped the rate of economic expansion. They therefore failed to meet their daily needs and certainly did not have enough to cover the cost of festivals, marriages and other such social expenditure. The growing liquor consumption and frequent visits to Mandya town by a large number of villagers has further increased their household expenditure. The poorer farmers who could not bear the burden of all this heavy expenditure and consequent increase in family debts were forced to sell some or all of their lands to rich Peasants.

Many of Wangala's *Adi Karnatakas* and Functionaries, who were also unable to cope with the increased family expenditure and high cost of cultivation, have likewise sold all or part of their ancestral lands. The prohibition of Transfer of Certain Lands Act of 1979 imposed restrictions on sales of lands granted to Scheduled Castes and Scheduled Tribes. Therefore, many Scheduled Caste households could not sell the lands earlier granted to them by the government.

Many Functionaries also sold their lands and became agricultural labourers. The village Potters faced difficulties in selling their earthen pots and hand-made tiles on account of the increase in demand for metallic and plastic products and machine-made Mangalore tiles. Consequently, they became redundant and gave up their traditional craft occupation. Increased family expenditure impoverished them and compelled them to sell their lands. Out of five Potter families, two have sold all their lands and have become agricultural labourers.

The remaining three families possess about an acre of wet land each. Similarly, many Goldsmith families also sold their lands and became agricultural labourers. Blacksmith Veerachari had sold part of his land holdings and his four sons now have no more than half an acre each. One of the two Washermen sold his land and became a Class IV employee in Mandya. Since Peasants and Functionaries are no longer fully interdependent the assured annual payments Functionaries used to receive in the form of food grains have gradually stopped; their economic conditions have thus considerably deteriorated.

The economic differentiation among Peasants, Scheduled Castes and Functionaries is reflected in their living conditions. The rich and enterprising villagers have improved their facilities and comforts, whereas the poor have to struggle to meet their bare necessities. Thus, the progressive rich are becoming richer while the unenterprising poor are becoming poorer.

FIVE

How Wangala's Political and Cultural Practices have Changed

THE POLITICAL SYSTEM

Hereditary versus Achieved Political Status

*W*angala's political system had earlier relied on hereditary succession to socio-political office from among the selected major Peasant lineage members. The *patel* was the officially recognised hereditary village headman. He helped the government in the collection of land revenue and census figures. He was assisted by a *Thoti*, a low-ranking village servant. The *patel's* post was considered an honour conferred by the government whereas the *thoti* was gifted some lands known as *Thoti Inam* lands. The *patel* belonged to the *Gowdara Vatara*, one of Wangala's major peasant lineages, which has been economically and numerically strong and enjoyed a hereditary socio-political supremacy for a long time. As village headman, the *patel* was respected. It was his responsibility to persuade land owners to pay land tax and other government dues. He also assisted revenue officials during their visits in the discharge of their duties in Wangala.

The traditional village council known as the *nyaya* panchayat was composed of the elders of the major Peasant lineages. The *nyaya* panchayat is an informal village council consisting of judicious individuals renowned for their wisdom and knowledge of traditional norms and social values. This council of Peasant elders settled intra-familial and intra-village disputes and dispensed justice, and also represented Wangala's major Peasant lineages on a hereditary basis.

The chairman of the *nyaya* panchayat was selected for his lifetime from among its members. He was considered to be the most judicious and wisest among the members and was respected by all villagers. The *nyaya* panchayat, apart from adjudicating village disputes, also decided on the observance of festivals, rituals and village ceremonies. The panchayat meetings were convened in the *Marichowdi*, the village deity's temple. The large open area in front of the temple enabled villagers to assemble and witness the proceedings. Decisions made by the *nyaya* panchayat were always strictly obeyed by Wangala villlagers. Prevailing traditions and customary adherence to social norms and moral values facilitated enforcement of panchayat decisions. The traditional hereditary Peasant panchayat has functioned virtually as 'village government' since time immemorial.

The Dawn of Elected Village Government

The enactment of the Mysore Village Panchayat and District Boards Act, 1952, was a major breakthrough in transforming the hereditary village government into a formally elected council. Initially, the new political system did not evoke much interest among villagers as they had strong affiliations to the conventional hereditary system. Only after the onset of economic development in Wangala and the gradual exposure to the new political system did villagers begin to adopt the notion of elected authority. The 1964 village panchayat elections heralded the process of change from hereditary succession to a democratically elected political leadership.

In the 1964 elections which followed the constitution of group panchayats, my father, who belonged to an unimportant minor Peasant lineage, was elected as member of the village panchayat along with some of the powerful major Peasant lineage members, such as, for instance, former chairman Kempegowda. The new Panchayat Act provided for grouping of a number of adjacent villages to constitute a panchayat area and reserved seats for Scheduled Caste/Scheduled Tribes and women. The chairman was elected from among the elected members following the democratic process. Thus, the Wangala panchayat then also included four neighbouring villages: Hebbakavadi, Lokasara, Thimmana Hosur and Marasinganahalli. As the majority of panchayat members belonged to villages other than Wangala a counsellor from Hebbakavadi village was elected as chairman, but the panchayat headquarters were in Wangala.

Dispute over Panchayat Headquarters

After the Hebbakavadi counsellor became the chairman, the majority of panchayat members passed a resolution amidst the walkout of the Wangala members to shift the panchayat headquarters from Wangala to Lokasara village which is located in the middle of the group panchayat area. Acting on this resolution, the Mandya deputy commissioner passed an order to declare Lokasara the headquarters of the group panchayat. This was strongly resisted by Wangala panchayat members who decided to boycott panchayat meetings. Meanwhile, my father along with other Wangala members filed a writ petition in the Bangalore high court and got the orders of the deputy commissioner of Mandya stayed. Subsequently, the high court decided in favour of Wangala. Wangala villagers remember to this day my father's efforts in protecting their interests by filing a petition and persuading the authorities to retain the panchayat headquarters in Wangala.

The enactment of a revised Panchayat Act in 1985 necessitated for administrative reasons the constitution of a larger panchayat area called *mandal* panchayat. The draft notification was issued by the deputy commissioner of Mandya in 1986. Accordingly, seven neighbouring villages, namely, Taggahalli, Haluvadi, Pura, Lokasara, Hebbakavadi, Thimmana Hosur and Marasinganahalli, were included in the Wangala *mandal* panchayat area with Wangala as its headquarters. This irritated the powerful villagers of Taggahalli who strongly objected to the notification. It created tension between Wangala and Taggahalli villagers. After the final notification, Taggahalli villagers challenged the notification before the divisional commissioner, Mysore. Taggahalli villagers were more united and had more resources than Wangala. They, therefore, could engage a competent lawyer to whom they paid heavy fees. Wangala villagers realising that the change of headquarters would adversely affect the status and importance of their village tried to defend the notification. But they could not mobilise sufficient funds to engage a better lawyer. A serious conflict and cold war developed between Wangala and Taggahalli villagers. By then, Wangala was in an advantageous position having already several facilities and an infrastructure which fulfilled the requirements of acting as panchayat headquarters. Finally, the case was heard by the divisional commissioner, Mysore; it went in favour of Wangala. Following the notification to this effect, elections were conducted in 1987 and the panchayat was constituted with Wangala's Shangowda as Chairman. Wangala elected four more panchayat members: two Peasants, two *Adi Karnatakas*.

However, this was not the end of the conflict and cold war between the two villages. It erupted suddenly like a volcano on the day the foundation stone of the panchayat offices in Wangala was laid. The Wangala panchayat members proposed to construct a new panchayat building in Wangala with the share of the village development funds provided by the government. This was strongly opposed by Taggahalli villagers on the presumption that once the building was constructed, the headquarters would remain at Wangala. But, Wangala went ahead with the proposed construction by arranging the foundation stone laying ceremony. For this they invited the then speaker of the legislative assembly and the local member of parliament. This infuriated Taggahalli villagers so much that they decided to altogether stop the construction of the building. They successfully persuaded the assembly speaker to refrain from attending the function on the threat of a law and order problem. The deputy commissioner and superintendent of police were also informed of the potentially critical situation. Meanwhile Wangala villagers continued making elaborate arrangements for the occasion. On the day of the function, large numbers of Taggahalli villagers came in a fighting mood to Wangala with their bullock-carts, tractors, scooters and bicycles. There was some altercation between the two sets of villagers. I had come as another official invitee to attend Wangala's function. As an experienced government officer having worked as sub-divisional magistrate I quickly sensed the imminence of a serious law and order breakdown. I assessed the situation, urged Wangala people to stop fighting with Taggahalli villagers and advised the function be postponed. Wangala villagers accepted my advice. My timely intervention helped to resolve the impending danger of an explosive situation. The Taggahalli villagers also agreed to return home peacefully. Some time after, when peace had been restored, Wangala people organised a programme for the construction of the panchayat building and got me to lay the foundation stone without any formal function. The construction of the building in Wangala was started in 1990 and completed in 1993 at a cost of about Rs 493,000. The Wangala panchayat utilised Rs 217,816 of government grants and the villagers contributed Rs 225,000 in cash and Rs 50,000 in kind, such as building material.

Wangala's New Panchayat

The 1985 Panchayat Act was amended again in 1991 to provide once again for smaller groups of village panchayats and Taggahalli became another panchayat headquarters. The Wangala panchayat was reconstituted as a unit including Hebbakavadi, Lokasara, Thimmana Hosur and Marasinganahalli villages, with Wangala as headquarters; elections were held in 1994. Most of Wangala's former members were re-elected. In the eighteen-member panchayat there were ten men and eight women, among whom five were from the Scheduled Castes and Scheduled Tribe communities and two were Lingayats. The chairmanship was reserved for the Scheduled Caste and Doddasiddaiah of Lokasara village was elected. As the vice-chairman's post was unreserved, M.H. Javaregowda of Wangala was elected. The reservation enabled some illiterate members, particularly Scheduled Caste and Scheduled Tribe men and women, to get elected. The new panchayat is now functioning harmoniously. With government assistance it has executed several village projects like the construction of a school complex and the panchayat building, the improvement of village roads, water supply and drainage facilities, the constuction of a compound wall for the school and hospital, the extension of street lights and other facilities. Wangala villagers have on their own account renovated many temples.

The reserved seats for Scheduled Caste/Scheduled Tribe men and women in panchayat institutions provided a greater impetus and new opportunities for these underprivileged sections of society to participate in the decision making process of their local government bodies. This important socio-political development has reduced Peasant dominance in Wangala and ushered in a new era of change.

A New Political Scenario

The younger among Wangala's elected Panchayat members formed what I came to call a 'core group'. A number of them are elected panchayat members; others are members of the traditional hereditary Peasant *nyaya* panchayat. This core group constituted by Peasants with a formal education has brought about an increased social cohesion in Wangala because of their keen interest in village affairs. There is now a better understanding between Wangala's elder statesmen on the one hand and the enlightened young leaders on the other. This is a significant and positive change in Wangala's political arena. The core group is more concerned with village development than the exercise of power politics.

This does not mean that in Wangala political parties are not active or influential; core group members are each affiliated with one or other of the major political parties. Some are staunch supporters of the Janata Dal, a national party which is presently the ruling party in the state; others support the Congress party, also a national party. Wangala's panchayat elections of 1987 were fought along political party lines. Shangowda won for the Janata Dal party and M.H. Javaregowda for the Congress party. Each had the support of their respective lineages and political factions. Before the 1980s village elders used to decide for which candidate from which political party the village electorate should vote. The village was then a major vote bank of the Congress party. Growing awareness of regional political developments and the influence of different political parties on village leaders and youths changed Wangala's political affiliations.

In the legislative assembly elections of 1983 and 1985, Wangala had two factions, one supporting the Congress party and the other the Janata Dal. However, unlike in many other villages in Wangala these factions never indulged in serious faction fights or violence. Wangala's political factions are composed of lineages that interact harmoniously. The village never witnessed any political group clashes or tension as an aftermath of elections. The enlightened village youth took an active part in the subsequent assembly and panchayat elections. They were largely responsible for electing the educated, enlightened and young panchayat members. This change in political leadership from hereditary succession to democratically elected young and better educated leaders has been a significant transformation in Wangala's political arena.

EXPANSION OF WANGALA'S PUBLIC FACILITIES

As already discussed, Wangala, though strategically situated on a major district road, remained backward for a very long time. Several rural development programmes launched both by the state and centre and the government welfare schemes hardly touched Wangala. Though the village is situated in close proximity to the district head-quarters, it was years before it obtained proper drinking water, health and education facilities. The conservative outlook of the tradition-bound social system, lack of initiative and villagers' apathy were largely responsible for Wangala's backward status. Subsequent population growth and rapid village expansion increased the need for essential civic facilities and services. The local members of the state legislative assembly and other elected representatives who were keen to help Wangala, provided the initiative and the mobilisation of resources. Successive members of the legislative assembly (MLA) have taken some interest in Wangala's development. In fact many facilities were sanctioned for Wangala with their support and recommendations. But initially, Wangala's lineage and political factions, in their attempt to establish socio-political supremacy, inhibited village development and faster growth of public facilities. These factions with their respective political alliances tried through their political bosses in Mandya to get facilities for Wangala. They could not fully succeed due to lack of unity in the village.

My Own Role as a Political Catalyst

My position as a senior government officer occupying important posts such as assistant commissioner and deputy commissioner helped me to mobilise the support of the villagers and the faction leaders. As a civil servant, I could not show allegiance to any political party. Hence, I stayed away from Wangala's political activities. But I was committed to promoting village development and therefore took the initiative to unite different factions and help them to form a strong village force to mobilise internal resources and to develop the village as an important growth centre. With that strong desire, I made frequent visits to Wangala and discussed with villagers the problems and prospects of getting various facilities. The villagers and leaders of Wangala's lineages and political factions responded positively to my suggestions and advice. My intervention and constant interaction with my fellow villagers and leaders of political parties over a period of time evoked positive responses. Gradual improvements in facilities created greater awareness which enabled them to understand and appreciate the advantage of being united for Wangala's overall development. Thus the core group that had emerged as a multi-party nucleus became the vehicle that initiated and promoted village development and the establishment of public amenities.

Wangala's basic requirements like potable drinking water, a higher secondary school, a hospital etc., were discussed with me during my frequent visits to the village. Proposals for sanctioning these schemes initiated by the villagers were followed up at the *taluk* and district levels. Moreover, I was in a good position to provide access for Wangala's representative to the appropriate authorities in Bangalore, the state capital. I am always happy to provide help for the benefit of my native village.

My Education: A Struggle for Excellence I was admitted to primary school in Wangala at the age of five. As a result of my interest and performance in school, I was promoted in one stroke from standards II to IV. After I completed primary school in Wangala my parents were reluctant to send me to Mandya's middle school because they faced financial and labour problems in cultivating our lands. The school headmaster and my uncle persuaded my parents to send me for further studies. In those days, buses to Mandya were not many and their timing was not suited to school hours. Therefore, I had to walk barefoot the distance of about 4 miles everyday from Wangala to Mandya on a mud road carrying my school satchel and lunch box. While other village boys were more fortunate and had bicycles, I had to tread a more strenuous path to achieve my ambitions. I had the strong urge and determination to overcome any obstacle. I completed my middle and secondary school education coming from Wangala everyday while also helping my family in agricultural operations. When I sat for my secondary school leaving certificate (SSLC) final examination in March 1963, the question papers of some subjects had leaked out ahead of the examination. This caused a big furore and criticism in the legislative assembly. Some other boys who had not taken the examination seriously succeeded in getting the question papers in advance, which enabled them to do well in the examination. However, things went in my favour: the government decided to conduct a re-examination. In the course of this re-examination I passed with distinction, whereas many others who had taken advantage of the leakage of questions failed. This constituted a turning point in my career. While I was studying in the college my mother passed away, leaving me depressed. My father felt helpless as there was no elderly person in the family to help him manage the household affairs and agricultural operations. He urged me to discontinue studies. However, the elders of the village and my relatives persuaded him to change his mind. Though my father was heavily indebted, he supported my graduation and post-graduate studies and I became the first Wangala boy to undertake post-graduate studies in the prestigious Central College of Bangalore University. My university studies were a real struggle for excellence; a large number of my classmates hailed from urban educated families and had studied in good schools and colleges of Bangalore. Many a time I felt the odd one out in the midst of well-dressed English-speaking young men and women in the post-graduate course. My rustic appearance must have amused many, but my self-confidence and determination to excel in studies resulted in my doing well. I completed my post-graduate degree in economics with distinction in 1970. Subsequently, I became a lecturer teaching economics at a private college of the people's education society in Mandya. It was during this time that I met Scarlett Epstein again during her revisit to Wangala and Dalena.

I enjoyed and appreciated my brief interaction with Wangala Kempamma (Scarlett Epstein). It further kindled my interest and determination to follow a professional career. During one of our meetings she advised me that having accomplished a post-graduate degree and having got a good job of which my fellow villagers were rightly proud, I should in turn take interest in their well-being and overall development. Following her suggestion I tried to fulfil at least some of what the Wangala people expected from me. I decided to join the administrative service. As a senior officer of the state government and member of the Indian Administrative Service (IAS), which is the premier service of the country, I have been able to help in Wangala's development.

Education

Education is the key factor influencing economic and social changes. Wangala people did not realise the importance of education in the earlier years of the post-independence period. Therefore, they were not keen to send their children to school. The overall literacy noted in the village was very low and educational facilities were inadequate. In those days, villagers failed to appreciate the importance of education. Most villagers considered education less important than agriculture or other allied activities. It was generally believed that only Brahmins who possess little or no lands should be educated and seek employment. Lack of awareness, poverty, ignorance and inadequate educational facilities were the main factors responsible for the earlier educational backwardness in Wangala. An increased interest in education was a slow and phased process.

Primary School   In 1955, Wangala had only a primary school up to class IV. The classes were conducted in the inner courtyard of the *Mariamma* temple. After Professor Epstein's departure, the primary school was upgraded to a higher primary school and shifted to the PWD bungalow she had occupied. Wangala Peasants were content with the primary schooling of their children and intended to involve them in farming and grazing of cattle. The Scheduled Castes were unable to send their children to school due to economic difficulties. Therefore, the policy of compulsory primary education had little impact on villagers; attendance was poor and the rate of drop-outs was very high. Only few Wangala boys attended higher secondary school in Mandya; girls were not sent at all to cities and towns for higher education. The *patel's* son Kempegowda became Wangala's first graduate in 1964; he started work as a high school teacher. Many others who did not continue their education took to farming.

I graduated in 1968 and completed my M.A. (economics), in 1970. In recent years, many more have graduated and some have even continued their post-graduate studies.

Higher Secondary School   Economic prosperity and population growth have increased the need for better facilities and higher education. This awareness among villagers was propelled by the educated young local leaders who helped in mobilising adequate support for starting a higher secondary school in Wangala. The villagers persuaded me and the local member of the legislative assembly to help them reach their objective. I was then special deputy commissioner (additional collector), Bangalore district, and had contacts with ministries. Inspired by Professor Epstein's earlier suggestion, I took this opportunity to help the villagers in getting the school by using my position and contacts. I pursued the proposal in the state secretariat and with the education minister. Finally, it was sanctioned on the condition that a building should be provided for running the school. I requested one of my uncles to spare his newly constructed house on the main road. He readily agreed and the government higher secondary school was sanctioned and inaugurated in 1984 by the then Education Minister, Sri B. Rachaiah, who later became the governor of Himachal Pradesh and Kerala states. After some time, the construction of an independent school building was taken up and completed with government assistance together with contributions from villagers. Now there are eleven rooms for the primary and middle school, seven rooms for the higher secondary school and a composite junior college. Four nursery schools are also functioning: two each in the Scheduled Caste and Peasant colonies.

The establishment of a higher secondary school in the village has raised Wangala's status in the neighbourhood. Boys and girls from Wangala and neighbouring villages were admitted and have completed their secondary schooling in the village. I am pleased to see that a large number of village girls completed their secondary schooling and some now even attend undergraduate and graduate courses. This I consider an important step in changing the socio-economic conditions of Indian villages. There are folk sayings such as 'a mother is the first teacher' and 'educating a girl is like opening a school'. I am convinced that girls' education is a necessary precondition of socially desirable changes.

A Government Junior College for undergraduate courses was started in Wangala in 1994. All these facilities provide a greater impetus and unleash opportunities for village youths to continue their education. Now there are more than fifteen graduates, eight post-graduates, about fifty undergraduates and 150 holders of a Secondary School Leaving Certificate (SSLC) among Wangala's young men and women. Some of them are employed in Bangalore and other places. Every year increasing numbers of boys and girls attend Wangala's higher secondary school.

A *Student Hostel* The growing enrolment of a large number of students from other villages necessitated the establishment in Wangala of a hostel for poorer students. Thus, in order to help the poorer Scheduled Caste and Scheduled Tribe students and other boys studying in Wangala, a government boys' hostel was started in 1985. It provides residential accommodation and boarding facilities for about fifty boys belonging to Wangala and other villages. Of them, thirtyfive belong to Scheduled Castes and Scheduled Tribes and fifteen to other castes. Today there are ten Wangala Scheduled Caste boys in this hostel. Presently, the hostel is housed in a donated accommodation. The building for the hostel is yet to be constructed. A warden is looking after the day-to-day functioning of the hostel.

Drinking Water under the National Rural Water Supply (NRWS) Scheme Potable drinking water was an urgent requirement for Wangala's large population. The water drawn from the age-old pond was often contaminated and caused severe health hazards. The village panchayat took up the matter with the district administration, supported by the local member of the state legislative assembly. The proposal for a borewell and power pump with an overhead tank for a piped water supply under the NRWS scheme was sanctioned by the state government in 1982 at an estimated cost of Rs 175,000. The work was started immediately. The borewell was drilled on the outskirts of the village. It yielded 10,000 gallons per hour of fresh potable water, which is more than sufficient for Wangala's population. Wangala villagers were jubilant, seeing the drinking water coming through taps at their doorsteps. Women in particular were greatly relieved because piped water freed them from the ordeal of bringing water from the village pond which is about half a kilometre away from Wangala's residential area. Borgowda, a small landholder, who was earlier employed at the Mandya sugar factory plantation, is now the operator of the water supply pump and the panchayat pays him Rs 600 per month for his job. The panchayat has maintained the village water supply since 1985. Gradually, the water supply has been extended to Wangala's new areas and presently, it has 370 house connections and an overhead tank of 20,000 gallons capacity. Because of the constant flow of water from the taps, drainage became an absolute necessity. Realising the urgency and importance, the panchayat began to undertake drainage work in a phased manner.

A Primary Health Unit

Earlier, Wangala villagers were using locally available medicinal plants and adopted native homeopathic methods to treat their minor ailments. Only in cases of severe illness and major diseases did they frequent Mandya's general hospital and private clinics. Poor farmers and landless Scheduled Castes suffered without proper treatment for fear of staying away from home and also due to the expensive treatment in the town. The government health care facilities in the villages were inadequate for treating major diseases. Therefore, Wangala villagers demanded a health centre with a doctor and nurses be established in their village. A proposal was sent with the recommendation of the local MLA to the state secretariat in 1984. The major problem encountered in this context was the precondition imposed by the government that the villagers must provide two acres of land free of cost and a substantial contribution for the construction of the health centre building and staff quarters. By then lands around Wangala had become very costly due to increased demand for house sites and cane crushers. Many land owners were unwilling to part with such a large area of land and there was no suitable government land available near the village. Wangala leaders were helpless to secure the land and were unable to mobilise adequate contributions to meet the cost of the land and the matching contribution for the building. They put these problems to me during my visits to Wangala. Coincidentally, I had helped Mallegowda, a Wangala youth, in securing a job in Bangalore. His wet land was situated on the main road to the south of the village. I persuaded the boy to part with his land at a reasonable price as he was an only son and now working in Bangalore. Members of the core group were enthusiastic and became active in mobilising adequate contributions from Wangala's rich peasants. The big land owners, the philanthropists and the owners of Wangala's cane crushers together contributed Rs 95,000 for the land purchase and initial payments to the government for building the health centre. The government matched this amount with a grant of Rs 110,000. After completion of the required formalities, the primary health unit was sanctioned to Wangala in 1985. India's former Prime Minister Shri H.D. Devegowda (then Karnataka's PWD minister) and the then Health Minister, Shri P.G.R. Sindhia (presently state's Transport Minister) with other ministers and MLAs came and inaugurated Wangala's health centre. It was initially started in an independent and spacious private RCC building that belonged to the late Ningegowda; he generously offered the building free of charge. Subsequently, a new building was constructed on Mallegowda's land earmarked for the purpose. The Wangala primary health unit now has a full time doctor and three nurses, plus a compounder and watchman. Its running cost is met by the government. It treats between fifty and a hundred ailing persons every day belonging to Wangala and surrounding villages. A proposal for a maternity unit is presently under consideration by the government. The villagers have already remitted their contribution of Rs 100,000 for this purpose.

A *Rural Veterinary Dispensary*

The establishment of a milk producers' co-operative society in Wangala in 1978 encouraged villagers to purchase a large number of milking animals including some high yielding crossbreed cows and buffaloes. The increase in the number of cattle, particularly of cross-breeds which are easily susceptible to disease, created an urgent need for a veterinary dispensary in Wangala. The proposal was sent to the government. I was then the Director of the Rural Development Department in the state secretariat. Fortunately, the then Minister for Rural Development, the late B. Basavalingappa, who belonged to the Scheduled Caste, held the portfolio for animal husbandry and veterinary services. When the proposals came from the department to the minister for approval, Wangala was not on the list of villages to get this facility. I had sent word to Wangala's 'core group' to come to Bangalore and meet the minister along with me; I appraised the minister of the need. He was convinced and jokingly remarked saying 'When did Thimmegowda become a social worker of Wangala?' The veterinary dispensary was sanctioned for Wangala in 1991. It is functioning in a private building with a compounder and a peon providing treatment for about ten animals a day. A veterinarian visits once a week and examines ailing cattle, which is followed up by the local staff. Cattle from neighbouring villages are also brought to this dispensary for treatment.

A Commercial Bank Branch and Private Finance Corporations

In consideration of Wangala's growth potential, a corporation bank branch was opened in December 1984 in the village. The bank gives loans at 12 per cent to 16 per cent annual interest for crops, pump sets, tyre-carts, small businesses, milking animals, poultry, agricultural implements, tractors, power tillers, etc. After the service co-operative society became defunct, poor and middle class Peasants turned to banks and finance corporations for short-term crop loans and other purposes. In addition to the bank, two registered financial corporations and a large number of unlicensed money lenders advance short-term credit at higher rates of interest on promissory notes and securities.

Post Office

A sub-post office has been set up in Wangala to provide postal services and savings bank facilities. Presently, it has 138 savings bank accounts, 275 recurring deposit accounts and 300 *Mahila Samruddhi Yojana* (women's prosperity scheme) accounts. *Mahila Samruddhi Yojana* is a new scheme introduced by the government for the benefit of women to encourage them to save. Under this scheme, each account holder contributes Rs 300 annually and the government adds Rs 75 as an incentive. The post office also disburses old age, widow and handicapped pensions at the doorsteps of the beneficiaries.

A *Village Library*

Literacy and education enabled Wangala to establish a village library in 1987. Now it has more than 800 books which include novels, poems and books on literature, science, history etc. It also makes available to readers newspapers, monthly and weekly magazines. A large number of educated village youths and students make use of the library. I have also donated some books and magazines to the library during my visits to Wangala. The vernacular version of Scarlett Epstein's two books on her South Indian village studies are also stocked in Wangala's library.

A *Fair Price Depot*

Wangala has a fair price depot for the supply of certain essential commodities such as sugar, kerosene, rice, wheat, clothes and edible oil at controlled prices under the public distribution system. Poor people were given green cards with which to get these commodities at subsidised rates. The saffron coloured cards are given to others who pay the market price. It is a boon to the agricultural labourers and migrants who can buy essential commodities much below the market price. Richer villagers buy kerosene, sugar and edible oil with their saffron cards.

A *Youth Association*

The educated and enthusiastic youths started a Youth Service Association in Wangala in 1989. It is affiliated to the Youth Service Department of the state government. The Youth Service Association organises felicitation functions, competitions of folk songs and *rangoli* for women. It sends teams of Wangala boys and girls to other *taluk* or district centres for competitions. The association also undertakes small public works such as drainage and compound walls on a work contract basis and mobilises funds for the Association. The Association organises *Shramadaan* (voluntary labour for public works), tree planting and distribution of prizes to meritorious Wangala students. It is recognised as one of the most active Youth Service Associations in Mandya *taluk*.

The fast growth of education, health and other facilities in Wangala during the last fifteen years has greatly elevated the status of the village in the neighbourhood. Wangala has now become the focus of attention in the surrounding area and shows signs of becoming a semi-urban settlement. Scarlett Epstein's expectations and those of Wangala people themselves about village development and the facilities and services have by now been almost fully realised. In 1954 when she spent one year in Wangala, Epstein became convinced of the need for improved facilities and services. This coincided with the aspirations of the villagers and has thus become a reality. I am proud to have been able to help my fellow villagers realise their aspirations.

CHANGES IN CULTURAL PRACTICES

Festivals

Festivals are important social events and account for considerable expenditure within each family. Important Wangala festivals apart from national and regional ones are *Mariamma, Kalamma* and *Mahalaya*.

The *Mariamma* festival is celebrated during the first week of March with great devotion and gaiety. Preparation for the festival starts with cleaning and whitewashing the houses and temples and painting doors and windows. New clothes are bought for men, women and children. The panchayat always meets a few days before the festival to decide about the contributions to be made by each household for the renovation and whitewashing of temples and also for the conduct of the rituals. On the festival day, the bullock-carts, *kondabandi*, are decorated with green mango and sugarcane leaves. The bullocks of some privileged Peasants, *Meerasu*, decorated with coloured gowns are tied to the carts and taken round the village streets in procession. Coconuts and camphor are offered in front of each house. After performing *poojas* (worship), they are let free to roam around the four corners of the village and afterwards are brought back having covered some distance. Then the folk dancing starts with young Wangala men dancing to the beat of drums in front of the village temple *Marichowdi*. At midnight, the Scheduled Caste families arrive in large numbers with

Arathi Tatti (a decorated *pooja* plate with a lamp on it). Beating drums they come to the *Chikkamma* temple situated in the main Peasant street adjacent to my house to take the holy pots. *Chikkamma* and *Huchamma* are sister goddesses, the former is worshipped by Peasants and the latter by the *Adi Karnatakas*. In celebrating this festival the ritual symbolises the unity and complementarity between the Peasants and the *Adi Karnatakas*.

An important feature of this festival has been that untouchability was not treated as a stigma. On this occasion Peasants and Scheduled Castes move around together freely in a procession. When I participated in the *Mariamma* festival of 1996, I was treated as a special guest by the Peasants and Scheduled Castes alike for all events of the festival right through the night. Some village enthusiasts organised folk dances to test my memory of earlier participation. I danced to the beat of drums along with panchayat members and some elderly Wangala persons. A large crowd cheered by clapping and whistling with joy. My dancing with the villagers was reported in the *Mandya District Headquarters Newspaper* under the caption, 'IAS Officer Participating in Folk Dance'.

The *Kalamma* festival is celebrated in the first week of April. A large number of sheep and goats are sacrificed in the name of the Goddess Durga and meat preparations are fed to large numbers of friends and relatives. Considerable expenditure is incurred for this festival. Now the village elders feel that this feast could also be simplified as has that of *Mahalaya Pitrupaksha*.

Mahalaya Pitrupaksha focuses on the worship of family ancestors. Normally, in most of the villages of the Mysore plains this festival is held every year on the new moon day of October. But, Wangala had the tradition of holding it on the next Wednesday after the new moon day. By then friends and relatives of other villages were free to attend in large numbers. This meant a heavy expenditure for the Wangala people. For a long time, the hereditary lineage elders did not agree to change the festival day to synchronise with celebrations in other villages. After the change in the political leadership and my constant urging, coupled with economic pressures, the people of Wangala began to think of reducing the expenditure. The villagers finally became convinced and for the last five years it is now being celebrated on new moon day. This has reduced the expenditure involved by almost 75 per cent for each household.

Thus, population growth and the consequent reduction in family incomes have also brought about significant changes in the observance of festivals. Now the customs and traditions are simplified to suit the family budget. Most of the small and middle class Peasants and agricultural labourers have reduced their expenditure for whitewashing, painting and buying new clothes during festivals.

Marriages and Dowry

Earlier, in Wangala, marriage rituals were held continuously for three days under the specially erected canopy at the bridegroom's residence. Meals were provided for almost all the villagers for three days during the celebrations. Most of the expenditure was borne by the groom's family. Now the system has completely changed. Marriages are celebrated either at the bride's residence or in the temple. The marriage expenditure is now borne by the bride's parents. Even an uneducated Wangala bridegroom demands dowry in cash or a scooter or a motorcycle and a substantial amount for clothes, jewellery, a wristwatch, etc. A minimum of Rs 30,000 to Rs 50,000 is required even by a lower middle class Peasant family to perform the marriage. Until not so long ago if the groom was educated and had a good job, the marriage cost and the dowry offered would have been far higher. More recently, people have begun to prefer simple marriages to minimise marriage expenditure and would rather help the newly-weds to get a substantial dowry in terms of cash, jewellery or property.

The emergence of the dowry system among Peasants and other castes in Wangala as elsewhere has adversely affected the economic conditions of many small and middle class families. They could hardly meet the required funds from their meagre income. Therefore, they borrowed at high rates of interest and got themselves into the debt trap. The loan repayment with interest adversely affected their living standards. Many a time they ended up by having to sell their lands and properties. The incidence of dowry is also responsible for suicide attempts and psychological stress in many families. Recently, the elder brother of one of Wangala's richest Peasants was driven by heavy debts to poison himself.

Demand and acceptance of dowry is an offence under law. But villagers do not attempt legal recourse for fear of spoiling the future life of their daughters. Only in cases of continued harassment and threat or danger to life are complaints filed with the courts as a last resort. Though Wangala villagers do not attribute girls' suicides to dowry demands, continued harassment has led to divorce and suicide among some young local girls. There are three cases of divorce in Wangala and two girls got remarried recently. Tugowda's granddaughter, i.e., his daughter's daughter, recently got a divorce decree from the courts. In the past, remarriage occurred only in a few cases; it was called *Kuduvali*, i.e., the union of a divorced man or woman with his or her new spouse. Widow remarriage is also taking place particularly if the girl is young. Recently, Doddichowdi, Badda's son-in-law, died in an accident and the young widow got remarried. Gradually, Wangala's traditional society is giving way to adjustments in its moral and social values influenced by the needs of the time.

Sanskritisation and Changing Attitudes

Better education and greater exposure to outside influences have radically changed attitudes and lifestyles of Wangala's younger generation. Most of them have adopted urban lifestyles, clothing and hairstyle. Previously, men wore long shirts and half-pants and a towel on their shoulders. Now they wear shirts, dhoti or trousers and *chappals* (sandals). Younger women have switched over from casual cotton sarees to chiffon, nylon or silk sarees.

As a small boy, I remember seeing large numbers of men with a tuft of hair on the back of their heads with crescent shaven heads. My father insisted on the traditional rustic hairstyle with half of my head shaven in the front and long hair in the back which sufficed for a tuft. This was the hairstyle of most Wangala men. During my school days I changed over to crop-cut hair. Gradually younger men also adopted urban hairstyles. Village men who earlier bathed only once a week are now bathing more frequently. They now wear ironed clothes and neatly stitched outfits. All these changes were part of the process of Sanskritisation with its adoption of urban lifestyles.

Economic prosperity and adoption of urban lifestyles have brought changes in the customary habits, rituals, ideas, beliefs and ways of life. The process of Sanskritisation which thus started among the wealthier and educated Peasants has penetrated into the lower strata and castes. Now, a majority of the Peasants, Functionaries and Scheduled Castes have adopted Brahmanical names without the suffixes of their castes. Unlike in the past, now many Wangala Peasant women have stopped carrying food to their menfolk working in the fields. These days they concentrate on their household duties such as cooking, cleaning, washing clothes and looking after their children's education and upbringing. Rearing milking animals and supplying milk to the village dairy co-operative has become an additional activity for many women. It enables them to earn extra income for better household management. Lately, large numbers of younger men and women frequently visit the nearby town of Mandya for shopping and entertainment. Cinemas, shopping centres and restaurants are the main urban attractions. On an average, a Wangala man goes to Mandya about ten times a month. The buses are always overloaded and often carry passengers even on the roof top.

Closer interaction and exposure to urban lifestyles has brought changes in village attitudes and behaviour which have had a profound impact on living conditions. Families now prepare better and tastier food at home and keep their houses neat and tidy. A greater awareness of the advantages of small families is noticeable among younger women. It is said that even if their husbands are reluctant, wives often volunteer to persuade their husbands to adopt family welfare measures. Wangala's educated girls now read magazines and books borrowed from the school and village library. A large number of households use modern domestic equipment such as electric fans, iron boxes, radios, television sets, grinders, electric stoves and mixers. Young mothers now take interest in sending their children to school. Consequently, the number of school drop-outs has considerably declined. Better education of girls in Wangala has helped them change their attitudes and behaviour. These positive changes in the attitudes of younger women instil the hope that they have greater potential and aptitude to initiate further beneficial socio-economic changes in the village. They only need better education and opportunities. Realising this, both the central and state governments have undertaken the implementation of a total literacy campaign to promote literacy and awareness among the illiterates in the age group nine to thirtyfive years of age and a large number of districts are covered in the country under the programme called Literacy Mission.

SIX

The Pros and Cons of Wangala's Socio-economic Development

*E*conomic prosperity and improved awareness have brought in their fold several social changes in Wangala, some for the better and some for the worse. Age-old customs, traditions and social beliefs have undergone revolutionary changes.

From Superstition to Rationality

Superstitions have given way to better understanding among the younger people. Illness and family problems earlier attributed to the anger of gods are now reasoned out and the treatment or solutions are more practical. Most of the educated and enlightened adopt a scientific approach in solving their personal problems. The best example in this regard is the voluntary initiative of restricting fertility by following family welfare methods. Their increased income has been invested in better living conditions, facilities and comforts, and an improvement of their social status.

Economic improvement enabled wealthier peasants to construct new houses and RCC buildings, to purchase scooters and motorcycles, radios and television sets, modern household equipment and kitchen aids. These facilities and comforts have heralded the adoption of new lifestyles and attitudes, particularly among younger people. The greater advantages that smaller families are perceived to offer have developed the tendency among both literate and illiterate young people to opt for independent living. In the process many have severed their family ties with their parents and brothers. The conflicts and tensions arising out of this individualistic behaviour create misunderstanding and separation. It is often said that the new daughters-in-law do not get along well with the family and thereby induce their husbands to insist on partitioning the joint family property. Thus the strength of the joint family system wherein the members had to show strict obedience and loyalty to the head of the family is threatened. A large number of these smaller families with more liberal attitudes and outlook became socially and economically vulnerable. Consequently, family cohesion and adherence to established social and moral values have been adversely affected.

Growing Social Unrest

Rapid population growth leading to poverty, unemployment and frustration among young people is reflected in social unrest and tension in the villages. A large number of educated and unemployed youth who could not settle down to farming are either engaged in village politics or idling their time. Many become liabilities to their families rather than contributing to family production or income; they take a lion's share out of the family income for their education and better living. This has caused resentment among other members of the family creating inter-personal and intra-family conflicts and misunderstandings. Respect and obedience to parents and village elders is gradually declining. The exposure to an urban lifestyle, individualistic behaviour and outlook of these semi-literates have led to the disintegration of the joint family system and division of property. Many such 'liberated' young unemployed and under-employed among the rich and poor families have become addicted to undesirable habits and lifestyles and anti-social activities that adversely affect and disturb village social harmony and moral values. The established traditional social norms and moral and ethical values which formed a solid foundation of Wangala's earlier social order are now disregarded and family tension and social unrest are common.

The Effects of Alcoholism

Alcoholism has caused severe damage to Wangala's economic and social life. Earlier, only some Voddas and Scheduled Caste people drank toddy in the village. Previously, it was taboo and socially unacceptable for Peasants to consume liquor. But now more than 50 per cent of the young and middle aged Peasants are addicted to liquor. Drunkenness has become a common feature in rural areas. Many families have been economically, socially and morally ruined on account of continued excessive drinking of arrack by their men. Children and women suffer mental and physical agony and torture at the hands of their drunken men. Wangala's liquor shops and non-vegetarian restaurants have become attractive places for those who have developed drinking habits. They spend lavishly, unmindful of their resource limits and borrowings, often taking away their wives' jewellery, utensils and other valuables to pledge or sell. Some have sold their landed property to clear their debts. Moreover, they also make a nuisance of themselves by starting quarrels in public. This is a common situation found these days in most of rural India. The labouring classes are in the habit of consuming arrack in the evening, after the day's toiling, as they claim that liquor provides great relief to their mind and body. Thus, most village labourers nowadays demand liquor as a supplement to their wage payments. Besides, they also spend a major share of their wages on liquor and are often unable to provide minimum subsistence for their wives and children. To ensure their family's subsistence women often have to work as domestic and agricultural labourers. Considering the evil effects of liquor consumption, the government has expressed its intention to impose a ban on the sale of arrack in Karnataka.

Changing Untouchability

. Wangala's Scheduled Castes still remain backward in education and social status. Their socio-economic dependence on Peasants, illiteracy and ignorance are largely the main factors that contribute to their continued backwardness. It has become a vicious circle such that unless they are educated and assertive, their socio-economic conditions will not improve. Education enhances the level of awareness to enable the Scheduled Castes to join the mainstream. In Wangala, out of the many graduates, undergraduates and students who completed their secondary schooling, only four graduates, two undergraduates and five SSLC educated belong to the Scheduled Caste category. There are two nursery schools in the Scheduled Caste colony. Some of them attend higher secondary and undergraduate courses. Many still live in conditions of social inferiority and meekly accept the customs and traditions. Reservation and the benefits the law provides are not fully utilised by them, and most of them are still in bondage to the Peasants. They do not realise that they could lead a respectable life, just the same as their Peasant masters. Indigenous social forces pose obstacles in the way of full implementation of legislative measures. The state government has enacted two important pieces of legislation, viz., the *Protection of Civil Rights Act of 1977* and the *Scheduled Caste and Scheduled Tribe Prevention of Atrocities Act 1989* to prevent the practices of untouchability and atrocities against the Scheduled Castes and Scheduled Tribes. Under these legal provisions untouchability is declared a cognizable and punishable offence. An official state directorate has been set up with senior police officers to enforce the legal provisions. Fear of punishment has a deterrent effect on the Peasants and other upper castes. But many Scheduled Castes are reluctant to take recourse to the courts largely because of fear of social and economic insecurity. Of late, the growing discontent and the strong urge among the educated Scheduled Caste youth to come out of traditional bondage and social stigma has triggered off their rebellious instinct; it is driving them to assert their rights and social status. A few of them who are young and educated are beginning to refuse to work as agricultural labourers, though hardly any of them have as yet succeeded in pursuing non-agricultural activities. One graduate is employed in Mandya and another is driving an autorickshaw. Others are now beginning to think of starting some businesses. Yet so far this has not materialised. The reservations in government jobs and other public bodies may help those who are better educated.

Some of the rebellious youth have formed associations to mobilise the strength and support of their caste people to assert their rights and status. During my recent visit to Wangala's Scheduled Caste colony, some progressive youths from among them have openly expressed their resentment and grievances in the presence of some of Wangala's Peasant leaders. Such instances had never occurred before. Education and exposure has created an awareness among youth about the need for improvements in their lifestyle. A growing number of young boys and girls now attend Wangala's primary and higher secondary schools.

Leaders of the *Dalit* (oppressed castes) Association are working out plans and strategies for educating and creating awareness among their caste people to fight for their constitutional rights and social status. Increased awareness has helped them to claim the benefits provided under various government programmes and welfare schemes. Some have already availed of the benefits provided by the government and have improved their living conditions. A large number of them have constructed tiled-roof houses with government assistance under the People's Housing Scheme. Water supply, street lights and drainage facilities have been provided to their colonies, and a community hall has been constructed to help them conduct social and cultural activities. A colour television has been provided by the government and a large number of men and women from the community watch programmes. After 1980, some Scheduled Caste men have performed a number of dramas in their colony as well as in front of Wangala's *Marichowdi* temple. In recent years many Peasants from Wangala and other villages attended these performances without resentment. This contrasts with the Peasant boycott of a Scheduled Caste drama performance in 1954, which Scarlett Epstein described in her 1962 book.

The Caste Barriers are Weakening

An important social development in Wangala in recent years is the broadening social outlook among progressive Peasants and educated youth; consequently the intensity of the stigma of untouchability has been declining. This liberalisation in caste discrimination is further promoted by legislative measures. The outlawing of social oppression accompanied by economic pressures induced many Peasant elders to change their attitude towards the Scheduled Castes. Their earlier segregation and distancing from Peasant residences is gradually disappearing. Many Peasants have constructed their new houses adjacent to the old Scheduled Caste colony. At the same time, some Scheduled Caste men have started to assert their self-esteem and personal dignity in their social interaction with Peasants. Their clothes, attitude and lifestyle have also undergone changes. In the towns and cities, in cafes and restaurants and in the buses and cinemas the castes now mix unhesitatingly. They eat and drink together from the same plates and cups. Younger Scheduled Castes and Functionaries are emulating Peasants in their dress, lifestyle, attitude and social behaviour. Many wear modern clothing and have adopted changed lifestyles.

Thus, socio-economic development and change have had a tremendous impact on the thoughts, ideas and attitudes of Wangala people over the last forty years. Their traditional outlook, customs and social beliefs have changed significantly. Education and exposure to modern life have created greater awareness and adaptability and have brought about changes—some for the better but also some for the worse.

Wangala's Changes in Retrospect and Prospect

Wangala's transformation from traditional subsistence farming to modern scientific agriculture is in conformity with the regional development of the Mysore plains. Post-independence development programmes like the Community Development Project and Intensive Agricultural District Programme and the new opportunities created by successive government welfare schemes have largely contributed to the overall development of Wangala. Village development and a fast growth of public facilities as well as population increase, migration and a strategic location have raised Wangala's status in its vicinity and accelerated its growth. The village has become a centre of attraction in the neighbourhood. Economic prosperity has brought changes in living standards and material improvement. Education and exposure to outside influences have broadened the outlook of many, particularly the younger villagers, and have changed their attitudes and lifestyles noticeably. The emergence of a new enlightened and progressive political leadership is significant for initiating further desirable socio-political changes in Wangala.

On the negative side economic development has brought in its fold greater economic and social inequalities. Enterprising rich Peasants became wealthier and thus socially and politically stronger. By contrast, a large number of middle and small farmers and agricultural labourers are struggling hard to maintain their subsistence. The conventional rigid caste structure and social discrimination have undermined creative instincts and suppressed the entrepreneurial abilities of the poor and the socially depressed classes. The decline of sound social and moral values has adversely affected the social fabric of village life. The dowry menace and spreading alcoholism have had devastating effects on the lives of many families. The growing number of unemployed and under-employed, whose productive capacity is being wasted, creates concern about their future. All these factors have contributed to increasing social unrest, disunity and decline in moral and ethical standards. However, education and positive changes in attitudes among the young and enterprising men and women offers some hope for stabilising these disruptive forces. The progressive village situation is likely to create better opportunities for educated and enterprising youth and should promote their entrepreneurship. Much depends on how the wider economy and polity will develop over the next decades.

The process of development triggered by economic changes does not necessarily have an altogether beneficial impact on the lives of villagers. Scarlett Epstein's micro-level socio-economic studies clearly establish the fact that in underdeveloped societies the interaction between economic variables on the one hand and attitudinal and cultural ones on the other have far-reaching effects on how development proceeds; these variables need to be flexible and in harmony to accommodate the process of change. She rightly observes that macro-analysis in purely economic terms cannot offer appropriate solutions to the many varied socio-economic problems faced by developing societies. Her pioneering study and analysis of socio-economic changes in Wangala and Dalena indicate an important lesson for policy makers and development planners.

A full understanding of cultural factors and grassroots level problems in all their economic, political and social dimensions is a necessary precondition of any successful development plan and activity.

T. Scarlett Epstein observing goldsmith at work (Wangala, 1955)

T. Scarlett Epstein chatting with Wangala villagers (1955)

Wangala panchayat headquarters (1997)

Milk delivery at Dalena's Milk Co-operative Society (1997)

Bicycle repair, Wangala (1997)

Sugarcane crushing, Wangala (1997)

Kempamma (T. Scarlett Epstein) with T. Thimmegowda, A.P. Suryanarayana and Gopalegowda addressing their Dalena Farewell Function in June 1997

PART THREE

A Researcher's Views

T. SCARLETT EPSTEIN

Acknowledgements: This part is the end-product of a life-time's research in South Indian villages. Over the last fortyfive years there have been so many individuals and organisations that have helped my efforts that it is extremely difficult to name each separately. Therefore, I herewith record my gratitude and thanks to all those who in their different ways have helped to bring my studies to fruition. I hope they will understand and forgive that I do not name each of them individually.

The greatest debt I owe of course to my many village friends for their boundless generosity: they took me into their midst, patiently taught me their ways of life and made me feel I belong—I only wish I could make them realise the full extent of the deep gratitude and warm affection I feel for them.

SEVEN

The Preliminaries of a Field Study

*T*his part discusses and analyses the dramatic changes that have occurred in Wangala and Dalena over the past four decades and outlines the manifestation of continuity within these radical changes as perceived by a now retired social scientist. To enable readers to evaluate any personal bias they may suspect in my presentation I begin with a brief statement of the factors that I believe influenced my career development in general and how I perceive my relationship with Wangala and Dalena villagers.

RESEARCHERS ARE SUBJECT TO MANY INFLUENCES

Often when I read social science books I cannot help but wonder what influenced the authors to present and analyse their materials in the way they have done and if someone else with a different background may possibly have treated the same data quite differently or focused on a different problem altogether. Social science studies invariably are subjective; this is illustrated not only by the different aspects of socio-economic change that have been studied by different researchers but also by the decisions made on what data to collect and also how to gather and analyse them. Some researchers are convinced that numerical data derived from questionnaire surveys based on random sampling and subjected to sophisticated statistical analysis provide the only reliable exposition of the topic, whereas others believe that qualitative materials collected by personal observation and/or in the course of interviews offer the best insight. Again others favour a combination of quantitative and qualitative research methods.

To explain my own approach to the study of socio-economic changes at the micro-level I begin here with a brief account of my personal and academic background so that readers will be in a better position to understand and evaluate why I collected what data by which method and why I present the account of rural transformation and its analysis in my own chosen fashion.

Personal Background

In my case it was emigration that exerted the dominant influence on my research focus and on the way I related to the different types among my informants.

As a refugee from Nazi oppression I was one of the small proportion of Jews who were fortunate enough to escape from Vienna to Yugoslavia and subsequently to Albania. During this odyssey of emigration I experienced extreme poverty and real hunger. This made a lasting impression on me. In 1939 shortly before the last war when I was sixteen years old I managed to get to England. While still in Vienna I had aspired to become a medical doctor. On arrival in London I had to bury this ambition and concentrate on earning a living. I found employment as a machinist making ladies underwear in London's Eastend. Since my schooling had not equipped me with any skills to earn my living I became altogether disillusioned with learning. It took some years before I got myself to re-start studying by attending night school where I got a diploma in industrial administration. Scholarships helped me to take up full time study again first at Ruskin College, where in 1950 I gained the Oxford University Diploma in economics and political science. At the age of twenty-eight I proceeded to Manchester University to read economics. In 1954 shortly before I was due to sit for my finals I suffered a serious burn accident which hospitalised me for ten weeks. Having set my mind on graduating I was determined to take the degree examinations, even if it meant doing so from my hospital bed. The hospital and university authorities rallied round and helped me reach my goal: the hospital gave me a private room for the period of the examinations, faculty members volunteered to act as invigilators and as I did not have the use of my right hand, departmental secretaries came equipped with a typewriter to take down my dictated answers to examination questions. For me it was all a great challenge. It reinforced my fighting spirit, which has stood me in good stead for the rest of my life. It has since given me strength to overcome many other difficulties I encountered. Altogether it made me tougher and more determined to succeed. I was of course overjoyed when word reached me in hospital that I had been awarded a II (i) B.A. (Honours) economics degree; under the circumstances I was proud of my achievement. It provided the basis for a research assistantship that enabled me to begin my doctoral studies in 1954 and with it my subsequent academic career.

The Influence of Supervisors

I consider myself fortunate in having had three supervisors each of whom not only influenced the conduct of my doctoral studies in his specific and positive way but also offered me personal help and support. They are each considered outstanding authorities in their respective fields.

While I was a graduate student my Professor, the late (Sir) W. Arthur Lewis, worked on *The Theory of Economic Growth* (1955), which has since come to be generally regarded as a classic in the subject. He sponsored my interests in Third World development and gave me my first training in development economics. He also taught me the strategic role of quantitative data in economic analysis.

The late Professor Max Gluckman enthused me about the method of social anthropology and convinced me of the insight qualitative case material collected by means of 'participant observation' can provide for the understanding of social change processes. He also helped me get a Rockefeller Research Fellowship to fund my field studies.

Professor M.N. Srinivas, the most eminent Indian social anthropologist, as a Visiting Professor at Manchester University in the early 1950s kindled my interests in Indian society and initiated me into South Indian cultures. Originating from Mysore he was familiar with the local scene and was therefore in a position to suggest the topic of my studies. His concepts of Sanskritisation and dominant caste helped me to understand cultural changes in South Indian societies. He was also instrumental in my settling into South Indian life and in the selection of Wangala as my first research site.

BREAKING NEW GROUND

All this should help to explain why as a student of economics I conducted two years of anthropological-style micro-level studies on the

'Impact of Irrigation on the Socio-economic System of South Indian Villages'. In my own research I attempted a synthesis of the different research focuses and approaches instilled in me by my three teachers, each derived from a different academic background. I thus crossed the conventional academic disciplinary boundaries and tried to develop a truly interdisciplinary approach to the study of socio-economic change at the micro-level.

For a student of economics my style of research then was a daring venture. It meant that in many cases I myself had to design without much guidance from anyone, methods of collecting, processing and analysing micro-economic data, such as household budgets, details of productive and non-productive household property, input–output of crops, etc. I often blush now when I think of how naive I was then, but in my own defence it must be said that it was not easy for me to work it all out by myself while living on my own in villages far from libraries and academic discussion. Even when I did put my problems in writing to some of the Manchester University faculty who worked in the field of rural development I got very little help. They admitted that they were themselves just then still trying to prepare procedures of tackling the problems I faced and expressed their interest in learning from my own experiences. Though this was flattering for a graduate student it did not amount to much help!

My earlier life as a refugee when I had personally experienced poverty and hunger made me empathise with the underprivileged and should help to explain my interest in and empathy with the poorest stratum in society.

I completed my fieldwork in the South Indian villages in 1956. The year after returning to England I married A.L. Epstein, a fellow anthropologist at Manchester University, who had done field studies in Central Africa for which he had already received his doctorate. In 1958 I was awarded my doctorate and in 1962 a revised version of my Ph.D. thesis was published under the title *Economic Development and Social Change in South India*. After having got my doctorate both my husband and I joined the staff of the Australian National University as research fellows. This provided us with a base from which to conduct more field studies in Papua New Guinea. I continued there to focus on socio-economic change processes and closely examined the impact of cultural factors which promote and also those that hamper response to new economic opportunities at the micro-society level. A few years later our two daughters were born. All this meant that for fifteen years after I had left India I was almost completely out of touch with my South Indian friends.

THE LOGISTICS OF MY FIRST FIELD STUDY, 1954-56

As a result of the influence my supervisors had exerted over my academic background I decided to settle in these South Indian villages to collect a great deal of micro-economic quantitative data as well as a lot of anthropological qualitative materials (for details of my research methodology see Epstein, 1973: 9) during my first spell of fieldwork.

Learning the Vernacular

The logistics of fieldwork posed the first hurdle. Before I could hope to get villagers to allow me to live among them and establish rapport with them I obviously had to know at least the rudimentaries of their language. Before leaving for India I thought of finding digs in Mysore city in the expectation that this would help me to pick up quickly the essentials of the vernacular. Alas, I had obviously been oblivious of the fact that orthodox Hindus consider us Europeans polluting because of our beef-eating habit; they are therefore not prepared to share their homes with any of us. Since most of the Mysore houses that were large enough to accommodate an additional person seemed to be owned by orthodox Hindus all my attempts to find digs were frustrated. After grappling with this problem for some time without getting anywhere a fortunate incident occurred. I was invited to stay with the family of one of the professors at Mysore University while he himself went for a few weeks to another university. The household was orthodox to the extreme but because the professor considered my presence auspicious, he invited me to join them during his absence. None of them could speak any English and in order to communicate at all I therefore had to learn Kannada, the vernacular. My hosts were very kind and took a lot of trouble to help me. They initiated me into the life of a Hindu household: I learned to take off my outdoor footgear and to wash my feet before entering the house, to wash my hands before sitting crosslegged down to eat on a mat on the floor. I learned to eat with my right hand while keeping my left hand behind my back. My hosts always took me along on their frequent visits to their many kin and in doing so taught me genealogical terms and the names of the various dishes I was offered. Then in the evenings back in the house they usually tested how much I remembered of what I had been told. During these sessions they often roared with laughter while I had difficulty in discovering the meaning of what I had said to amuse them so much. Learning a language in this way is often tough but it is also very effective. After three weeks of this intensive language learning I felt I was ready to start my fieldwork.

WANGALA, MY FIRST STUDY SITE

I had already prepared a specification of what kind of research site I wanted: it had to be a multi-caste village with about 200 households, some irrigated lands with a place for me to stay. Through the kind intervention of Professor M.N. Srinivas, who was well familiar with Mysore's rural areas, I managed to find Wangala. It fitted my specifications perfectly and even had a disused Public Works Department (PWD) bungalow which was made available to me. He also helped me find a research assistant by introducing me to Professor A.P. Srinivasamurthy, whose younger brother A.P. Suryanarayana— called Suri for short—had just completed his M.A.(statistics) and was prepared to venture into village life to work with me. This was the beginning of a close friendship between Suri and myself which has lasted now over four decades. As there were no Brahmin households in Wangala to accommodate Suri, we decided that he and I should share the little house allocated to me. Since this meant a sacrifice for him in return I undertook to keep a Brahmanical style vegetarian kitchen and engaged a cook accordingly.

Suri proved himself very efficient not only as research assistant but also as household manager. As a graduate student who had faced a hard time in England trying to live on a meagre scholarship I found it strange to be all of a sudden expected to employ several servants to do our various household chores. But Suri patiently explained that besides the cook we needed another three servants: one woman to fetch water for us from the nearby well, another one to clean the front of the house and a sweeper to clean the pit latrine at the back. As soon as I agreed Suri took over the employment procedures. The village headman recommended a number of villagers for the jobs. Suri interviewed them while I watched intently. I listened with amusement to the ongoing bargaining process. From what I gathered Suri obviously thought their individual demands excessive; he was convinced that they asked twice as much pay from me than they could expect from a local employer. When I calculated the sterling equivalent of the differences involved I was amazed by the pittance. Though my scholarship funds were strictly limited I had a budget for household expenditure. Therefore, I tried to dissuade Suri from bargaining. As I found out only later, he rightly insisted that our relationship with villagers should start on the right footing rather than for us to be treated as wealthy outsiders. It made me appreciate there and then that poverty is culture-specific and in general a relative concept. In England before leaving for India I ranked as a 'poor' student. Yet when I moved into Wangala and unpacked my belongings villagers who had come to watch this novel process marvelled at seeing my various items of camping equipment—such as a plastic wardrobe, bucket shower, etc. It all seemed to them to indicate that I was a person of considerable wealth. Chatting to each other I heard them say that they thought a rich *maharani* (queen) had moved into their village, which greatly amused me. The bungalow we had taken over was pretty dilapidated: the roof leaked, the interior walls were pitch black. Yet we were lucky to have found a roof over our heads. I was determined to get the walls cleaned; I bought a bucket, brush and whitewash and we put a man on the job. This was a most frustrating experience. As soon as the walls dried they were as black as they had been before. I had no idea how we could solve this problem. Then the late Mr B. Dasegowda, Manager of the Mandya sugar factory, drove up in a big limousine which looked quite out of place in front of our little old house. He had heard that a strange white young woman had moved into Wangala and he came to see whether I needed any help. I pointed at the black walls and enquired what we could do to clean them. He smiled and responded 'you foreigners frown at our ways of doing things, so I don't think there is any point in my advising you', to which I immediately responded that I believe while in India do as the Indians do! He then told me that to get the walls clean they must first be sealed by the application of cowdung and only then whitewashed. We followed his advice and I was pleasantly surprised when our walls turned out sparkling white. This incident taught me another early lesson: I began to appreciate the advantages cowdung offers and why it plays such an important role in rural India.

At first the villagers were understandably curious to know why a young white woman had decided to settle in their village and learn about their lives. They seemed pleased when I explained that I intended to write a book about their village and a number of them impressed on me that in my write-up I must mention their real names rather then the nicknames by which they were known in the village.

FIELD STUDY AND WHAT IT INVOLVES

Suri and I kept an open house and let it be known that we always welcomed visitors. Villagers took advantage of the cool shelter our bungalow provided and the *beedis* (country cigarettes) that we offered them. Thus besides our more systematic data collection we gained a lot of insight into the local culture just by listening to their gossip. Many nights we stayed up late with them as our visitors appeared to enjoy the bright light from our pressure lamp. As I kept to the rule of writing up always all the data I had gathered during the day before going to sleep, I often did not get to bed before the early hours of the morning.

Together with Suri I attended all the functions and ceremonies that were taking place in the villages. During the wedding season in Wangala eleven marriages took place each lasting three days. Suri and I always noted down separately our observations of the same events. Though enjoyable to watch the colourful ceremonies it was also pretty exhausting to take note of everything that was going on. In the evenings when we often got back late to our house we always compared our notes. Often we discovered discrepancies in the various data we collected which then led us to cross-check with informants to enable accuracy and reliability.

Though I found this kind of life quite demanding I also enjoyed every moment of it. Living in the midst of a small society does not only provide an excellent base for learning about different cultures and ways of life, which I found fascinating, but also at a personal level it offers the pleasurable experience of belonging; of shared joys and shared sorrows. Wedding ceremonies were joyful occasions, sickness and death brought sadness. A typhoid epidemic broke out in Wangala during my stay. Realising it I rushed to the Mandya health authorities requesting them to come and inoculate the villagers. A doctor arrived pretty quickly and I encouraged my village friends to have themselves protected against typhoid. Many did, but quite a few did not. There were then a few deaths in the village, which made us all very sad. One of those who had died was a young girl. Her kin blamed her death on the fact that she had failed to observe her menstrual taboo. Observing her funerary rites I had difficulty in keeping back my tears. As is the custom her elder brother walked round her body lying in the grave carrying a mudpot full of water; his younger brother broke a hole into the pot every time he passed him. The gushing of the water from the pot as the young man carried it round the grave appeared a symbolic sign of the ebbing away of life.

There were of course also many pleasurable occasions. For instance, I clearly remember after all these years the day I had gone to the weekly Mandya fair together with some of my Wangala friends when a crowd of town beggars noticing my white face began to surround me asking for money. At first I felt a bit worried being engulfed by this crowd of relentless beggars. But my villagers soon pushed them aside shouting at them to go away, 'she lives with us and is *one of us!*' This spontaneous response was music to my ears and made me feel really good.

There were of course also times when I found life in the village difficult. The continuous presence of villagers who obviously did not appreciate my need for privacy often made me feel claustrophobic. To get over it I went for walks, but even then I was followed by well-meaning and friendly villagers and crowds of children, all of whom wanted to know where I intended to go. On such occasions it took me all my time not to lose my temper. But such negative feelings were far outweighed by the joy of experiencing the warmth of belonging. This was a particularly thrilling experience for someone like me, who at an early age in Austria, the country of my birth, had become rootless because of Nazi persecution.

THE IMPORTANCE OF A FRIENDSHIP NETWORK

Some of the hardships of fieldwork I experienced were also ameliorated by the kindness shown me by the Van Ingen family, who as European taxidermists had lived in Mysore for many years and spoke the vernacular fluently. The late John D. van Ingen, one of the Van Ingen brothers, was so worried about my isolated lifestyle and what would happen if I needed urgent medical help that he kept telling me to invest in some means of transport. I could see the sense in his arguments but my limited funds allowed me to buy only a second-hand bicycle. At first I cycled happily along the unsealed and narrow mud roads, but soon I began to fall off my cycle when facing cattle not prepared to give way to the cyclist. My cycle therefore was not much use and certainly would not enable me to get quickly to Mandya if I needed to do so. Realising my financial problems Mr Van Ingen then kindly offered to make available to me for the duration of my stay a second-hand car as long as I could pay the running expenses.

This was too good an offer to refuse. He gave me the use of an old Hindustan car, which I called *Sangi* and which helped me to get about easily; it was also of course a great attraction for my village friends,

who regularly joined me on my trips to the weekly fair in Mandya
town. Each member of the Van Ingen family helped me in their specific ways. For Christmas 1955, I joined the whole Van Ingen family
in their customary festivities including a duckshoot and a memorable
picnic at one of Mysore's idyllic spots besides a large pond. Barbara
van Ingen, John D's sister-in-law, also became a good friend of mine.
As the daughter of Mr Flagherty, the pioneer film maker who had
made the film *Elephant Boy* in Mysore with Sabu as the star per-
former, Barbara had become an expert photographer. Being a sensi-
tive person she always felt reluctant to photograph people without
their expressed permission. On her frequent visits to my village home
my local friends were keen for her to photograph them, which
pleased her greatly. Thanks to her photographic skills and her generosity I accumulated a lot of excellent photographs of my many
village friends.

The year I had allowed myself to stay in Wangala passed far too
quickly. The day before we moved out of Wangala I presented *veelya*
(areca nuts and betel leaves) to each household, which is the customary farewell by a young girl when she moves to her husband's village
after marriage. The emotional scenes on that occasion have remained
deeply imprinted on my mind ever since.

As much as I would have wanted to stay on in Wangala my research
focus required me to study not only a village that had benefited from
irrigation but also another one with dry lands. Thus to conduct a valid
comparative study of the impact of irrigation I had to find a village
similar to Wangala in all aspects except for access to irrigation.

It was of course a lot easier to find a second village than it had been
to find my first field site. During the one year I had spent in Wangala
I had established good relations not only with local villagers but also
administrators and dignitaries in Mandya.

Because of the novelty of a young European woman living by herself in an Indian village, my fame seemed to have spread wide and afar.
Many federal and state ministers as well as senior administrators came
to see for themselves how I managed to live. At first I was a bit shy
on these occasions but I soon got used to receiving such dignitaries.
Sometimes when the chairman of the Mandya sugar refinery visited
Mandya, he sent his driver and car with a note inviting me to join him
and some of his friends for dinner at the town guesthouse. I gladly
accepted and always dressed in my best sari for the occasion; it made
me feel like Cinderella on her night out.

OUR MOVE TO DALENA

By the time I moved to a new village I already knew quite a lot of the local language, which to the greatest amusement of my urban Indian friends I spoke with a broad village dialect. With the help of my many Indian friends we found Dalena where lands are above canal levels and therefore have remained dry. Dalena is very close to Wangala—only 6 miles distant as the crow flies. Both villages are situated near Mandya town and are part of Mandya *taluk*. Dalena was slightly smaller than Wangala in 1955 but both were multi-caste villages where Peasants formed the dominant caste and owned a large proportion of lands. In Dalena we rented the tiled-roof house of one of the villagers and arranged for the installation of electricity. Suri and I were thrilled when we could switch on the light after dark and no longer had to go through the tedious nightly process of lighting our pressure lamp. Thus Dalena exceeded my expectations of what I intended to find in a dry land study site.

However, although Dalena people on the whole also made us feel very welcome I often felt homesick for Wangala. I guess one's first field experience is like one's first love—one never gets it completely out of one's system. While staying in Dalena we often returned for a visit to Wangala. On such occasions I always felt as if I were return-ing home. Some of our Wangala friends ventured to visit us in Dalena. To my surprise their behaviour clearly indicated that they felt alien vis-à-vis Dalena villagers whereas they so obviously felt at home with Suri and myself.

Even only a brief visit to Dalena indicated that it differed signifi-cantly from Wangala. Dalena appeared lifeless during the day. There were hardly any people to be seen walking around the village in con-trast to Wangala where there were always lots of people, cattle and bullock carts throbbing through the village streets. This immediately posed the question: what are the reasons for this difference? During my eight-month stay in Dalena I think I managed to find the answer.

Having completed my field studies on South Indian village develop-ment I was keen to discover the impact of Community Development Projects. These projects were then considered by many as the panacea for all of India's rural sector problems. I therefore decided to spend a few weeks in Malavalli before leaving India.

My first fieldwork in South India was thus composed of one year in Wangala, a wet land village, eight months in Dalena, a dry land village and six weeks in Malavalli observing the work done in the pilot Community Development Project.

VILLAGE STUDY EXPERIENCE AND THE ADVANTAGES IT OFFERS

Looking back at these two years they represent the highlight in my career. I am now convinced that the anthropological style fieldwork I conducted constituted an apprenticeship that has stood me in good stead for the rest of my life; it has helped me to grasp the interaction of economic, political and social variables in individual and group behaviour at the various levels of society. For example, when in the 1970s as a member of the UK–UN Social Science Advisory Committee I was asked to attend UNESCO meetings in Paris and present the UK's views on the UNESCO Five Year Plan I listened to the discussions and was reminded of the many nights I had listened to village council discussions in South India and Papua New Guinea. It made me realise that the same attempts are dominant; namely, to try and reach a unanimous decision under conditions when unanimity is difficult to achieve. Although this was my first experience of addressing one of the large UN meetings, my speech, in which I related my village study experiences and their relevance, was hailed as path-breaking by many Third World delegates who then queued up for copies of what I had said. Though I understandably found this flattering, in my own mind I thanked my many village friends, who by sharing their lives with me had helped me to gain insight into the factors that affect social behaviour at all levels.

EIGHT

The Impact of Canal Irrigation on Wangala and Dalena, 1954-56

*B*efore canals reached Mandya *taluk* in 1934, villages in the area had largely subsistence economies. Uncertainty of rainfall and poor quality of soil restricted local ryots to subsistence cultivation of dry land crops; small scale sericulture and sheep-breeding provided the only village sources of cash income. Thus it was reasonable for me to assume that in pre-irrigation days, the economy of Dalena was almost identical with that of Wangala.

WANGALA AND ITS UNILINEAL CHANGES

The advent of irrigation upset the balance of these almost stagnant economies. To Wangala, irrigation brought one dominant new opportunity: the growing of cash crops such as sugarcane and paddy. To Dalena farmers, irrigation presented no such single outstanding opportunity. I looked upon my village studies as a piece of 'detective' work; namely to collect data from different sources about different phenomena and piece them together to present a meaningful analysis of the different socio-economic change processes apparent in Wangala and Dalena.

I began my field studies in Wangala by preparing a sketch map of the residential area (see sketch map 1955). This was an excellent way to get acquainted with the local scene. Suri and I walked around with paper and pencil drawing symbols for whatever we encountered: a square denoted a tiled-roof house, a triangle a thatched-roof hut and so on. Wherever we went we were always followed by crowds of children who turned out to be excellent informants. From them we learnt the caste and names of the different household heads as well as their lineages and many other relevant details. We also overheard a lot of interesting local gossip. We soon discovered that the caste settlement was separated by an area of waste land from that of the Scheduled Castes, then referred to as *Adi Karnatakas*. Different groups of children belonging to the respective settlement took us over in the two separate parts of Wangala. When we crossed from one to the other the children did not come with us, but others joined us. The caste barrier was then still strictly separating castes from Scheduled Castes and the children were obviously fully aware of it.

In trying to discover the impact of irrigation I had to learn not only about conditions as I found them but also what life had been like in these villages before the advent of canals. This meant collecting present day materials as well as all the available relevant historical primary and secondary data. My studies clearly indicated that canal irrigation had made Wangala altogether much more prosperous. Farmers were able to grow the more valuable crops of paddy and sugarcane. These crops required more labour than their traditional dry land millet crops, which meant more employment for local landless labour and also attracted migrant labourers to settle in Wangala during the agricultural peak seasons. Irrigation had thus raised Wangala's income with one stroke onto a higher level, though the degree of improvement in levels of living differed considerably between landowning farmers and landless labourers.

Tradition versus Modernity

The changes within Wangala resulting from irrigation strengthened the ties between Peasant caste farmers on the one hand and their landless Functionary caste and Scheduled Caste clients on the other. It thereby reinforced the traditional intra-village social system. At the same time external forces were trying to break these hereditary dependencies. India's independence in 1947 had set in motion a process of radical socio-political changes aiming at transforming India's hierarchical caste societies, which emphasised status ascription into egalitarian democratic social systems with universal adult franchise. For instance, legislation introduced democratically elected village panchayats with reserved seats for Scheduled Castes. It thereby

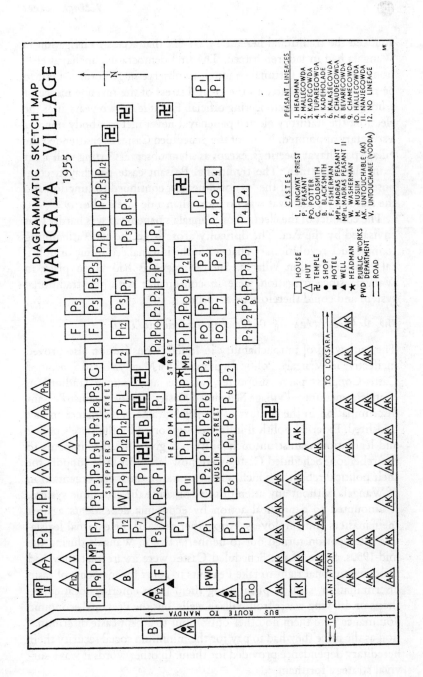

DIAGRAMMATIC SKETCH MAP
WANGALA VILLAGE
1955

CASTES
L. LINGAYAT PRIEST
P. PEASANT
PO. POTTER
G. GOLDSMITH
B. BLACKSMITH
F. FISHERMAN
MP. MADRAS PEASANT I
MP.II. MADRAS PEASANT II
W. WASHERMAN
M. MUSLIM
AK. UNTOUCHABLE (AK)
V. UNTOUCHABLE (VODDA)

PEASANT LINEAGES
1. HEADMAN
2. MALLEGOWDA
3. KADEGOWDA
4. TUPAREGOWDA
5. KADEHOLADE
6. KALASEGOWDA
7. CHAUDEGOWDA
8. BEVAREGOWDA
9. CHAMEGOWDA
10. HALLEGOWDA
11. NANJEGOWDA
12. NO LINEAGE

□ HOUSE
△ HUT
卐 TEMPLE
● SHOP
■ HOTEL
★ HEADMAN
PWD PUBLIC WORKS
       DEPARTMENT
═══ ROAD

SHEPHERD STREET
HEADMAN STREET
MUSLIM STREET

BUS ROUTE TO MANDYA
TO LOKSARA
TO
PLANTATION
N

attacked the traditional hereditary system that access to irrigation in Wangala had in fact reinforced. The first democratic panchayat elections which I was fortunate enough to observe in 1955 turned out to be no more than a farce to the great distress of the revenue inspector who was also the electioneering official. For at least two years after the election, the statutory elected panchayat never met as a body nor was a secretary appointed. None of the Scheduled Castes ever attended the village panchayat meetings, except as silent observers sitting well apart from the caste men. The traditional Peasant caste panchayat, composed of the elders of the 'major' lineages, continued to function and the statutory panchayat was no more than a de jure authority.

The conduct of the election of Wangala's panchayat was hardly that envisaged by the Act. The difficulty arose from the state attempting to introduce revolutionary changes in the internal economic or political relations within villages. Such changes as had taken place in Wangala since irrigation were in consonance with the traditional system and could therefore be absorbed in it.

The Difficulties of Outlawing Untouchability

The outlawing of untouchability in India's Constitution also proved ineffective in Wangala. Political agitation by a Mandya based Scheduled Caste Congress party supporter, who as an absentee landlord in Wangala encouraged village Scheduled Castes to rebel against Peasant discrimination in the context of the 1955 drama performance in fact backfired. External political influence supported by the state's policy and legislation against untouchability had given the first impetus to the rebellion. Scheduled Castes were now left with little support for their political rebellion which was an attack on the social organisation of Wangala without any attempt to re-organise the economic system. It amounted to a political action by economic dependents against their masters and employers. Altogether most of the external legislative intervention turned out to be ineffective in Wangala during the mid-1950s. Some of the Scheduled Castes were aware that they had the constitutional right to take Peasants to court for incidents of caste discrimination, such as prohibiting them from entering local coffee shops or drawing water from village wells, but the Peasants' economic dominance gave them no other option but to accept caste discrimination as the price they had to pay for the minimum social security their hereditary dependence provided for them. In other words it was a survival strategy for them.

All this made me analyse the impact of irrigation on Wangala's socio-political system in terms of unilinear changes in the sense that the new opportunities were in line with the former mode of economic organisation and therefore reinforced the traditional socio-political system to such an extent that it could withstand external interventions.

DALENA AND ITS MULTIFARIOUS CHANGES

On moving into Dalena I was immediately struck by how much it differed from Wangala. Dalena displayed much more radical socio-political changes than had taken place in Wangala, although it remained a dry land enclave in the midst of an irrigated belt. Dalena land was actually traversed by a canal yet remained completely dry. Across the canal Dalena farmers could see immediately before their eyes the benefits resulting from irrigation and exactly what was involved in growing cash crops. This spurred some of them onto efforts leading to their own economic progress, and encouraged them to participate in the economic growth resulting from irrigation in the region.

Dalena villagers, like Wangala people, referred to the advent of irrigation as the turning point in their history. Alternative economic opportunities which occurred in the new wet land region made dry land farming comparatively less advantageous to Dalena farmers.

Realising that economic development could only take place by reaching out into the wider economy they looked for opportunities outside Dalena. The village dry land continued to be cultivated, but mainly by female labour. This allowed men to take up other income-earning opportunities. Since they could not grow cash crops in their own village, many purchased newly irrigated land in neighbouring villages, where they would then grow crops for sale. Many Dalena families were shrewd enough and tried to marry their daughters into neighbouring irrigated villages to make sure they would be the first to hear whenever land came onto the market there. By this and other methods they managed to acquire a considerable wet land acreage outside their own village. In 1956 as much as 73 per cent of Dalena households owned and cultivated wet lands in the vicinity. Their extra-village network of relations put them into a strategic position to venture also into work outside farming. A fair number of Dalena ryots acted regularly as contractors for the building of canals and the accompanying road system. Most of Dalena's poorest farmers and landless have worked at one time or other as labourers for private contractors or for the PWD directly. Their contact with the administration made Dalena people realise the importance of literacy in particular and education in general. Accordingly, a few sent their sons to secondary school in Mandya and two of these students subsequently secured jobs in the Mandya administration. They worked in 1955 in the town's agricultural office and transmitted the latest techniques of farming to Dalena ryots. The *patel* was thus encouraged to experiment with the Japanese method of paddy cultivation on wet land he cultivated in neighbouring villages. Surprising as it may seem, as a native from a dry land village he won the prize for the best irrigated paddy cultivation in the region in 1954.

Their many extra-village contacts enabled Dalena men to take advantage of the new economic opportunities resulting from irrigation in the region. In 1956 altogether twentysix men (13 per cent of the male working population) were employed in Mandya, most of them worked as labourers in the sugar factory; others were clerks, orderlies or drivers. Dalena men also helped to provide the services needed by neighbouring irrigated villages. Some bought carts and strong bullocks and transported cane from nearby villages to Mandya's refinery at a daily hiring charge. Others again became cattle traders and/or middlemen in bullock sales.

Diversification of Economic Activities

By providing these services they enabled farmers of recently irrigated lands to concentrate on cultivating their lands. In doing so Dalena men first of all helped to extend the benefits of irrigation even to villages situated at the margin of the canal system; second and more important they spontaneously promoted the development of a regionally integrated economy. Farmers of irrigated lands were able to concentrate on farming, their traditional occupation, while Dalena and other like dry land villages provided them with the various new services irrigated crops require, such as access to purchasing strong bullocks, transport of their sugarcane to the Mandya refinery, cane-crushing and flour-milling facilities, etc. The development of this regionally integrated economy offered the advantages of specialisation and the division of labour. This desirable by-product of large irrigation schemes appears to have eluded the planners of the overall canal irrigation scheme and still seems to be ignored by planners of large irrigation schemes. This became apparent in talking in 1976 with a Filipino economist. As one of the expert consultants of the Asian Development Bank's updating of the Second Asian Agricultural Survey I was in Manila at the time of an IBRD (International Bank for Reconstruction and Development) feasibility study of a proposed large irrigation scheme. When I asked the Filipino economist who was involved in the study whether in their cost/benefit analysis they were taking into account also the benefits dry land villages at the mꞏr-gin of the scheme can derive, he looked a bit puzzled and did not quite understand what I had in mind. I then told him a little bit about the findings of my own studies of the impact of canal irrigation on wet and dry land villages in South India. This made him think and after a little while he answered 'we cannot take them into account because we cannot quantify these benefits!', which seemed a rather strange attitude to me.

The Disappearance of Traditional Hereditary Patron-Client Relationships

The diversification of economic activity which occurred in Dalena as a result of the advent of irrigation in the region was reflected in the village's social and political system. In contrast with Wangala where irrigation had reinforced the traditional hereditary labour relation-ship between Peasant farmers on the one hand and Functionaries and Scheduled Caste landless labourers on the other, in Dalena this relationship had already completely disappeared by 1955. This was so because local Peasant patrons who were already operating in the wider economy found the hereditary labour relationship with their clients inefficient and the annual reward in kind that it involved an unnecessary burden. They preferred to employ labour on a contract basis to work on their wet lands in neighbouring villages. Dalena's Scheduled Castes had no option but to accept the Peasants' decision to discontinue their customary relationship. For them it meant losing the assurance of a minimum of social security. The only way they could show their dissatisfaction with the turn of events was by dis-continuing to perform their traditional ritual services for their Peasant patrons. Already in 1956 I found a striking difference between the social matrix that existed in Wangala and Dalena. Dalena's social system did not operate any longer on the basis of the hereditary principle; panchayat membership was no longer based on hereditary elders, nor were relations between Peasants and Scheduled Castes based on hereditary links. Greater individualism had entered Dalena's social system since the diversification of its economy.

The broadening of Dalena's economic horizon also broadened villagers' political horizons. Unlike Wangala, where nobody read papers and only few were aware of the wider political issues, Dalena commuters were members of trade unions; as factory workers they not only participated in a strike but also became familiar with elected authority and majority decisions, political arrangements which differed radically from their customary hereditary succession in particular and ascribed status in general.

VILLAGE FACTIONS

In Dalena as in Wangala, there existed two factions organised on the principle of lineage with a floating support oscillating between the two major opposing factions. In the analysis of my 1954–56 research I considered the two factions in terms of the opposition between 'progressive' and 'conservative' village interests. In both villages one faction was led by men whose main concern was to preserve the traditional village system. They looked down upon their progressive entrepreneurial opponents, who in turn were keen to translate their economic success into ritual and political status; they considered them as 'nouveaux riches' without roots in the village society. Factions became operative on occasions of Hindu festivals when the ritual unity of the village was at stake. Wangala's factions were much less rigid than Dalena's simply because Wangala's progressives were all still full-time farmers just like the conservatives. Whenever there was a drought, or a cattle or crop disease, all villagers—disregarding which faction they supported—were equally affected and they all joined efforts to avoid the disaster. By contrast, in Dalena there were far fewer occasions which affected all villagers jointly and thereby served to unite them. Consequently, sectional interests outweighed joint interests. Dalena's progressives were also still farmers, but the major part of their income originated from activities carried on outside their own village. The *patel*, who was the leader of Dalena's progressives, was an outstanding innovator who ran commercial and industrial businesses. By contrast with Wangala, Dalena progressives did not seek ritual status in the village. Their faction represented a new element in village organisation; a break-away section which undermined the traditional unity of the village. To Dalena's *patel* the village ceremonies were no longer of great importance; he was much more interested in the wider political and social system in which his economic interests had come to be vested.

The hereditary principle of social organisation appeared to be compatible only with a closely integrated society, in which economic, political and ritual relations were concentrated within the boundaries of the village. Once the range of these relations was extended beyond the limits of the particular society, the dependence on fellow-villagers diminished and the personal character in the indigenous relationships gave way to an impersonal one. My 1954–56 study of Wangala's and Dalena's socio-economic systems thus provided interesting comparative data. I then argued that the impact of irrigation on Wangala produced a unilineal change by strengthening the farming economy and therefore also reinforcing the traditional socio-political system; whereas Dalena's diversification of economic activities represented multifarious changes. I argued that these multifarious economic changes that had taken place in Dalena since irrigation reached the area triggered off a more radical socio-political transformation. The diversification of Dalena's economy widened the economic horizon of the Dalena villagers and consequently also their political horizon. Already in 1955 they had so many different economic links with the regional economy that their political attitudes and social relations had changed accordingly.[1]

NOTE

1. For a detailed account of changes that had occurred in Wangala and Dalena by 1955 see Epstein, T.S., *Economic Development and Social Change in South India*, 1962, Manchester University Press; republished 1979, Media Promoters and Publishers Pvt Ltd, Bombay.

NINE

Re-exposure to Mysore Villages in 1970

$\mathcal{A}$mong economists the re-study of the same social micro-universe in the 1970s was then and still is a rare phenomenon. By contrast there existed already in 1970 a considerable number of anthropological longitudinal micro-studies. These longitudinal studies were of different types: some involved *continuous research* in the same small society over a number of years, others were *periodic re-studies* of the same society at regular or irregular intervals; and still others were *re-exposure* after a lengthy interval of time since the original study.

ADVANTAGES OF RE-EXPOSURE

My own re-exposure in 1970 to the societies I had studied intensively many years earlier was a fascinating experience. It convinced me that such re-exposure is the most effective means of studying socio-economic changes. It offers several major advantages: first of all, it makes researchers much more aware of the changes that have occurred than continuous studies are ever likely to do; second, it can build on earlier relationships and does not necessitate spending time on building rapport with informants, therefore a lot of data can be collected in a relatively brief period; third, the earlier experiences and readily available baseline data can result in sound comparisons over time viewed by the same researchers; and fourth, by extrapolating from past trends of change it is possible to try and predict future socio-economic changes. Noticing the result of changes that have accumulated over a longer period of time is obviously much more striking than to observe slow and incremental socio-economic changes. It is therefore likely to lead to more insightful analysis of change processes.

Most social anthropologists dream of the opportunity to return some day to their field of study after years have elapsed just to see how the people and the place have changed. I too cherished the dream of re-visiting South India but had little hope that it would ever come true. The invitation to return to Wangala and Dalena, which I received quite unexpectedly from Mr S. Schoenherr, my German colleague, early in 1970, gave me the unexpected chance to realise my secretly-held desire and return to the very same villages where I had done my first piece of fieldwork from 1954 to 1956. Having found that my 1962 book contained valuable background material he had been attracted to conduct his doctoral studies in Wangala and Dalena. Mr Schoenherr invited me to return largely because many of my village friends kept telling him that they were eager to see me again.

Fifteen years had passed since I left South India. In the meantime I had taken up a research fellowship at the Australian National University and conducted socio-economic studies among a New Guinea tribal people—this overshadowed my interest in India. I had also lost such command as I had had of the language. Therefore, on receipt of Mr Schoenherr's invitation I was worried that it would be a long and difficult task for me to re-establish my relationship with my many South Indian village friends after such a long absence. Yet I was overjoyed at the chance of re-visiting what I had come to regard as 'my' South Indian villages. Much as I would have liked to spend another two years in Wangala and Dalena, personal circumstances made a long spell of fieldwork impossible—I could spend no more than five weeks in the field.

As I left for my re-study I took with me a lot of the data I had collected earlier: the tattered village sketch maps which used to decorate the walls of my village home, a list of my sample households and the processed details I had calculated for each of them, sets of blank schedules, which I had used in 1954–56, one copy of all the notes I had collected then and so on. I also took along a copy of the volume I had published in the meantime to prove to my village friends that I had kept my promise and written a book about their way of life. When I left South India in 1956 none of them was literate in English. I could not communicate with them in writing nor did I see any point in sending them a book about their villages which none of them would be able to read. When I returned in 1970 I had my first chance of showing the book to them. Though they still could not read it they were happy to know that their village had been immortalised in book form and also took pride in their photographs that appeared in my book.

Suri, who by the time I reached South India in 1970 was working with the Bureau of Statistics in Bangalore, had managed to get leave so that he could come with me for our re-study.

A Royal Welcome

While driving back to the villages I was wondering all the time how my village friends would receive me and kept hoping they still remembered me. I need not have worried: I received a truly royal welcome. Having been told that on my first day back in Mysore the daughter of one of Dalena *patel's* younger brothers was getting married, we first called into Dalena. The welcome I received from the Dalena villagers was indeed overwhelming. My fears of having completely forgotten their vernacular were soon dispelled: as they surrounded me, many of them chattering away at the same time, I began to answer their questions and in turn put many to them. After the warm reception I had in Dalena I began to expect big things from Wangala too. The warmth of their welcome exceeded even my highest expectations. The old headman, Chennamma, his distinguished-looking wife, Tugowda, the enterprising leader of what I used to call the 'progressive' faction and many of my old friends who were now in their seventies, gathered round me and took it in turn to touch my toes and their eyes three times in succession as a sign of respect. Many young men now in their late teens or early twenties crowded round to shake hands with me. Karegowda, who was about four years old in 1954 and who was then my special favourite in the village, rushed up to me and we embraced in a way quite uncommon among South Indian villagers. He kept muttering how much he had missed me throughout the years and how happy he was to see me again. Altogether, my return to Wangala and Dalena provided some of the most moving experiences I have ever had.

To my greatest regret on my return in 1970 I could not arrange to settle in the villages for my brief stay. Together with Mr Schoenherr's research team we found suitable accommodation in the Mandya Sugar Refinery Guesthouse. I designed a research plan together with Suri.

Thanks to Mr Schoenherr and his team's willing help as well as the villagers' readiness to answer our searching questions we managed to collect a multitude of information which enabled me to publish a book and several articles.

Reconnecting

Every day early in the morning Mr Schoenherr drove us either to Wangala or Dalena; we usually returned only after dark. In the evenings we compared our records and I typed my field notes. Thus we worked seven days a week often ten to twelve hours a day. Needless to say we found this intensive concentration pretty exhausting. Yet we loved every moment of it. We were happy not only with all the fascinating data we were collecting but more importantly we enjoyed again the 'warmth of belonging' I had already experienced during my first spell of fieldwork. Our village friends were genuinely pleased to have us back in their midst. They had come to regard Suri and myself as an inseparable research team. They kept telling me that during the fifteen intervening years a number of my kin had visited them. At first I was puzzled by this statement, not being aware that any of my kin had ever ventured to South India. But I soon realised that they were using the classificatory system of kinship terminology. I knew that a considerable number of anthropologists when travelling between Bangalore and Mysore had made the effort to visit 'my' villages about which they had read in my book. The villagers classified men and women of my own generation as my siblings and younger researchers as my sons and daughters. Although they realised that Mr Schoenherr was not my biological offspring they referred to him as my 'son'. They took no account of the fact that I had never before met Mr Schoenherr or any of the other researchers who had come to see them. Meeting again my South Indian village friends after a lapse of fifteen years has made me feel much more humble vis-à-vis them and made me change my personal values and sets of priorities. This lesson was dramatically brought home to me when on my return to Wangala I sought to meet again one of my closest village friends who in the intervening years had gone almost blind; when I approached him he fumbled with his hands reaching out to me; when I took his hands in mine he said quietly and with great dignity: 'Now that I know you are still alive and have come back to see me again I can die in peace.' I felt very small indeed.

NEW ECONOMIC OPPORTUNITIES IN MANDYA DISTRICT

The years between 1955 and 1970 saw a considerable economic expansion of Mandya district's integrated regional economy, the formation of which I had noted in my earlier studies. The authorities realised the area's overall economic potential and consequently in 1962 it was included in the All-India Intensive Agricultural District Programme (IADP). The programme aimed at, among other things, maximisation of production by providing facilities such as supplies of improved seeds, fertilisers, agricultural credit and technical know-how and marketing to all the participating farmers. The state authorities devoted considerable amounts of money and effort to promote agricultural development in Mandya district. During the year 1970–71 public expenditure on agricultural development per head in Mandya district was more than three times that in the neighbouring Mysore district: in the former it was Rs 1.60 while in the latter only Rs 0.50, although the amount spent in Mandya district on rural development was still considerably less than what the state spent on industrialisation.

The further opportunities which had come within reach of Wangala and Dalena by 1970, I discuss under the headings: (*a*) Agricultural Productivity; (*b*) Cane versus Jaggery; (*c*) Regional Growth; (*d*) Educational Facilities; and (*e*) Education and Urban Orientation.

Agricultural Productivity was increased through extension of irrigation and also by higher per acre crop yields. Between 1955 and 1970 Wangala's wet land area increased by as much as 69 per cent; 88 per cent of this extension of irrigation benefited villagers and outsiders acquired the remaining 12 per cent of wet lands. In 1955 slightly more than half of Wangala had access to canal irrigation; by 1970 as much as 80 per cent of Wangala's lands were irrigated. Rising wet land prices reflected the increase in agricultural productivity of irrigated land. In Wangala wet land prices increased by about 330 per cent between 1958 and 1971 while the consumer price index for the same period amounted to about 280.

The use of highyielding variety (HYV) seeds and fertiliser made available to farmers on credit through village co-operative societies further promoted higher crop yields. Between 1955 and 1970 in Wangala average cane yields increased by 5 per cent and paddy yields by 38 per cent. Dalena farmers also increased their average yield per acre of wet land situated in neighbouring villages by 11 per cent for cane and 15 per cent for paddy, but the benefit they could derive from increased productivity of wet lands was obviously limited by the wet land acreage they managed to acquire outside their own village.

Cane versus Jaggery   South Indian cane growers have the option of supplying their cane to a refinery where it is purified into white sugar or, of processing it into cubes of jaggery for sale as brown sugar. For many years prices paid by the refinery for cane exceeded jaggery prices. Therefore, except for rare occasions in 1955 cane farmers wanted to sell their crops to the Mandya refinery and were keen to take advantage of the crop contracts this arrangement involved. They often tried to sell to the refinery cane they had grown without a contract; it was difficult for the refinery to refuse such illegitimate supplies.

All this changed drastically after the stricter enforcement of prohibition in Mysore state and throughout most other parts of India in 1962. This was so simply because jaggery lends itself readily for illegal distilling. It became a highly desired and highly priced commodity in people's attempts to circumvent prohibition laws. Intermediaries in these illicit transactions toured sugarcane areas and offered premium prices for jaggery. Wangala farmers were quick to respond to this attractive new opportunity; the total area under cane cultivation increased by as much as 55 per cent between 1962 and 1963. Farmers not only planted larger areas under cane but they also underfulfilled their contracts with the factory. The greater comparative advantage which jaggery offered over cane sales adversely affected the Mandya refinery. In 1966 it incurred a deficit before tax of Rs 21,444. The refinery losses were the village cane crushers' gains. Soon after one of Wangala's magnates had opened the first cane crusher in the village jaggery prices almost doubled. High jaggery prices increased the demand for village cane processing facilities. Dalena's enterprising headman established a cane crusher and a flour mill at a strategic road junction along the Mysore highway. At the same time his younger brother decided to move his machinery from Dalena to a site on the main road. Wangala farmers also were keen to share in this jaggery boom. By 1968 there were as many as eight crushers in the village. To the great disappointment of some of these new Peasant entrepreneurs, the Mysore government decided just then to remove prohibition once more from most parts of the state. This resulted almost immediately in a severe fall in jaggery prices. Consequently, selling cane to the refinery instead of processing it into jaggery became once more comparatively more attractive to cane producers in the Mandya region. In turn this reduction in the demand for jaggery led to village cane crushers standing idle for many months in the year and hence a loss to their owners. The jaggery boom brought more lasting gains to Dalena than to Wangala entrepreneurs, simply because they were able to establish their cane crushers and rice mills by the side of the main Mysore highway, where demand for their services continued although at a reduced rate. After the removal of prohibition lorries were no longer prepared to tour the rural areas for jaggery and therefore Wangala's cane crushers, which produced in excess of local needs, remained idle for many months in the year.

Regional Growth   Mandya district's integrated regional economy grew at an increasing rate between 1955 and 1970. Irrigation and the sugar refinery triggered off the establishment of several other industrial enterprises. This led to a considerable increase in the population of Mandya town, which almost trebled between 1951 and 1971. This influx of people created further economic opportunities: new houses were being built and more cafes and other amenities opened up to meet the increasing requirements of the growing population. In 1956 there was only one cinema hall in Mandya; by 1970 there were four. The weekly fair in Mandya attracted growing numbers of sellers and buyers from a widening area. The opportunities resulting from Mandya's economic expansion attracted not only immigrants from near and far in search of work but also many small and marginal farmers as well as landless labourers within a commuting radius who sought urban employment and travelled daily for work from their village homes.

The numerous Dalena wage earners provided a good example of such village commuters. The experience of urban employment widened the horizon of these commuters which was reflected in their *village extroversion.*

Educational Facilities   increased considerably between 1955 and 1970. The 1961 Mysore state Compulsory Primary Education Act provided the establishment of primary schools within a walking distance of 1 mile from every child in the state and made parents responsible for sending their children to school. Compulsory primary education led to a high enrolment rate of children, but attendance rates still left a lot to be desired. After eight years of primary education successful students could go on to a four-year high school course. Between 1944 and 1966 the number of high schools in Mandya district increased from two to fifty. Tertiary educational facilities also expanded considerably during this period. In 1962 the Mandya Intermediate College was upgraded to a First Grade College offering B.A. degrees in arts subjects and B.Sc. degrees in science subjects. Moreover, there was also one college and one polytechnic offering courses in civil, mechanical and electrical engineering.

There was thus a substantial increase in educational facilities available to people in Mandya district between 1955 and 1970. However, the overwhelming majority of students belonged to the dominant Peasant caste. The state's attempts to encourage Scheduled Caste children to take advantage of education by the provision of scholarships, hostels and reserved places in colleges were not really successful, largely because of economic factors.

Education and Urban Orientation By 1970 Wangala also had five university graduates and four undergraduates. None of these young men was prepared to use their education for the benefit of their native village. All of them perceived their future in terms of urban professional employment. Education certainly furthered individual achievements but was it promoting rural development? State education seemed to suck the brightest out of the rural areas, who then became so alienated from their natal villages that they refused to return. Yet the development of India's rural areas which still house the large majority of the population was still a major problem. It made me wonder how anybody could expect the rural sector to progress while education denuded it of its brightest young people.

In 1970 I discussed this problem with Wangala's T. Thimmegowda, taking advantage of his fluency in English. He was then a junior lecturer at a Mandya college after having been awarded a first-class master's degree in economics at the University of Bangalore. We explored whether the young educated coming from a rural background should use their skills to help improve their native villages and if so how they should set about it. He understood perfectly well what I was driving at, but kept repeating over and over again that he felt too alienated from rural life ever to be prepared to settle back into a village. He demonstrated his alienation by walking around Wangala dressed like a city dweller wearing shirt, trousers and shoes, in sharp contrast to what ordinary young village men wear. The attitudes he then expressed were those of a young man rebelling against his elders and trying to establish his own identity.

*How and Why Wangala and Dalena Changed
between 1955 and 1970*

Both villages changed considerably in appearance. The most striking feature was the increased economic differentiation. It was not even necessary to collect statistical evidence to substantiate the claim of polarisation that had gone on between 1955 and 1970; it was so obvious. The lifestyle of the wealthier had considerably improved in every aspect: they had better housing, wore better clothing and looked better nourished. By contrast among landless labourers and marginal farmers housing had deteriorated, their clothing looked more tattered and their bodies seemed more emaciated.

The households with larger wet land acreages were strategically placed to improve their economic position; the more acres of wet land a family owned the greater was its overall income. During the fifteen years that had elapsed since my first field studies in Wangala and Dalena a decline in real wages had led to a deterioration in the levels of living among all those households that depended on employment for most of their income. On the other hand the wealthier parts of the villages had access to more and better facilities. Dalena had already been connected in 1955 with the state power supply; Wangala installed electricity in 1963 mainly to operate power cane crushers but also benefited from street lighting. A few of the village magnates, who had built for themselves nice modern two-storeyed houses by the main road passing through Wangala, formed a roadsite elite. The Scheduled Castes' settlement consisting mainly of landless labourers presented a stark contrast to the increased wealth among Peasant farm households. There poverty was glaringly obvious.

Wangala's Village Introversion

In 1955 I analysed the change that had taken place in Wangala as a result of the advent of canal irrigation in terms of a unilineal process. I was struck by the continuing effect of this process expressed in terms of resistance to outside interference in intra-village affairs even fifteen years later. I then decided to refer to this social phenomenon as *village introversion*.

Wangala's traditional social system on the whole continued unimpaired by exogenous attempts to bring about changes through more and more pieces of liberalising legislation offering the underprivileged positive discrimination. The rising rewards to be gained from wet land cultivation encouraged landowners to concentrate on maxi-mising crop productivity. To do so they needed ready access to labour which the local Scheduled Castes were keen to provide. This resulted in a further strengthening of the traditional hereditary labour rela-tionship between Peasant patrons and their untouchable client house-holds and was accompanied by continuing caste discrimination. When I enquired from the Scheduled Caste headman whether they were still performing dramas in the village he raised his eyebrows and said, 'you yourself saw what happened in 1955; it taught us a lesson and we therefore stopped our drama performances ever since!'

An Aborted Adi Karnataka Rebellion   The Scheduled Caste head-man bitterly complained that there had been hardly any changes in the discriminatory attitudes displayed by Peasants towards them in spite of all the legislative measures that outlawed caste discrimination. In support of his statement he quoted a recent incident:

A young Wangala Scheduled Caste had ordered a cup of coffee from one of Wangala's cafes. As it was handed to him outside in a glass specially kept for members of his caste, he saw that the cafe was empty and dared to go and sit inside. He was obviously aware of his constitutional right of access to coffeeshops and other like premises. However, unfortunately for him his hereditary Peasant patron just then happened to pass by. He was enraged when he saw that his Scheduled Caste client had dared to break traditional caste rules. He immediately ordered him to leave and threatened that he would hit him if he was not quick about it. The young man somewhat lin-gered whereupon the Peasant got hold of a coconut and indeed hit him good and proper. Being physically hurt and mentally humili-ated, he threatened to complain to the Mandya police about the assault. A few of the traditional Peasant caste panchayat members who had been attracted to the scene by the shouting immediately held an ad hoc meeting. The Scheduled Caste headman was called and it was pointed out to him that if his young subject insisted on taking his complaint to the Mandya police this would seriously upset the good relations which existed in the village between Peasants and Scheduled Castes. The Peasant who had committed the offence insisted that he had been justified in hitting the Scheduled Caste men for breaking customary caste rules and most Peasants gath-ered agreed with him. What had probably been quite an innocent action on the part of the young man came to be regarded as the heinous act of a rebel and he was treated as such. His Peasant master made it clear that if he insisted on taking the case to the Mandya police, he in turn would insist on immediate repayment of all the money the Scheduled Caste's family owed him. This finally clinched the matter. The young Scheduled Caste men accepted the situation and the whole matter was hushed up.

The event continued to feature prominently in Scheduled Caste gossip. Its account became increasingly more devoid from reality. One of Mandya's Scheduled Caste Congress party politicians distorted the story by telling us that the Wangala Peasant had actually been imprisoned for having hit one of the village's Scheduled Caste. What happened in fact was that the Peasant master decided some months after the incident to sever his hereditary relationship with the young man's household. Another local Scheduled Caste family stepped into the breach and this new labour relationship soon took on the character of a hereditary link. As a result the young rebel's household was deprived of one of their hereditary Peasant masters and consequently of one lot of annual rewards in kind. In this case, as in the drama incident of fifteen years ago, Peasants used economic sanctions to maintain their socio-political dominance in the village and the Scheduled Castes had no option but to accept their dependency.

Ascribed versus Achieved Status   The state's attempt to change Wangala's traditional political system of status ascription into a village democracy with universal adult franchise apparently failed to succeed in Wangala. The Mysore Village Panchayats and Local Boards Act, 1959 which ushered in a new system of panchayati raj hardly affected the traditional hereditary village political system. Presumably to make for more effective village government the minimum size of population for a village panchayat was raised to 1,500 and the maximum to 10,000. This meant that in many cases several villages were expected to join together under one group panchayat. Accordingly, Wangala was grouped together with four neighbouring villages into one panchayat. As long as Wangala was chosen to house the panchayat headquarters villagers were prepared to go along with the new arrangements. However, when it was decided to shift the administration to one of the other four villages which was more conveniently situated, Wangala residents got so upset that they decided to abstain from participating in the official local government. During the group panchayat elections

held in 1968 no one from Wangala contested nor were residents prepared to pay government taxes. They argued that their village was sufficiently big to have its own local government and they saw no reason
why councillors from much smaller neighbouring villages should have
any say in matters which are the concern of Wangala residents only.
Their numbers in fact already slightly exceeded 1,500, the minimum
population stipulated in the Act for a separate panchayat. Village
elders went as far as to file a writ-petition with the Mysore high courts
asking for Wangala to be declared a separate and independent electorate. Wangala's refusal to participate in the group panchayat was
another obvious sign of village introversion.

Increased Wealth, Women's Work and Education   Higher crop
incomes reduced farmers' dependence on subsistence labour, which
they replaced with hired labour. In fact it became a matter of prestige
for Peasant farmers to claim that their womenfolk no longer had to
perform agricultural labour, even if this was not really true. The
increased wealth was also reflected in a considerable increase in school
attendance.

In 1955 most Wangala Peasants still needed their son's help in cultivating their wet crops. Accordingly, even those boys who by then had
attended school beyond primary education were expected to take up
farming as soon as they turned fourteen. The continuing increase in
Peasant wealth was reflected in 1970 by their greater preparedness to
have their sons continue with further education. There were then,
besides the few graduates and undergraduates, also seventeen high
school students. Wangala's increased involvement in education was
not reflected in an increased absorption in the wider society. Their
economic interests were in 1970 still firmly focused on intra-village
activities which remained reflected in their village introversion.

Dalena's Village Extroversion

In contrast to Wangala, Dalena's multifarious style of economic development had continued in a big way. The socio-political system had
changed more radically since I lived there first. Increasingly Dalena
villagers looked to the wider economy to improve their standards of
living. Realising this I decided to refer to this process as 'village extroversion'. The number of Dalena men in regular employment outside
increased between 1955 and 1970 from twentysix to fortyone, of
whom 80 per cent were members of the dominant Peasant caste and

the rest were Functionaries and Scheduled Castes. All Peasant workers owned some land in Dalena—for them wages represented a necessary supplement to their small subsistence output. All the Functionaries and Scheduled Castes were landless and depended solely on wages for their livelihood.

Education, the Passport to Employment The government policy to increase the proportion of Scheduled Castes and Scheduled Tribes in public service to 18 per cent had obviously not succeeded very well in Dalena. There were signs that the slow absorption of Dalena Scheduled Castes into public service jobs was representative of what had been happening in Mysore state as a whole. In government white collar jobs the percentage of ex-untouchables employed has fallen far short of the quotas. Government spokesmen complained that they could not fill the quotas because of the lack of suitably qualified applicants. In other words low levels of education among ex-untouchables prevented them from benefiting from the positive discrimination the state had introduced in their favour.

Increasing Economic Differentiation and Decreasing Caste Discrimination By 1970 the economic difficulties of Dalena's Scheduled Castes had considerably increased: they had lost the minimum social security the traditional hereditary labour relations used to offer them, the demand for their labour within the village had decreased, and their lack of education prevented them from taking up the public service positions the state offered them. While their economic position had deteriorated their social status had improved. The more liberal attitude by Peasants towards them that was already noticeable in 1955 had continued further. They were allowed into local cafes. In 1955 none were allowed to enter a Peasant home; by 1970 the Scheduled Caste postmaster was able to conduct his activities in a Peasant house. The increasing social acceptance of Dalena Scheduled Castes by Peasants was, however, not accompanied by improvements in their standard of living. Their growing economic problems outweighed their appreciation of their increased social acceptance. They themselves complained that 'you cannot eat social acceptance'. More Dalena men and their families had by 1970 left the village and taken up residence near their place of work. The majority of these emigrants still owned some land in Dalena. They kept their ties with the village. This resulted in a new type of family which I call the 'share family'.

The share family differs from the joint family in as far as the family no longer lives under one roof; it differs from the elementary family because it involves a number of kin—agnatic or affinal—each living separately with their families, but who agree to share the responsibility for their incomes as well as their expenditure. The share family constitutes an example of the adaptation of their conventional institutions to the new economic circumstances.

Dalena's network of relations which extended well outside the village was reflected in a greater preparedness in the village to adopt new legislative measures. Unlike Wangala, Dalena readily accepted the linkage with three neighbouring villages into the group panchayat. At the 1967 elections Dalena accepted the reserved seats for women: eight candidates were nominated, all of whom were Peasants and three were women; only one was a hereditary lineage elder. Each candidate was motivated by different personal factors. They all electioneered on the basis of personality and reputation, rather than on policy issues. Two men and one woman were elected to represent Dalena in the group panchayat. They soon became disenchanted with the functioning of this elected body, mainly because of its lack of funds and restricted powers.

In the period between 1955 and 1970 the factional opposition among Dalena's Peasants continued to intensify. In this dry land village economic progress could be achieved only by reaching outside the village; by participating in the regional expansion. There were, therefore, hardly any occasions which affected all residents alike and would unite them. Consequently sectional interests came to outweigh considerations of overall village welfare. The *patel* faction operated on the basis of different premises from those of their opponents. The *patel* who continued to be the outstanding entrepreneur in Dalena was more and more absorbed by the wider society. His chief concern was to succeed in the wider economy; he thus did not attach much importance to social recognition within Dalena. He and his followers felt more at home with exogenous institutions. They turned to urban courts for settlement of village disputes and called in the state police to protect a procession held within the village. By contrast the opposing faction led by the chairman was still wholly village-oriented. The chairman was a full-time farmer and his main concern appeared to be the continuous reaffirmation of his political prestige within the village. He had a wealth of knowledge about Dalena's past and was therefore well qualified to act as arbitrator in disputes. The *patel* hardly ever participated in any of the small informal ad hoc panchayats composed of hereditary Peasant lineage elders; these meetings were invariably conducted by the chairman.

Interest in educational achievement was promoted by Dalena's multifarious style of change and in turn reinforced the village extroversion. Their linkages with the wider economy made Dalena farmers realise the importance of education in the generation of income. The success of those with education encouraged others to follow suit. Dalena landowners could more readily spare their sons for education, simply because their labour was not essential for intra-village dry land farming or for wet land cultivation outside. Therefore, an increasing proportion of Dalena's young men sought further education in different fields; there were for example already some Dalena graduates in physics.

Neither in Wangala nor in Dalena did villagers place any importance on educating women; the proportion of females above the age of six with any schooling was in 1970 no more than 7 per cent.

TEN

Predictions Based on Micro-society Studies

$\mathcal{A}$ll macro-development planning obviously involves predictions of change. In 1970 I found that most of these predictions made by economists, who worked as planners or advisers with national governments (see Planning Commission, Government of India, 1952, *First Five Year Plan*) or international agencies either ignored the impact of social and psychological variables or were based on purely hypothetical assumptions of how these variables affect economic motivations. I then fully realised that many more macro-surveys and micro-societal studies were required before sufficient relevant and reliable data on the interaction of economic and socio-cultural factors in the context of change would become available. This would then enable developers to include sound social and psychological considerations in the planning process. In my own longitudinal micro-society studies I had focused on the impact of irrigation on the socio-political system of villages. I thought that in the interest not only of improving understanding and general scientific knowledge but also to increase the efficiency of the planning process it would be useful if I tried to extrapolate from the past and predict how Wangala and Dalena are likely to change by the year 2000. I knew there and then that at best only a part of my predictions will prove to be accurate. I reasoned that even if I had predicted wrongly my kind of interdisciplinary and longitudinal socio-economic micro-studies of Mysore villages might provide useful base data for development plans. This may then help to increase the effectiveness of such plans.

To help readers evaluate my predictions in the light of our 1996 findings I quote here extensively the relevant part of my *South India: Yesterday, Today and Tomorrow* (1973):

> Wangala and Dalena can be regarded as representing two types of village in an irrigated region. Therefore a reasonably accurate forecast of their future development may throw light on the changes that can be expected in similar villages in the rest of South India. Rural development must necessarily be viewed within the framework of the interaction between the modern development-oriented and egalitarian all-India policies on the one hand and traditional socio-economic organisation on the other....

> *Dalena: Tomorrow* Dalena's population has increased at an average annual rate of at least 2.5 per cent over the last fifteen years. Family planning, though widely advocated in Mandya district, has not been accepted by many villagers.... Therefore we must expect natural population increase to continue at least at its present rate. Unless migration takes on unprecedented proportions, Dalena's population is likely to double within the next thirty years. There is little chance that within this period, if ever, canal irrigation will bring water to Dalena land, though of course there is always the possibility of more efficient pump irrigation being introduced to irrigate the village dry land and thereby increase agricultural productivity. If this were accompanied by the introduction of high yielding varieties of millet and paddy seeds comparable in result with the high yielding wheat varieties, Dalena might be able to produce overall sufficient crops to feed its population for the next ten or fifteen years. However, in view of past trends these favourable expectations seem over-optimistic.

> More realistic is the assumption that population will continue to grow much faster than the increase in village food production. Wealthier farmers may succeed in buying more wet land in neighbouring villages, but the area involved will be decreasing over the years as the demand for wet land is growing, and altogether it will add only little to the total village product. In view of their partible inheritance the increasing population will be reflected in more and more subdivisions of estates which will make the size of individual farm units smaller and less economic.

The decreasing supply of farm output per family in Dalena will put increasing pressure on a growing number of households to seek income from other sources. This is likely to lead to greater economic diversification among villagers. More and more of the smaller Peasant farmers will seek income other than from cultivating crops. Assuming that the regional economy continues to expand, Mandya will probably have a population of over 150,000 by the year 2000. This urban growth is bound to concentrate along the already existing major highway, which will mean that before too long Dalena is going to be swallowed up by urban suburbs in very much the same way as villages which used to be in the vicinity of Bangalore have by now become part of the city. The greater productivity of irrigated land and its consequently higher value will prevent urban settlement from expanding over much of the nearby wet land. Therefore Dalena and similar dry land villages near Mandya will offer ideal conditions for urban growth. Some of the village land will probably remain devoted to agriculture while the greater proportion of it will be bought by urban developers on a larger scale or sold or rented in small plots to individual settlers.

Dalena's change from being a separate village to becoming an urban suburb will, however, be a slow process. In the meantime every year more villagers will seek and possibly get regular urban employment. Younger men will probably predominate among those who get regular work outside agriculture. If, as is likely, the greater proportion of them... remain village-oriented, this will lead to the spread of share families as well as a new type of progressive faction in Dalena. The present progressives are all entrepreneurs; by contrast, the new type of progressives will be workers. Thus there are indications of the development of intra-Peasant caste cleavages emerging along class lines....

It will be interesting to see what form and what expression class cleavages within the Peasant caste in Dalena will take... by past experience it is likely that the leaders of Dalena's peasant workers faction will be readier to make concessions to the demands of the more conservative Peasant farmers than will the entrepreneurial faction. It is possible that the entrepreneurs may want to opt out altogether from intra-village political competition and instead concentrate all their interest and energies on establishing a firm foothold in the wider polity. However, in a democratic political system, wooing of the electorate is an important part of political activity. Should Peasant entrepreneurs therefore ignore intra-village politics altogether they will make the cardinal mistake of any politician who loses the support of his home base.

There will be for a long time to come in Dalena a group of Peasants who will be predominantly conservative and who will continue to regard as the good old days the time when their village was a separate socio-political entity. At the same time the new progressive Peasant worker faction will want to maintain and reinforce much of village custom to keep the old ritual prestige structure alive and to secure a high place within it. As the older Peasants, who have most knowledge of their traditions, die, it is reasonable to expect that it will be the new workers' faction which will take over the role of conservatives in trying to resurrect their old village society. This will probably sharpen the intra-village conflict between progressive Peasant entrepreneurs and Peasant workers.

Simultaneously, other forces will be at work helping to bridge this intra-caste class conflict. The growing need for more Peasant farmers to seek income from outside agriculture will reinforce intra-Peasant caste loyalty. The network of a Peasant's relations with fellow caste men will be widened and each link strengthened and manipulated as the need arises. As long as it is legitimate for Peasants to claim certain benefits on the basis of being members of a 'backward community', caste differentiation will gain in strength. However, even if all benefits to 'backward communities' were to be removed and the concept of 'backwardness' altogether abolished, there is very little chance of caste disappearing within the foreseeable future as a basic principle of socio-economic organisation in the Mandya region.

The persistence of a caste-conscious society will have the worst effect on AKs in Dalena. In the traditional village system AKs certainly always formed the poorest section, but... inequality must not be confused with exploitation. The system used to assure subsistence to each proportionately to his status.... Past economic changes have already removed this minimum social security for AKs in Dalena and nothing positive has been put in its place. Unless increasing population in the region should be offset by an equal or greater rate of overall economic expansion, competition for employment will be intensified. AKs will be at a disadvantage in this competition, even though legislation lays down that they are to receive preferential treatment at least in public employment. Only if official policy changes to using economic criteria instead of caste as the decisive qualification for favoured treatment may the poorest villagers be able to secure regular employment. In the meantime their best chance of earning wages will be as casual agricultural labourers. As we have seen, the supply of labour in agriculture has increased much more than the demand for it. This has led to a reduction in real wages which was facilitated by inflation: rising prices enabled farmers to reduce real wages without reducing the money wage, thereby they avoided certain socio-economic resistance that they might otherwise have had to face. Since we must expect population increase and inflation to continue in South India in the near future, real agricultural wages will continue to fall until they reach bare subsistence level, unless drastic steps are taken to prevent a further deterioration in the standard of living of the poorest landless labourers.

To summarise the way I see the near future of Dalena: an increasing economic diversification reflected in an intra-Peasant class cleavage and a further deterioration in the economic conditions of the local AKs. These economic changes are likely to be reflected increasingly in more radical socio-political changes. Discrimination by village Peasants against AKs may become considerably less as their economic interdependence disappears. Yet the social distance between them is likely to remain as big as ever.

Wangala: Tomorrow Wangala's population, like Dalena's, must be expected to continue growing. Wangala men are even less interested in family planning than are their Dalena counterparts.... Wangala's population will probably double in about twentyfive years. If in the meantime a high yielding variety of paddy can be successfully introduced this will obviously increase the carrying capacity of irrigated land. Otherwise at least 800 wet acres will be required by the year 2000 to produce enough food to feed Wangala's population with its staple diet of rice and ragi alone. In view of their subsistence orientation farmers will replace cash crops by subsistence crops as population pressure necessitates a greater food acreage. At least, past indications point to such a trend. Though Wangala has been incorporated in the cash economy, farmers are still only secondarily cash croppers; their first concern is to grow sufficient subsistence food. Only if they have more wet land than is required to feed their household do they plant cash crops.

A decline in the acreage under cane will reduce the villagers' cash income. The few wealthiest Peasants will be least affected: though they too will devote an increasing acreage to subsistence agriculture they will still have surplus wet acres to plant cane. Caste middle-farmers will be the most affected group; the extent to which individual households will be impoverished will depend on the size of their wet landholding and the rate of increase in the size of their families. The continuing splitting up of joint families and the increasing number of nuclear households which will emerge will lead to smaller and smaller estates. The smaller the individual farm unit the greater will be the pressure on the farmer to seek income from sources other than cultivating his own land. Some of these impoverished Peasants, particularly those who will have received secondary education, will seek regular employment. However, bearing in mind their strong attachment to the land, they will continue to keep a stake in the rural economy in the way we have seen Dalena urban workers do. Therefore, it is likely that an increasing number of share families will be formed among this section of Wangala Peasants. The magnates, on the other hand, will continue to keep their families 'joint' for as long as possible so as to avoid the splitting up of their estates.

Wangala magnates will remain concerned predominantly with organising the cultivation of their wet land, and with operating crop processing plants in their own village. Consequently, they will continue to concentrate their political interests on intra-village problems. The wider polity will remain of marginal concern to them only. If the state offers help or services which Wangala Peasants find useful they will be prepared to co-operate; otherwise they will continue to mind their own business. This isolationist attitude is likely to come under attack from those Peasants who will have secured regular urban employment in the meantime. However, since the majority of these too will probably be concerned with preserving village traditions, as their Dalena counterparts still are, they will not press their demands too hard. As long as the richest Peasants derive their wealth from village land, intra-village factions will follow a cyclical course of about two generations' depth.

It is of course always possible that external democratic influences may help to separate the village power structure from its economic base. In Wangala Peasants have what Srinivas calls decisive dominance, which is unlikely to be challenged by the only other sizable, but still much smaller, AK community. Therefore, in Wangala, even the adoption of a truly democratic political system is unlikely to upset the traditional power structure controlled by Peasant magnates.

University graduates from Wangala are unlikely to exert much influence over village affairs. Most of them will probably seek regular Public Service or teaching appointments outside. The indications are that, unlike their less educated fellow villagers in urban employment, the graduates will sever their ties with the village completely and become contemptuous of the village way of life; they will try to become fully-fledged townsmen. The few graduates who may be attracted back to the village will probably be sons of established magnates or they will use their broader education to try and join the wealthiest. They will therefore reinforce the traditional socio-economic system of the village.

Wangala's increasing population, accompanied by a swing to food production and a declining cane acreage, will automatically reduce the average number of labour days per resident. Mechanisation of agriculture may further reduce village labour requirements. This will make Wangala a less attractive place for migrant labourers and may once more result in a greater reliance by Peasants on their local AK dependents. Consequently traditional hereditary relationships which exist between Peasant and AK households might again be strengthened. Wangala AKs will therefore continue to enjoy a minimum social security. Their income will probably fall back to mere subsistence level. An increasing number of village AKs will seek regular urban employment nearby, but unless conditions radically change in the regional employment pattern only very few, if any, are likely to succeed in getting such jobs.

....Wangala AKs are understandably reluctant to risk jeopardising their assured minimum survival by migrating in search of work in a completely unfamiliar environment. They therefore tend to restrict the radius within which they look for regular employment to commuting distance. They have not yet had a chance to develop faith in the stability of urban employment: they know that if they move into the town and then lose their job they will have a very hard time scraping enough food together to keep themselves and their families alive. While in the village they feel reasonably secure that in the last resort they can always depend on their local Peasants' charity.

This basic feeling of security influences Wangala AKs to accept their low ritual and social status in the village against which they may otherwise be tempted to revolt. There is hardly any danger of Wangala AKs taking any violent action against their Peasant masters in the near future. There may be a few occasional rebellious attempts by local AKs against Peasant dominance, but judging by past events these are likely to be easily squashed by their economic masters. The biggest problem facing Wangala AKs is the fact that not only are they inferior in terms of economic, ritual and socio-political status, but even in terms of numbers they cannot constitute a viable challenge to Peasant superiority. Therefore, even if Wangala Peasants adopted democratic village government based on universal adult franchise, local AKs have no hope of securing a majority of councillors so as to have their interests adequately represented.

Thus on the whole I do not envisage any radical socio-political changes taking place in Wangala's foreseeable future. Unless alternative sources of income reduce the pressure of population on landed resources and/or a new high-yielding variety of paddy can successfully multiply the productivity per unit of land, there is going to be a steepening decline in the rate of economic growth per head. Economic differentiation will be heightened: the few wealthiest Peasant farmers will become richer, while caste middle-farmers will become poorer and AK labourers may be reduced to a minimum subsistence level. Except for a limited number of Peasant farmers who may secure regular urban employment and commute from their village home, intra-village agriculture will remain the dominant economic interest and activity of Wangala residents. This economic introversion will be reflected in continued political isolationism (p. 233–42).

ELEVEN

Another Re-study in the 1990s

CONTACT WITH SOUTH INDIA SINCE 1970

After two years of my return to Dalena and Wangala in 1970 I moved with my family back to England where I took up a professorial fellowship at the Institute of Development Studies of the University of Sussex. This enabled me to get back to South India more often. I thus met T. Thimmegowda in Bangalore again in 1974. Having sent him a copy of my *South India: Yesterday, Today and Tomorrow* (1973) I was worried that he would complain that included in my book was what he had told me in great confidence. Though I referred to him by a pseudonym, Kempa, I remembered how guilty I felt when using his case to illustrate how education sucks the brightest out of India's rural areas and alienates them from their rural villages. However, Thimmegowda's struggle to succeed illustrated, at least to my mind, far too important a feature of India's rural development not to alert the powers in being to the obstacle the existing education system created in the path of rural advancement. I was thus pleasantly surprised when Thimmegowda greeted me saying: 'I like your second book about our villages even better than your first'. He went on to say that he had taken to heart what I had written about him and had seriously searched within himself whether he should go back to Wangala. Yet he felt that his university studies had urbanised him and made him feel too alienated from village life to return to his native place. He smiled as he told me that he had done what he considered second best: he had joined the

State Development Administration. At the time I agreed with him that under the circumstances his decision represented a compromise solution. Little did either he or I realise in 1974 what an important role he would come to occupy in Wangala's development. Being a very capable and hardworking public servant he quickly rose to the ranks of an IAS officer. His continuing and overriding commitment to helping his fellow villagers has proved a great bonus for Wangala. Aware of the legal rights and duties of villagers he provides an essential link between Wangala and the state authorities. As I met Thimmegowda more recently I realised that what we had initially considered a second best choice was the best thing he could have done to promote Wangala's development. With hindsight what he might have done to help develop his village had he settled there would have been nowhere near as effective than what he managed to do as a senior IAS officer in Karnataka.

Planning to Update the Studies of Wangala and Dalena

Whenever I come to India I try my best to get to Karnataka. I am always keen to go back for however short a period to 'our' villages. I had come to regard them as my 'spiritual home'. Together with Thimmegowda and Suri I usually go on a day's trip to Dalena and Wangala. This gives us just enough time to see some of our old friends again and have a brief look round the villages. On these short return visits it became pretty obvious that rapid change was taking place together with a great deal of continuity. But of course these one-day visits did not enable me to update my earlier data and to test how much of my earlier predictions had materialised or failed and why.

At the end of 1992 when I happened to be once more in Karnataka Suri, Thimmegowda and myself sat together in Bangalore after another of our one-day visits to the villages and jointly decided that it was high time my earlier studies were updated. I would have liked to spend at least a few months in the villages, but health and family commitments did not permit this. So we decided I should set out the data we needed for Suri to collect with Thimmegowda's help. They would send the material to me in England where I would analyse and use it as a basis for updating my earlier publications. I was not happy with the idea of remote control research but realised it was the only way I could update my village studies. Nevertheless, the more I thought about the proposition the more excited I became.

I prepared a list of what I thought I needed to discover what changes had taken place in the villages since 1970. Suri, who had been my research assistant every time I conducted my earlier village studies in Mysore was already pensioned in 1992. He therefore had time to get back to the villages to collect more data. Having seen him at work on previous occasions and cross-checked the data he collected I was confident that he would again conscientiously collect reliable information. Thimmegowda volunteered to help Suri with the logistics and arranged for him to have access to relevant official statistics and helped him to get accommodation in Mandya town.

Suri and Thimmegowda were so enthusiastic about our update studies that I asked them to become my co-authors. I pointed out to them that a book including different perceptions of the rural transformation that has taken place in 'our' two South Indian villages over the past forty years is likely to have wide appeal. Each of us obviously observed the changes from a different angle. Suri as research assistant and statistician, Thimmegowda as the villager who had become a high-ranking public servant, and myself the retired expatriate social scientist. I put it to them that if we worked together we might produce a book with a difference—they agreed. By targeting developers in particular and the wider public in general we may help to improve the understanding of the kind of changes a large canal irrigation scheme is likely to bring about. Although no two societies respond exactly in the same way to the same stimulus we considered that there are certain constants and that Dalena and Wangala can to a certain extent be regarded as representative of dry and wet land villages situated near or within large canal irrigated areas. Therefore, this may enable planners of future rural development to learn from the experience of what had gone on in our South Indian villages.

During the early months of 1993 I heard from Suri that with Thimmegowda's help he had found suitable accommodation in Mandya and collected much of the data I had requested. For several weeks he daily went by motorbike to Dalena or Wangala and sent data to me. This included information such as village sketch maps, data on population, land-holding, cropping pattern, and household budgets.

Some of my English academic colleagues warned me of how difficult it has become to find a publisher for a village study. But we were extremely fortunate in arranging fairly quickly a contract with Sage Publications (India) on the basis of a brief synopsis. A Sussex University student volunteered to process the various basic numerical data I received from Suri. As many more questions arose in my mind, I sent them to Suri, who replied quickly. When Suri and Thimmegowda sent me the first draft of their contributions, this raised even more questions. It convinced me that only by spending at least a few weeks myself gathering selected case studies in the villages, would we produce the kind of book we had in mind. Fortunately, I managed to secure fairly quickly a 'Small Nuffield Foundation Research Grant' which financed my return to South India. I could only stay away from home for four weeks, but that brief period was such a wonderful experience that I will remember it as long as I live.

A Further Re-exposure in 1996

The flight to Bangalore in June 1996 was pretty exhausting. Travelling by Air India from London I had to change planes in Bombay and Madras with a long wait in each place. I kept wondering whether I would still be able to withstand the physical strain of fieldwork. Would I remember any of the vernacular? How many of the villagers I first met in 1954 would still be alive? How would those who had never met me before behave? These and many other questions were buzzing in my head. By the time I arrived at Bangalore airport I was mentally and physically exhausted. But the warm welcome which awaited me helped me to recover quickly. Thimmegowda and Suri greeted me with a big sandalwood garland, and whisked me off to a hotel.

I stayed two days in Bangalore, making courtesy calls on a number of officials before setting off for Wangala. The drive immediately brought back many memories. We passed through Chennpatna where many years ago I had often stopped to admire the craft items that are a local speciality. Of course there were also many new and unfamiliar landmarks, such as a folk museum and a school for the blind.

As we approached Mandya I began to see how much the town had grown since 1970. There are now a number of new large hotels, many more restaurants and coffee shops and a much larger residential area. Thimmegowda gave us the option of staying in a spacious Mandya factory guest house or in a small town house with enough room for Suri and myself. We opted for the house, which was next to the family of Dr Srinivasan, Professor of Commerce at Mandya College. As close friends of Thimmegowda they were prepared to cater for all our needs. Then Thimmegowda took us to meet his in-laws, who belong to Mandya's elite and live in a large, well-furnished house. His brothers-in-law all spoke fluent English, whereas their wives did not, only the young daughters, who were studying—one of them intends to become a doctor—spoke English. This indicated to me the impact education is

having on the position of women in Indian society. After a lavish meal
we left for Wangala.

I was amazed to see that the road to Wangala was now tarred, which
made travelling easier for motorised vehicles but also more difficult
simply because villagers used it to dry their harvests. When I asked if
farmers were allowed to obstruct the road I was told that it is illegal
but officials are not prepared to enforce this law because the local
politician representing their area in the Legislative Assembly puts
pressure on them not to alienate his voters. This is why at harvest
time drivers have to avoid crushing heaps of drying crops, which
every few hundred yards make driving very tricky.

An Overwhelming and Memorable Welcome

In Wangala On the way to Wangala I remembered the welcome I
was given there in 1970 and was wondering whether it would be similar this time. On arrival at the outskirts of the village my doubts
vanished. Crowds of villagers were lining both sides of the main street;
it looked as if the whole village had turned out to greet us. A banner
across the street welcomed back their 'Wangala Kempamma (Scarlett
Mother)', the name by which villagers knew me. We were each gar-
landed; the local children neatly dressed in their school uniforms led by
their school band headed our procession along to the panchayat hall.
Many of my old friends came up to me to shake hands; Karegowda, the
little boy who I came to love when I was first in Wangala in 1954, and
who is now married with children of his own, again dashed up to me
and we walked arm in arm happy to be reunited once more. We passed
the school compound which includes the bungalow we occupied fortytwo years ago; it still looked very much like it had done then. But I was
struck by the large boards advertising different kinds of shops, such as
a cycle repair shop, a finance corporation, a fertiliser and seed distri-
butor and a stationary retailer.

In the recently constructed panchayat building the big hall was
decorated with flowers and there was a table for the three of us. The
schoolchildren settled down on the floor with their elders behind
them. The large hall proved too small to accommodate all those who
wanted to join in. Those who could not get in queued outside and listened to the proceedings through the open door. Thimmegowda was
the first speaker. He stressed at great length how through my studies
and publications I had put their village onto the world map; 'even in
America people now know about Wangala!'. Villagers can be proud

of their Kempamma. He explained to them that Suri and I had come to update our village study and appealed to them all to co-operate with us and give truthful answers to all our questions. Then Suri said a few words expressing our pleasure at being once more with our village friends. Though I would have liked to be able to address this gathering in the vernacular I just did not feel up to it. So I began my speech with '*Nanu Wangala Kempamma*' (I am Wangala Kempamma). This was the way I really felt then. I was overtaken by a strange sense of belonging. I do not know whether the audience realised what was going on inside me but they applauded enthusiastically. I continued in English while Thimmegowda translated. Our speeches were followed by a number of speakers including Shangowda, who as the grandson of the shrewdest village moneylender fortytwo years ago is now one of the few young, educated and committed village leaders; he is an active member of Wangala's core group (see p. 60) and one of the village councillors. He said that 'in Wangala political allegiances do not tear the village apart as they do in many other villages; political parties are important to us only immediately before elections. They cease their importance the moment the election booth closes and we all then feel reunited again'. I came to appreciate only later the significance of what he said after I learnt about how political party opposition often leads to violence in other villages nowadays. After our formal reception we strolled through the village followed by the crowd. However poor some of the houses looked everybody was keen to make us offerings of bananas and/or milk. As we were offered much more than we could possibly accept we gave the surplus to the children crowding around us. Altogether this welcome was a lot warmer and more demonstrative than the one in 1970. It was indeed overwhelming and I found it difficult to suppress my tears.

In Dalena   The following day when Suri and I—Thimmegowda had to return to Bangalore—went to pay our respects to our Dalena friends Thimmegowda's role in orchestrating our welcome in Wangala became glaringly obvious. In Dalena only a few people gathered to welcome us. It was just as I remembered it from years ago: during the day the village streets looked deserted. A few elderly men came to shake hands with us. We went to see the house I had rented from a Dalena Peasant in 1955. To my surprise in 1970 I had seen a Scheduled Caste postman conducting his business from here. In 1955 my landlord was always upset when I asked Scheduled Caste persons to visit the house; he then kept telling me that I should not allow these 'dirty people' inside. I used to reply that according to our rental agreement I was entitled to keep an open house and to offer a welcome to anybody who cared to visit me. To console my landlord I added that after my departure he would be free to ritually clean the pollution I might have caused. By 1970 he was obviously no longer so worried about allowing them into his house, though he still stressed that he would not have them anywhere near his kitchen. On our return in 1996 we heard rumours that in 1986 the old man, because of quarrels over land with his sons, committed suicide by jumping into a well. A few years later his elder son's wife also killed herself together with her four small daughters by jumping into the same well as her father-in-law had done. Apparently she had been unhappy about her husband's family complaints over her failure to bear a son; a quarrel with her husband over Rs 5,000 he wanted to give to his younger brother was the final straw, inducing her to drown herself and her daughters. When we entered the house the sons seemed to be pleased to see us and offered us bananas and milk, particularly the younger one; in 1955 he was a lovely little boy of whom I had taken many photos. It gave me a queer feeling to find myself again in the same house where I had stayed for about eight months many years ago. It was familiar yet strange: familiar because the layout had remained unchanged and strange to be there again after so long.

As we came out a young man dressed in trousers, shirt and sandals approached me introducing himself in broken English as the son of Halli, the Mandya refinery worker, who in 1955 took our mail to and from Mandya. He immediately asked for my help to find him urban employment. When after my enquiry about his father he told me that he was busy working his cane crusher on the outskirts of Dalena, I asked him whether it would not be better for him to help his father instead of seeking urban employment. He replied 'I have been employed as a clerk in Bangalore and do not feel at home in the village any more. I am desperately trying to find another urban job!' All this sounded so familiar to me. It symbolised precisely the kind of village extroversion that I had already noticed in 1955.

Then Palgowda, a young solicitor with an office in Mandya and a home in Dalena, came to greet us. He was another Dalena man who spoke English, only much better than Halli's son. I was pleased to have with me a villager with whom I could freely converse in English. He told us that a few weeks ago Thimmegowda had sent word of my planned return and had even let him have a copy of the vernacular version of my *South India: Yesterday, Today and Tomorrow*, which he read before my arrival. He repeatedly told me how happy he was that I had decided to update my study of Dalena and that he would make sure that villagers would co-operate with our enquiries. When we walked through the village a number of older widows appeared outside their houses or thatched roofed huts asking me for photographs of their now dead husbands. I felt I could not disappoint them by admitting that I had no idea what their men had looked like, but promised to see what I could do. One elderly lady shook my hand warmly and told me that she well remembered me from when I first stayed in Dalena. She herself was then the young mother of a small child. Now she walked bent with a walking stick. With her toothless mouth she asked with a broad grin 'how did you manage to keep all your teeth, while I have lost all mine?', to which I replied with amusement 'I see my dentist regularly, this is the secret of my success!' She shook her head disbelievingly and walked away.

Dalena villagers left us in no doubt that they too were pleased to see us again. But their welcome was not as warm as Wangala. There appeared to be a much stronger social unity in the wet than in the dry land village. Dalena's appearance had not changed as much as Wangala's. What seemed different in Dalena was the size of the residential area; population there too had increased considerably. But unlike in Wangala, hardly any new amenities had been added.

These rather superficial first observations gave me the impression that my earlier contrast between Dalena's village extroversion and Wangala's village introversion might still be valid and made me eager to discover how much of what I predicted in 1970 had turned out to be correct.

Research Methodology

We tried as much as was possible within the limited time at our disposal to collect the same data in the same way as from 1954–56 and then in 1970. Further details of our research methodology can be found in my 1973 book. Suri had already prepared the sketch maps and collected a lot of the statistical data on population and landholding, selected household budgets etc. On our return in 1996 we tried to update what he had done in 1993. But time constraints made it impossible to conduct a sample survey, or a 100 per cent village socio-economic census. Therefore, we decided that the most effective use of our time would be to concentrate on focus group discussions and individual case studies and try to support our quantitative data with as much relevant qualitative data as possible. In this way we might be able to show what if any changes had taken place in Dalena and Wangala since our last study in 1970 and why they occurred.

The presence in Wangala of a junior college was obviously a recent phenomenon. We took advantage of it and got permission from the principal to request some of his more advanced students to write about how they perceive the past, present and future of their own village. Some of these bright students even wrote poems for us (see p. 154).

Fieldwork Routine

Our neighbours in Mandya, Dr Srinivasan and his family overwhelmed us with their conventional Indian hospitality. They also arranged our daily transport: early in the morning Dr Srinivasan drove us either to Dalena or Wangala according to our plan. We arranged with him what time he should collect us and he was always there when we wanted him. All this we greatly appreciated.

Every time before we set off for our data collection Suri and I made a tentative plan of research for the day, though we often had to change it for lack of the appropriate informants. Suri and I spent the evenings separately writing up our field notes and then compared them. We noted any questions that arose and tried to follow them up the next day. As in the 1950s and in 1970 we worked long hours on each day of the week; it was pretty tiring but we were so thrilled with the way the villagers responded to our enquiries that we collected a great deal of information in a short time. Suri kept telling me: 'Your presence makes all the difference; villagers always respond positively to your request for information; when I approach them on my own they usually tell me that they have better things to do than to sit down and answer my many questions'. Unfortunately, since 1970 my knowledge of the vernacular had further deteriorated. Therefore, most of the time I had to stay with Suri when he interviewed informants. Seldom was I able to speak directly with villagers. But I understood more than I could say. Listening to what villagers were saying made me seek more information through Suri. In Wangala the only English speaker was one of the schoolmasters, who volunteered to act as my interpreter while Suri had to absent himself for a funeral. On one such day Dr Srinivasan insisted on helping me in Wangala. We sat down together in the panchayat offices and held a focus group discussion. Surrounded by a group of villagers we investigated the operation of village finance corporations. Dr Srinivasan seemed very surprised about the unbusinesslike way in which they were run. Kin and friendship relations seem to play an important role in these W.angala finance corporations (see p. 170). In Dalena I coped more easily without Suri: there were always a number of villagers who knew at least a smattering of English and of course there was Palgowda with whom I could speak English without any difficulty. This made me appreciate the advantages that village extroversion in South India offers an expatriate researcher!

TWELVE

How the Two Villages have Changed

OUTWARD CHANGES

$\mathcal{W}$e began our re-study by intensive observation in Dalena and Wangala; comparing our earlier records with what we saw. The tremendous expansion of residential sites was what struck me immediately. From the demographic details Suri had collected we already knew that the population had grown considerably (see p. 29). But what I saw far exceeded my expectation. Already by 1970 population and residential sites had increased. But, the increase was far greater between 1970 and 1996. An ever increasing amount of land became housing sites.

Wangala

On approaching Wangala from Mandya we first noticed that where in 1970 there were on the right side of the road about twenty small thatched huts occupied by Vodda migrants, today those huts are replaced by some cane crushers and flour mills. Since 1955 when almost all houses in Wangala were on the east of the main road passing through the village, housing now extends to a considerable distance on both sides of the road. The whole area is built up. The space that years ago clearly separated the caste from the Scheduled Caste settlement is no longer so obvious. A few years ago near Wangala's border and at a distance from the main village residential area a new colony with small RCC structures for landless households was

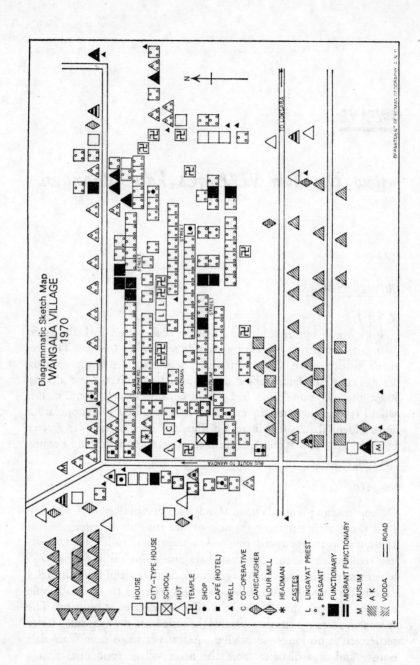

Diagrammatic Sketch Map
WANGALA VILLAGE
1970

N

TO GODGERI

BUS ROUTE TO MANDYA

SHEPHERD STREET

HEADMAN STREET

MUSLIM STREET

| HOUSE |
| CITY-TYPE HOUSE |
| SCHOOL |
| HUT |
| TEMPLE |
| SHOP ● |
| CAFÉ (HOTEL) ■ |
| WELL ▲ |
| CO-OPERATIVE C |
| CANECRUSHER |
| FLOUR MILL |
| HEADMAN ✳ |

CASTES
L	LINGAYAT PRIEST
°	PEASANT
■	FUNCTIONARY
‖	MIGRANT FUNCTIONARY
M	MUSLIM
⧄	A K
⬡	VODDA

= ROAD

DEPARTMENT OF HUMAN GEOGRAPHY A.N.U.

established (see sketch maps). In this colony there are about fifty households, the majority of which are Scheduled Caste. But there are also a few Peasant and Functionary caste families residing there. The number of houses in Wangala has greatly increased (see sketch maps) and their appearance has changed considerably. Many now are urban-style, well-furnished two-storeyed structures with modern facilities, private water taps and some even with latrines; some also have tele-phones and/or television sets. Moreover, there are public water taps so that all households have easy access to water. The housing of the poorest too has improved greatly; there are now fewer conventional small thatched huts as these have been replaced by RCC structures. Street lights and drainage are also important innovations which most houses have access to. This has done away with the earlier stench of the streets and makes the village healthier and cleaner looking.

The hustle and bustle around Wangala's main road—where most Peasants still reside—gives the impression of a small but thriving urban settlement. Indeed I heard people refer to their village as 'Little Mandya', a small replica of Mandya town. The headquarters for the village council are housed in a substantial structure consisting of a large meeting hall and three rooms with a telephone. Besides Wangala, the village council includes four neighbouring villages. This means that many government officials as well as residents from other villages frequently call at the council offices. Throughout the day buses, cars, scooters and bicycles stop off in Wangala on their way to other destinations. Such busy traffic was unknown in 1955.

Many village buildings carry boards with big lettering indicating the nature of their business. As was to be expected the most solid and impressive building is occupied by the branch of the corporate bank. This bank also caters for neighbouring villages and therefore attracts many visitors. In the morning when school begins and in the after-noon when it ends crowds of boys and girls neatly dressed in uniforms stream through the village streets; many go to the shops and treat themselves to snacks. Small specialist shops and restaurants cater for a variety of consumer requirements. They all appear well frequented throughout the day.

Dalena

To approach Dalena one has to go south of Mandya along the major highway connecting Bangalore with Mysore. In 1955, 4 miles of open countryside separated the town from Dalena. Since then Mandya too has grown a great deal and residential areas extend in all directions.

Along both sides of the highway south of the town many colourful advertisements try to attract the passers-by to the numerous small shops and restaurants along the roadside; there are cane crushers and flour mills, and mechanics provide bicycle and car repair services. These buildings now extend all the way to Dalena. The village lands situated to the west of the highway used to be open fields. I was surprised to find a church and other nice buildings including a health clinic there. Next to the missionary complex there is an industrial estate. Opposite, to the east of the highway there is now a line of buildings including a post office, small restaurants and various shops selling a great variety of goods. Much traffic passes along the highway. Buses travelling in both directions stop at Dalena. This creates the impression that by now Dalena is almost a suburb of Mandya. On turning left into the village, I spotted the primary school building which had looked nice and new in 1970. Now it was run down and badly in need of renovation. In front of it a water tank has been constructed to provide piped drinking water. There are eleven public water taps in the village and a number of houses have their own private taps. When we got to Dalena the main village square was just then being sealed to facilitate the traffic of cars and trucks. Bordering on the square and between a small temple and the house we occupied in 1955 there are now the offices of the Dairy Co-operative Society, which buys milk from the villagers. The Anjeneya temple near the square also looks completely renovated with attractive, colourful decorations. Along one of the village streets the old *Marichowdi* temple which in 1955 housed the local primary school was undergoing renovation. We spotted a few new elaborate and urban-style houses, but far fewer than in Wangala. The majority of Dalena's improved houses were in the Scheduled Caste settlement at the back of the Peasant residences. A lot of the old thatched huts here have been replaced by RCC structures. Most houses now benefit from drainage—another welcome innovation. At least four Peasant households have built their own bio-gas plants to provide fuel for cooking. The increase in the number of houses has greatly over-shadowed the separation between the various caste settlements which still existed in 1970 and some Peasant residences extend even behind the lower caste settlement which is now sandwiched between caste houses. Judging by appearances, the lifestyle of Dalena's Scheduled Castes has improved considerably in terms of housing, clothing and nourishment than what I remembered from 1955.

Dalena's residential area is obviously growing in all directions. There is now another new road lined with many recently constructed houses. It leads from the village square to the canal. Though this is still illegal besides the canal there are now pump sets and bore wells used to irrigate some of the village dry lands. Trucks pass through the village carrying cane to crushers in Dalena and/or delivering the processed jaggery to buyers.

Altogether there is no doubt that both Wangala and Dalena have grown considerably during the past forty years. This was to be expected. Yet I found a noticeable difference in the way the two villages appeared to have changed. This raised questions in my mind for which I felt I needed answers.

FACTORS RESPONSIBLE FOR THESE CHANGES

After we finished stocktaking the outward changes we concentrated on a detective-like investigation to discover what caused the changes. We perused all relevant available data and asked searching questions in the course of numerous focus group discussions and individual depth interviews. I sifted through all the materials thus gathered and pieced them together like a jigsaw puzzle. I sought to identify some of the most important factors responsible for the changes that have occurred in Dalena and Wangala during the past forty years. It turned out that population growth was obviously *the* factor responsible for the large expansion of residential areas. But there are also a number of other factors which caused the outward changes we spotted in the villages, such as for instance, the narrowing in the social distance between the various caste groups. For analytical purposes I categorised these factors each under a separate heading:

- Social Change Factors:
  Population growth
  Decentralisation of education
- Economic Change Factors:
  Agricultural technologies
  Urban impact
  Commercial opportunities
  Financial opportunities
- Political Change Factors:
  Socio-economic legislation
  Village government and party politics

Yet discussing change factors individually is not meant to imply that the different factors operate in isolation from each other; they in fact usually interact. For example, farmers have adopted new *agricultural technologies* not only because they have become available, but also because *population growth* made increased crop productivity a vital consideration. Besides, better *education* helped farmers to appreciate the importance of changing their conventional cultivation practices; and *commercialisation* has been accompanied by the establishment of different institutionalised sources of credit. The Manager of the Wangala branch of the corporation bank told me:

> Lingayats and Scheduled Caste farmers have the lowest loan recovery rate. They borrow money for the purchase of seeds and/or fertiliser and then fail to repay the money. Unlike informal money-lenders or financial corporations who ensure loan recovery through personal contacts, banks have no other options but to take bad debtors to court. We find it impossible to get satisfaction in the courts in cases involving Scheduled Caste debtors because they enjoy preferential treatment according to *socio-economic legislation*. Similarly, Lingayats enjoy *political protection* because theirs is the dominant caste in Karnataka.

This example neatly illustrates the interdependence of the different factors that have brought about changes in Dalena and Wangala.

SOCIAL CHANGE FACTORS

Population Growth

The expansion of residential areas is a sign of population growth. Between 1955 and 1970 Wangala's total population had increased from 958 to 1,603 and to 2,616 by 1991. Wangala's average annual compound rate of population growth during the earlier period was 3.15 per cent and fell to 2.28 per cent between 1971 and 1991. Dalena's rate of population growth was lower than Wangala's. Its population increased from 707 to 1,072 by 1970 and to 1,566 by 1991 at an average annual compound rate of 2.73 per cent and 1.78 per cent respectively. These rates differ by about 0.5 per cent from all-India rates of growth for the same periods. But this difference does not necessarily represent different rates of natural increase for it is also influenced by migration.

Migration Wangala's rather high rate of population growth between 1955 and 1970 was greatly influenced by immigration. People were attracted by the employment opportunities irrigated farming offered during the peak agricultural seasons. These migrants constituted a pool of labour which helped to meet peak labour requirements. Local farmers were pleased to have ready access to contractual labour that did not involve any long-term commitments on their part. Therefore, they did not object to the establishment of a migrant housing colony at the outskirts of the village. The number of Vodda households increased from seven to twentythree between 1955 and 1970. The Voddas were migrant labourers who, as hereditary stone cutters, had become redundant and lost their livelihood in their places of origin. Therefore they roamed the countryside in search of employment. Similarly, Functionary caste households such as Blacksmiths and Carpenters migrated to areas where irrigation increased the demand for their services. In 1970 there were eleven such households in Wangala. As compared to 1955, migrants made up at least 12 per cent of Wangala's population in 1970.

The decline in Wangala's average annual rate of population growth between 1971 and 1991 reflects both a decrease in fertility (see p. 151) and a fall in the demand for migrant labour. The adoption of agricultural machinery made a lot of rural labour redundant. Many migrants had to move on in search of employment elsewhere. On the other hand, only very few natives of the village have moved elsewhere since 1970. Without a 100 per cent census, which time constraints prevented us to conduct, it is impossible to gauge separately the relative importance of natural increase and migration. Yet in the course of our discussions and individual depth interviews it emerged that Wangala still attracts outsiders but for different reasons. Some come to pursue profitable non-agricultural activities others to ensure political protection, as emerges clearly from what a Vodda man told us.

Thus, one day while Suri and I were talking with a young Vodda lady shopkeeper who was telling us that she makes a reasonable living out of her shop a Vodda man in the crowd around us insisted on relating his own experience. He said:

During 1993 I was doing contract work in a village in Chickmagalur District when because of the Cauvery Water Dispute between Tamil Nadu and Karnataka violence erupted and many Tamilians, like we Voddas who now reside in Karnataka villages were attacked by the local population. This made a number of my Vodda friends return to Tamil Nadu. I too was afraid of what might happen to my kin and friends left in Wangala. But we turned out to be very fortunate. Mr T. Thimmegowda who originates from Wangala and happened then to be District Commissioner in Chickmagalur District immediately phoned his Mandya District counterpart and requested to ensure that the Tamilians residing in Wangala should be given protection. Because of Mr T. Thimmegowda no Vodda in Wangala came to any harm. This gave us all reassurance and we Voddas now feel safe in Wangala.

We also met an older Vodda man who showed us round the structure of the house he had recently constructed with government support and proudly pointed out the extension he was in the process of building for himself. He is one of the earlier migrants who stayed on and has been absorbed into Wangala society. Such instances show how immigration has become accepted in Wangala. So much so that adolescents even expect an increasing number of migrants which will make their village grow into a town within the not too distant future. A Wangala student outlined in his essay entitled 'Wangala, Past, Present and Future' his vision of Wangala in the year 2006:

> Wangala will be a town with many facilities. The number of labourers will have decreased and many people will have taken up business. The population will become 10 to 15 thousand and it may become the fifth largest town in Mandya District.... The rural environment will change to an urban setting.... I definitely want to remain in Wangala and work for the welfare of my people. Personally I would like to become a film script writer; through stories I hope I shall succeed to enlighten villagers. If I cannot become a writer I think I shall become a social worker. I am determined to do something that will help to ensure our society's well being.[1]

It seems that the many urban-style amenities Wangala's youth can now enjoy in their own village have strengthened their social identity. This has led them to expect that their village is destined to grow into a thriving town very much along the lines of what they know has happened in Mandya.

Dalena presents quite a different picture from Wangala. The diversification of economic activities and focus on professional and vocational education has created many links between the villagers and the wider economy. Several of them have moved with their families to their urban places of employment and have cut their links with Dalena. There are signs that this trend will continue to increase. More young men from Dalena seek urban employment. Those that succeed will soon want to settle near their place of work. Thus in Dalena the desire for emigration is shared by a growing number of villagers while only a few individuals have moved into the village over the past forty years. In Wangala the exact opposite pertains; most villagers, especially the younger ones, want and expect their village to grow into a town by immigration; very few display any interest in moving elsewhere.

Natural Population Increase Fecundity and mortality rates together determine the natural rates of population growth. Unfortunately, I was not able to collect the basic data necessary to calculate these rates for Wangala and Dalena. All I did manage to get are details of family planning adopters in Wangala. Better education among Wangala villagers is reflected in their attitude towards family planning. Many men and women mentioned to us their worries about their society's rapid population growth and stressed the importance of family planning. From what they told us the number of children young couples desire is no more than two, though there is still emphasis on having at least one son. The doctor at Wangala's Primary Health Centre proudly told me that as many as 71 per cent of Wangala's eligible couples have adopted family planning. The preferred method is tubectomy. There have only been fortysix births among all the 371 eligible couples in 1995. In both villages there is obvious concern about the problems caused by the large increase in numbers. More and more villagers display interest in family planning.

Palgowda emphasised the importance of keeping Dalena's population within manageable limits (see p. 157) Nelgowda, one of Dalena's elected members of the *grama* panchayat also stressed the urgency of reducing the rate of population increase:

> Our growing population constitutes a serious disadvantage, as lands are strictly limited and our dry land is not very productive. We have to take steps to have fewer children. We now arrange for our daughters to get married when they are a little older. We advise young couples to adopt family planning. Many of them attend the clinics located within the vicinity. We therefore expect that a

smaller family size will before too long reduce population pressure on our limited lands.

Nelgowda is about 45 years old and has studied up to School Leaving Certificate level. As the son of Dalena's previous entrepreneurial and now deceased village headman he lives in a big urban-style house to the West of the highway next to his cane crusher and flour mill. He repeatedly emphasised that he himself has only two children—both boys. He fully approves of his fellow villagers who decide to live and work outside Dalena and does not even contemplate the possibility of his village growing larger by future immigration. The decline in social cohesion that has accompanied Dalena's further integration into the wider economy does not seem to worry Nelgowda in the least.

Decentralisation of Education

In 1955 most Wangala villagers still regarded education as a luxury they could not afford. Rural households depended on their children to help with farm and domestic work. Children looked after farm animals, collected firewood, fetched water, etc. Dalena households could then even more easily spare their sons, because their labour was not essential for dry farming in the village or for wet cultivation outside. The many links these villagers had with the wider economy made them appreciate the importance of education. Many wanted their sons to secure positions in the state public service. In their eyes education provided a passport for such jobs.

Therefore, already in the mid-1950s there were a number of Dalena men who were literate in English. One young Peasant was already a student of physics at Mysore University. Though the educational differentiation was much greater in Dalena than in Wangala, the overall literacy rate was very similar in the two villages—in Wangala and Dalena only 12 per cent over 5 year olds were literate. On our return in 1970 we found a new primary school building in Dalena. It had been put up in 1960 before the introduction of group panchayats when it was still left to the individual village to decide on priorities in capital expenditure. Dalena villagers attached great importance to education and therefore invested in a school building. Only a small proportion of children of school age attended the classes which were conducted in the village temple. Since caste discrimination debarred Scheduled Castes from entering the temple none of their children attended school and only very few girls were sent to school.

The 1961 Mysore Compulsory Education Act aimed at enforcing education by making primary education compulsory and free for all children. It took years before the Act had the desired effect. At first it made villagers register their children at their local school but this did not make them attend classes. In 1955 only some 40 per cent of the boys of Wangala between the age of five and fourteen years attended school; not one above that age was at school. By 1970 as many as 52 per cent of the boys between six and twenty years attended school. Seventeen of a total number of 174 school-age boys attended high school, of these only two were Scheduled Castes. Not a single Wangala girl went beyond primary education as the education of girls was seen as a waste of time. Wangala's primary school had moved from the temple to the disused Public Works department bungalow I had occupied during my earlier stay in the village. When I visited Wangala's primary school on an ordinary school day I counted thirtysix children, of whom only two were Scheduled Castes. These numbers, the head teacher assured me, represented only about one-third of the total enrolment. He went on to say 'attendance is not very regular and generally far from 100 per cent'. A few of the Wangala boys who in 1955 came regularly to me for help with their English homework continued their studies. It took Wangala longer than Dalena to appreciate the advantages of education. Thimmegowda was the first Wangala man to have attained a post-graduate degree. His subsequent position in the administrative service coupled with his commitment to improving his native village have helped to bring about many of the changes that have taken place in Wangala. His fellow villagers are all very proud of him and grateful for his help. Older men and women who remembered earlier times when they lived without the various facilities now available to them in their village kept telling us: 'Without our Thimmegowda we would not have managed to enjoy all these amenities.' Some of Wangala's younger educated men told us that T. Thimmegowda inspired them some years ago to start a Youth Association. Its President, who has a B.Sc., said:

Our Youth Association has become a thriving organisation. We now have thirtyeight male and two female members; their ages range from eighteen to thirtyfive years. We pursue cultural activities, such as observing Independence and Republic Day as well as other regional festivals. We do a lot of voluntary work: we have constructed a flag pole, a drama stage and even have helped with drainage. We are proud of our achievements and hope our organisation will continue to grow and prosper!

The commitment of Wangala youth to improve their village and their admiration for T. Thimmegowda's part in this emerges clearly from a poem written by a student at Wangala's Composite Junior College:

Our Village Son

This sprouting village has been putting down a
strong root
It tried to grow into a big tree.
This big tree had no branches,
branches have now been added
and life is being filled
So that the tree can grow further
With the help of T. Thimmegowda
our village son and our pride[2]

It seems that every village needs a Thimmegowda...

To raise educational levels involves a long-term investment. This can be seen clearly in Wangala, where villagers' education has extended at both ends of the scale. By 1996 there were nurseries staffed with trained pre-school teachers. There were also many well-educated men living in the village, who had attended the university and had vocational training in skills such as printing and bookbinding.

Educational facilities have been decentralised for the benefit of rural areas. Mandya now offers a great variety of tertiary education. This enables students from the surrounding rural areas to take advantage of higher education without having to go to the big cities like Bangalore or Mysore. Almost all those Wangala men who pursued higher education between 1970 and 1996 obtained their degrees and diplomas in Mandya. Their studies did not take them too far away from home so that they did not lose their rural identity. They are putting their education to good use in developing their village. Wangala's overall literacy rate increased from 19 to 48 per cent between 1970 and 1996; it is still much lower for women. Many villagers now read newspapers. The effect of education is also noticeable in village politics. A number of Wangala's elected councillors have university degrees. They are impressive orators who present their arguments convincingly.

The importance the people of Wangala these days attach to education is shown by the impressive educational complex, which now employs as many as seventeen teachers. It caters not only for the youngsters of Wangala but also for those from surrounding villages. Every morning boys and girls dressed in neat school uniforms approach the school from different directions. The proportion of female and Scheduled Caste students is still well below the proportion they occupy in the total village population, but at least there already are some of both. Their proportion declines with higher levels of schooling: girls make up 57 per cent of the first standard in the higher primary school, 38 per cent of the standard eight students and only 30 per cent of pre-university college students. Yet it is encouraging to see so many youngsters and in particular so many girls and Scheduled Castes attending school regularly. This is a new phenomenon which in my 1970 re-study I failed to take into account. Much of the teaching in village schools is still a legacy of British days. In 1955 I saw the teacher explaining to Dalena school children how to add in pound, shilling and pence, something they would never be expected to do. Today these children still learn more about England than about their own local environment. Some children in Wangala showed me their school books. I spotted among the first few pages a map of England and photos of London buildings but I found no map of India or Karnataka in the rest of the book. There may of course be other books devoted to teaching children about their own country which I did not see, but they certainly did not learn anything about the history of their own village. I established this after questioning both teachers and students. In 1996 Dalena had two nurseries but still only the government higher primary school in the building which had been put up as long ago as 1960. Its appearance showed that it had seen better days; it needed a new coat of paint and looked badly run down. There are still only three class rooms in which seven standards are taught by three teachers. There too the proportion of female students declines with higher standards: in the 1995–96 school year there were 60 per cent girls in standard one and only 38 per cent in standard seven. Dalena youngsters wanting to study beyond standard seven have to attend school outside their village; most of them go either to Yeleyur, which is situated to the West of the highway 2 kilometres away or travel to Mandya.

There are now many well-educated Dalena men. When we tried to establish their exact number our informants failed to reach a consensus. This was because a large proportion of them have left and do not have any contacts with their native village any more. Dalena people therefore disagree on who they still consider as one of their villagers. We accepted the numbers on which most of our informants agreed:

two have medical degrees, two have legal qualifications, six have post-graduate degrees, twenty have first class degrees and four have technical diplomas. However, unlike their counterparts in Wangala most have studied either at Mysore or Bangalore University and are now working and often also residing far away from their village. I got the impression that Dalena's educated men do not see any possibility of putting their training to their own benefit or that of the village by settling in Dalena.

The only exception is Palgowda. He is about 50 years old and is a qualified solicitor. With encouragement and financial support from his father's brother who worked as agricultural officer, Palgowda studied at Mandya High School before going to Mysore University. After he qualified he returned to Dalena but worked in Mandya. For some years now he has worked as an independent advocate specialising in motor accident claims. His main objective in life seems to be to breathe some new civic sense into Dalena society through political manoeuvres. I quote what he told me at length in fairly fluent English because I think his account illustrates several important features of Dalena's changes since 1970:

In 1978 shortly after I returned to Dalena some villagers suggested that I should become a candidate for the forthcoming panchayat elections. I agreed just for the fun of it, but did not canvass at all. To my own surprise I was elected. Then in 1986 the Karnataka government appointed me as member of the Committee empowered to select village accounts for Mandya district. Many candidates offered me large bribes to secure jobs—I could have collected as much as Rs 300,000—but I made it clear to everyone that I was not prepared to accept bribes; I rather made sure the jobs went to deserving candidates. Through this I established my reputation as an honest and upright person. It gives me confidence that if I decide to enter the political field I can beat any competitor and that I can ensure the election of any candidate I decide to support! I personally know Mr Devegowda, the present Indian Prime Minister [1997] and our local Member of the Legislative Assembly (MLA) who belongs to the Janata Dal party. Politically our village is divided into two factions: the larger proportion of villagers under the leadership of Chikkachennegowda support Janata Dal and a smaller number led by Woddetimmegowda support the Congress party. Our factions are organised along lineage lines. There are lots of disputes between these two opposing factions. I myself am one of the elders of Woddetimmegowda's lineage. Though my faction supports the Congress party, as an educated man I keep good relations also with many Janata Dal party politicians.

The lineage composition of the two opposing factions has remained unchanged over at least seventy years. I can show you a document dated 1927 to prove it. This document was left to me by my father's father Puttaswamygowda. It illustrates the opposition between the same two major lineages that are still operative today. In the 1920s there were plans to build a temple in the centre of the village.

Chikkachennegowda's paternal ancestors wanted its use to be restricted to their lineage, whereas my paternal grandfather insisted that it must be open to all Peasants. The dispute was taken to the British court; while it was pending the idol was taken to Yeleyur, the neighbouring larger village. The court ruled in favour of my grandfather and the temple was finally built in 1949. I am proud to belong to Woddetimmegowda's faction. Though it is much smaller than its opponent, most Dalena educated men belong to it.

There have been no outward changes, no development since 1955 in Dalena. All that has happened is we have grown in numbers and there are now many more houses. But also more families have left the village and more men are employed outside Dalena. Admittedly, some attitudes have been changing. For instance, Dalena Peasants have begun to take food from Washermen kitchens. If this trend continues it may not be long before we shall accept food also from Scheduled Castes. Who knows?

I am worried that if our village population continues to increase, things will get worse and worse here. I therefore try to encourage our young couples to take advantage of family planning. There seems to be a growing interest in family planning among them: many women have had the tubectomy operation—only few men are prepared to have a vasectomy. Only future will tell how successful family planning has been in keeping our population at a reasonable level.

Our village has been allowed to run down. The public buildings have been sadly neglected. The primary school building badly needs to be renovated, and our temples have been allowed to deteriorate. In 1978, I made it my first job to renovate the Anjeneya temple at a cost of Rs 40,000. Hardly any of Dalena's villagers were interested in this venture; they refused to contribute towards the expense. This made me decide to raise the necessary funds mainly from outsiders. At the time entrepreneurs from outside Dalena wanted my intervention to help them purchase some Dalena lands for industrial sites. I refused their offer of large commission but told them I was prepared to accept their donations as contribution for the temple renovation. Not all of these outsiders were Hindus; some were Muslims or Christians. Anyway, with their financial help I managed to complete the temple repairs. I am happy that the temple again looks very attractive. I now want to see all the other temples also renovated and more facilities made available within Dalena. I am trying to do the same for Dalena what T. Thimmegowda has been doing for Wangala. He is more fortunate in gaining the support from his villagers. In Dalena they show no interest in improving their village environment. I have to do everything myself: I have taken on the chairmanship of the Dalena Dairy Co-operative Society and of the school committee. None of the other board members seem to take any interest. A Youth Association existed in Dalena for about one year; it had no civic support and did nothing. Members then decided to wind it up. The total lack of civic sense is very disappointing. Each family is concerned solely with its own economic future and devotes all efforts to securing jobs outside Dalena for its younger members. They could not care less about their own village! All this makes me feel very frustrated and depressed; so much so that I often contemplate moving out of the village and leaving Dalena people to fend for themselves. If things do not improve soon I think I shall leave Dalena with my wife and children before too long....

Palgowda's sad tale is very revealing. It clearly illustrates the important role of education as an agent of change. In both villages it has brought about an awareness of the problems created by rapid population expansion and consequently an interest in family planning: in both villages an educated man is using his influence to promote village improvements. Wangala's T. Thimmegowda is more effective because of his position as IAS officer whereas Dalena's Palgowda has to rely on his personal relations with politicians and other outsiders to support his efforts within his village. In Dalena, city-based further education has made villagers more village-extroverted which is reflected in the decline of civic identity. By contrast, in Wangala, town-based tertiary education has reinforced civic commitment.

NOTES

1. The essay was written in the vernacular by D. Nanjundaswamy and translated by A.P. Suryanarayana.
2. The poem was written in the vernacular by D. Nanjundaswamy and translated into English by A.P. Suryanarayana.

THIRTEEN

Economic Change Factors

Agricultural Technologies

*W*ith population growth and limited availability of lands the average per capita land area has declined in Wangala by about 55 per cent and in Dalena by about 45 per cent. But Wangala's wet lands permitted the application of new agricultural technologies which improved crop productivity.

In discussions with farmers it emerged that many single out the change in cultivation practices as *the* most important change that has taken place over the past forty years. Most Wangala farmers these days plant high yielding varieties of seeds and apply fertiliser to their irrigated lands. Much agricultural labour has been replaced by mechanisation. Different types of capital assets are now available to farmers: for instance, besides the numerous cane crushers and flour mills, there are now irrigation pump sets, power tillers and tractors. One Wangala farmer told us:

About four months ago I managed to get a loan of Rs 70,000 at 14 per cent interest from the Wangala branch of the Corporation Bank. This enabled me to purchase a power tiller, which I now use on my own lands, but I also offer it for hire. With my power tiller it takes about three hours to plough an acre of land. I charge Rs 125 per hour. I am pretty confident that there will be sufficient demand for my power tiller to enable me to repay my debt within about two or three years. Once I am in the clear I can then continue earning quite a bit of money out of hiring my power tiller.

To meet the higher costs of agricultural inputs farmers can get credit from different sources. By paying Rs 10 and thus becoming a shareholder of the Wangala co-operative society a farmer qualifies for credit on the security of his land holding. If he wants to get seeds or fertiliser he can get it through the co-operative society. He has to pay only 20 per cent cash down; of the remaining amount he gets 60 per cent in kind and 40 per cent in cash. Farmers can purchase fertiliser on credit also from private traders at government controlled prices. Only when traders have access to certain kinds of fertiliser that are temporarily in short supply while farmers are eager to get hold of some quantities, do they get away with charging higher prices unofficially.

Urban Impact

The recent commercial and industrial development of Mandya, the headquarters of Mandya District, which is within easy reach from Dalena and Wangala, has had an important impact on its rural hinterland. Mandya's population has increased manifold from about 6,000 persons in 1951 to 120,265 in 1991. This large population growth resulted of course mainly from urban migration. Increasing numbers of villagers not only from Mandya's immediate vicinity but also from much further afield have been attracted by the income-earning possibilities the growing town offers. The town has over the years developed into a thriving commercial, industrial and educational centre.

Travelling through the various parts of Mandya it becomes apparent that its development has been accompanied by a distinct class division. An area with substantial residential buildings, each of which is surrounded by large and well-tended gardens, manifests the presence of wealthy households. The presence of a sizeable middle class is indicated by a sprawling area with smaller but also nice looking bungalows each standing on a separate plot. A large mass of unemployed unskilled labourers mostly stay in small thatched roofed huts or in temporary and improvised accommodation.

Mandya's rapid urbanisation has had numerous repercussions in Dalena and Wangala. It provided a demonstration model for village development. In terms of lifestyles this is reflected not only in the many recently built urban-style houses in the villages but also in the furniture now part of many such houses and altogether in the availability of amenities such as television sets and telephones. In 1955 these were luxuries of which villagers would not even have dreamt; now they have become an accepted part of village reality. Economic activities and economic diversification have also been shaped by Mandya's development. Though this process has occurred both in Dalena and Wangala it has taken different forms in the two villages.

Many researchers and developers complain that they have to rely mainly on macro-surveys for information on non-agricultural activities in rural areas; they often bemoan the lack of relevant micro-studies, saying:

> It is likely that the decentralisation of certain industries together with relatively short distances and better transport facilities may have made it possible for many members of rural households to shift to non-agricultural occupations without changing residences.... Unfortunately, we do not have any data to assess the quantitative significance of such phenomena (Basant and Kumar, 1994: 111).[1]

These researchers might be well advised to take a look at Dalena and other similar type villages. Dalena's location near the town of Mandya and other expanding industrial and commercial areas enables villagers to commute. The constraints of dry land have forced them to seek incomes from other sources outside their village: skilled mechanics and electricians work on nearby industrial estates, building contractors build houses in neighbouring villages and towns, horticulturists work for the Bangalore and Mandya departments of agriculture; cane crushers process cane grown outside Dalena, carpenters make the more elaborate carts now wanted by better-off farmers in neighbouring irrigated villages, buying agents and merchants operate at Mandya's jaggery auction and many villagers are employed at the Mandya refinery. Dalena shops and restaurants by the side of the highway cater mainly to passing traffic—they sell for instance bottled petrol. Dalena villagers own four lorries which fetch the cane to the crushers and take the jaggery to buyers. About fifteen households own scooters. A few houses have their own telephones. There are eight small shops and as many small restaurants catering to villagers' requirements but none of the many specialist services that are now available in Wangala. Dalena's internal market is too small for much specialisation to meet local demand; villagers have to export their skills and services to secure and/or improve their livelihood. This has meant that they have turned more to work in secondary than tertiary industry, because in doing so they encounter less competition for employment in the wider economy. Some 65 per cent of Dalena men within working age are engaged in non-agricultural work outside the village and about 60 per cent of these pursue industrial activities. Also a considerable number of professionally trained Dalena men have already left the village with their immediate families to work and reside elsewhere. They appear to have severed their links with their native village and are likely to be forgotten soon by the people of Dalena.

By contrast Wangala's access to irrigation and the consequent increase in crop productivity and rural incomes has created a sufficiently large internal demand to promote non-agricultural activities within the village. There are vegetarian and non-vegetarian small restaurants all of which appear to be well-frequented by Peasants. Most of them have sheltered seating accommodation outside, so that customers can take their drinks and food while enjoying a bit of the breeze. There are also many small stores (see p. 52). One engineering and two cycle workshops offer hire and repair services. A post office provides, among other things, savings arrangements. A corporation bank branch offers general banking facilities and two finance corporations offer credit. Two private fertiliser businesses and one general farmers' co-operative as well as a dairy co-operative together with tractors, power tillers and harvesters on hire and many cane crushers provide the goods and services farmers need. Those craftsmen like the Potters whose products are no more in demand have had to turn to other work. One Wangala Potter does tailoring and another has acquired a motor rickshaw with the help of a bank loan; he runs it as a taxi. Almost all Wangala individuals who pursue non-agricultural occupations work within the village; the activities of about 60 per cent of them can be classified under tertiary industries; the rest are mainly craftsmen like the Blacksmith and Carpenter whose hereditary skills are essential in making and repairing agricultural tools and equipment. Most of the goods and services villagers require are now available within Wangala and this attracts neighbouring villagers to avail themselves of Wangala's facilities. The expanding market induces craftsmen from outside to move to Wangala and some of them have settled in the village recently. Wangala's non-agricultural activities are almost all directly or indirectly connected with village agriculture. Significantly, when I asked what changes they would like to see in the near future the Wangala men invariably said, 'We need a factory in Wangala that will manufacture agricultural implements'. Thus, whereas Dalena villagers concentrate their non-agricultural activities in secondary industries and meet the needs arising outside their immediate rural environment, Wangala's non-agricultural activities tend to relate in one way or another to intra-village requirements and agriculture.

Commercial Opportunities

The railway line and the major highway connecting Bangalore with Mysore pass through Mandya. There is now quite a substantial industrial estate to the west of the railway line. The sugar refinery was the first factory established in Mandya. It set the pace for the town's subsequent rapid expansion. By now there are many other industrial and commercial establishments that flourish in Mandya. Over the years the refinery's fortunes have depended not only on the productivity of cane crops which in turn largely depended on availability of water in the irrigation canals, but even more so on competing cane sale outlets.

The jaggery boon of the 1960s obviously alerted farmers to the possibility of alternative sales outlets besides the Mandya refinery and they never forgot it. There has been a growing demand for jaggery for sweetening purposes in different parts of India. The demand for jaggery therefore continued even after the 1960s, though the abolition of prohibition considerably reduced its level (see p. 115). This meant that buyers continued to tour with their trucks the cane growing areas to buy jaggery from local farmers. Many farmers and even some of the buyers complained that this was an inefficient and unsatisfactory marketing system.

In some cane producing states of India there already existed official Agricultural Marketing Corporations where jaggery was successfully auctioned. In 1989 the then Mandya District Commissioner decided to sponsor the establishment of such a corporation in Mandya. It now occupies a large area by the side of the town's main road where there are many go-downs and where jaggery auctions are held daily. This corporation operates through licensed agents and licensed buyers. The agents establish go-downs on the grounds of the corporation; they form a relationship with specific farmers and take care of their jaggery delivery and see it through auction. The cane supplier ultimately receives the total amount the buyer offers. The buyer has to pay 103 per cent of that amount: 2 per cent goes to the agent and 1 per cent to the Agricultural Marketing Corporation. The jaggery auctions have considerably improved cane farmers' bargaining position and have resulted in a mushrooming of village cane crushers, as can be seen in Dalena and Wangala.

The two villages were, however, affected differently by the commercialisation of jaggery sales. In Wangala, rising jaggery prices encouraged extension of cane cultivation besides the establishment of more cane crushers. By contrast Dalena villagers did not have the option of extending their cane cultivation on their own village lands. Instead some enterprising men sought a niche for themselves as agents or buyers. One morning when we arrived in Dalena we encountered Kenchegowda, a bright young man who was just about to set off on his motorbike to take his 8-year-old daughter to school in Mandya. I was both surprised and impressed when I heard him welcome me in reasonably good English by my full name. When I enquired how he had come to know my name he showed me his personal diary where he had written down a copy of my visiting card. When I enquired about his occupation he explained that he was a merchant buying jaggery at the Mandya auction and selling it in other parts of India. He went on to tell me that:

> There are four varieties of jaggery, three of them are used for sweetening, but come in different sizes and texture; the fourth variety is inferior and almost black, but demands a much higher price simply because it is used for distilling into alcohol. Seventyfive per cent of jaggery is sold for sweetening and 25 per cent for alcohol. Before the establishment of the jaggery auctions in Mandya I used to tour the cane producing areas around Mandya and buy jaggery direct from villagers. Cane auctions have put farmers into a stronger bargaining position. At the Mandya auction there are about twentyfive merchants bidding for jaggery. Jaggery fetches higher prices than what it used to do. But of course we merchants try our best to pass these price increases onto our own customers in other Indian states.

Commercialisation of the jaggery trade has led Dalena entrepreneurs to extend their commercial links way beyond the boundaries of Karnataka. As jaggery merchants they have to take higher risks. When bidding at the auction they must already have in mind potential buyers and an estimate of the price they will pay.

Wangala cane farmers now try to keep themselves informed about jaggery prices and compare them with what the refinery pays for contracted cane. When jaggery prices are more attractive than those paid for cane by the refinery, many farmers are tempted to default the cane contracts they have entered into with the refinery. This poses serious problems for Mandya's refinery because it makes its planning extremely difficult. The Refinery Manager related:

> We continually face unexpected fluctuations in the volume of cane supplies. In 1992–93 competition from jaggery auctions was largely responsible for the refinery making a loss of over Rs 22,000,000. Between 1991–92 and 1992–93 the metric tonnage of cane the refinery crushed fell by 12 per cent from 664,329 to 591,229 and the price paid per ton increased by 7 per cent from Rs 390 to Rs 420. During the same period the average price per quintal of jaggery rose by as much as 43 per cent from Rs 440 to Rs 630 and the quantity of jaggery auctioned increased by about 10 per cent. Significantly, farmers attracted by the higher jaggery prices delivered to the factory in 1993 only 76 per cent of their contracted quantity.

The refinery's profitability thus is strongly influenced by what farmers decide to do with the cane they grow, i.e., either to supply it to the refinery or sell it as jaggery. When I further discussed this problem with the Refinery General Manager he complained that:

> Farmers use the factory as a backdrop. To be on the safe side they always seek contracts with us. But whenever they consider jaggery sales a more attractive alternative they reduce their supplies to the factory. Then when they do not have such option they try to exceed supplies of their contracted cane tonnage. During the cane glut of 1995–96 farmers tried hard to sell us more of their cane. We tried as best we could to help them until we reached the limits of our crushing capacity and could accept no more cane. Without any sales outlets many farmers considered it not worth while to harvest their cane and allowed their crops to dry in the fields. I can sympathise with them and understand that they are now very upset. But they only have themselves to blame. If they had not been induced by rising jaggery prices to extend their cane acreages by so much they would not now find themselves in this predicament. Yet they do not seem to realise this and quite unjustly blame us for their difficulties. They expect us to buy from them whatever quantity of cane they decide to sell to us. They fail to appreciate how difficult it is for a large refinery to adjust to such great fluctuations in cane supplies.

Environmental conditions have influenced different responses to this commercialisation. Wangala farmers, who in 1955 were all risk minimisers and struggled to secure contracts with Mandya's refinery are now prepared to take more risks. They produce a much larger quantity of cane than they contract with the refinery in the hope that they can sell it as jaggery at attractive prices. They are happy as long as the going is good, but complain bitterly if the jaggery market fails. Having become aware of the bargaining strength they can derive from facing competing buyers they have learned to choose how and where to sell their cane with a view to optimising their returns. Wangala's thirtytwo cane crushers clearly indicate that many farmers consider it an economic advantage to process the cane they grow. They have taken to vertical integration like fish take to water. Yet they still do not appear to appreciate the impact on prices of increasing volumes of supply. High jaggery prices induce many farmers to put more acreage under cane cultivation. They do not consider that when many farmers do likewise the jaggery market will be flooded and prices will fall.

For Dalena, where lack of irrigation does not offer farmers the option to extend their cane cultivation on their own village lands, jaggery auctions have led to further economic diversification. There are now more cane crushers in this dry land village that service neighbouring irrigated villages; some have become jaggery merchants while others act as buying agents. This has required agents to build relationships with local cane growers and merchants to develop a wide network among suppliers of distant buyers. In doing so, Dalena's village extroversion that already existed to a certain extent in 1955 and which had developed further by 1970 is reinforced.

Mandya's jaggery auctions organised by the Agricultural Marketing Board have thus not only strengthened the links between the town and its rural hinterland but they have also helped to further the process of commercialisation in villages like Wangala and Dalena.

Financial Opportunities

The introduction of new and costly capital assets to farming and the expansion of non-agricultural activities could not have taken place without improvements in savings and credit facilities. In 1955 most villagers were indebted to informal money lenders; only the largest landowners qualified for bank credit. Nowadays many villagers have savings in appropriate institutions and have access to credit from various sources. Their financial position has thus greatly improved, though of course this does not apply to the same extent to all villagers.

Post Offices in Wangala and Dalena, besides postal services, also offer savings facilities. There are now numerous Recurring Deposit Accounts at Wangala's post office worth altogether about Rs 150,000. These accounts are meant for long-term deposits and carry an interest ranging from 10.5 per cent during the first year to 12.5 per cent during the fifth year. There are also about fortyfive short-term savings accounts worth altogether Rs 100,000 earning 5 per cent interest. Half of the savings belong to the Wangala school complex and the other half belong to individuals. The post offices also distribute government pensions and welfare payments.

Wangala's Corporation Bank Branch provides only savings and credit facilities, and current cheque accounts; it serves all the villages included in the Wangala *grama* panchayat. In 1996 Wangala villagers had some 1,200 savings accounts with a total of about Rs 950,000; about 125 of these savings accounts are held by women without their husbands' knowledge and twentyfive are in the names of widows, who receive a monthly state pension of Rs 150. There are eightyfive current accounts with a total of about Rs 100,000 and 105 fixed deposit accounts worth a total of some Rs 530,000.

The earnings of members of Wangala's Dairy Co-operative Society are paid directly into their bank accounts. Every month the President of the Co-operative Society hands the bank manager a cheque with a list of the amounts to be paid to individual suppliers. This explains the large number of small savings accounts. The average yearly earnings per milk supplier amount to about Rs 850.

The Bank also offers credit, but only on the basis of security of land, jewellery or third party guarantee. The Bank Manager explained:

The government provides a subsidy for agricultural development loans ranging from 50 per cent for Scheduled Castes/Scheduled Tribes to 15 per cent for other borrowers; the bank lends the remainder for which debtors have to pay interest. In 1995–96 the total government subsidy at Wangala was Rs 115,000. We gave one Peasant farmer a loan of Rs 4,000 to buy a buffalo; the government subsidised it by 33 per cent and the rest was bank credit at 12.5 per cent interest. We calculated that the buffalo will yield an annual income of Rs 850 which should enable the debtor to repay his loan in four years. However, the overall loan recovery rate is very poor; we have many large outstanding loans. Eleven court cases are pending; three of them involve Wangala individuals who altogether owe

Rs 34,000 for five years already without even having yet paid any interest. In 1995–96 we recovered only Rs 1,300,000 whereas our break-even rate is Rs 1,600,000. Our branch thus runs at a loss. If we were a private bank we would have already been closed down. But as we are a government institution we can continue incurring losses.

As I sat listening to his tale a well-dressed man, who had arrived in his own private car, walked in. He was warmly welcomed by the bank manager who introduced him as Mr Raj, a 'model' bank customer. Mr Raj proceeded in perfect English to tell me why he is considered such a good customer:

I am a Sindhi born in Mysore fifty years ago. I studied journalism and only one month after attaining my university degree when I was no more than 21 years old I got married. This meant that I had to earn some money to provide for my wife. Seeing it was not easy to earn a living as a young and unknown journalist I decided to open a cloth shop in Mysore. Though it was not doing too badly I was not really happy with it. When the Mandya refinery auctioned its Wangala plantation land in 1967 my father bought eight acres of wet lands at Rs 5,000 per acre. Do you know how much such an acre is worth now? As much as Rs 160,000!!! My father made an excellent investment. The land remained idle until 1988 when I decided to move to Mandya with my family and start cultivating it. I did not know the first thing about farming. So I learnt from books and from talking to experienced farmers. I then also met the bank manager. He seemed to think I had entrepreneurial talents and encouraged me to develop the 8 acres of wet lands. He generously let me have a loan of Rs 650,000 at 15 per cent annual interest. In Mandya I joined a club and altogether tried to extend my network of relations as widely as possible. In doing so I also managed to establish good contacts with the management of the Mandya refinery. Thus with the borrowed money I hired labourers and machinery and cleared the lands. In the beginning to reduce the risk in my novice farming I planted a large part of the land with cane on contract with the refinery. This enabled me within four years to repay almost two-thirds of my bank loan, which greatly pleased the bank manager; he felt his faith in me had been justified. I then thought it advisable to diversify my crop cultivation and investigated market demands for different crops. When I discovered that there is a growing export demand for copra and mangos I planted coconut palms and mango trees. I now look forward to getting into the export trade in about two years when my first crop of mangos will mature. I always keep an eye on the changing market demand for the different agricultural products. I am convinced that only by doing so will I make my farm into a profitable venture!

Mr Raj's account greatly impressed me, particularly his interest in diversifying his crop cultivation in tune with market demands. I suspect that many Wangala farmers could benefit a lot from the systematic way he sets about farming his wet lands.

Finance Corporations, of which there are two in Wangala, were started only within the last two years. They are registered as co-operative societies. Each corporation has six partners and was started with a share capital of Rs 90,000 contributed equally by the partners. One of the founding members of the Soudhardha Kougaroda Finance Corportation related:

> We saw the numerous finance corporations that have been established in Mandya and are registered as co-operative societies allowed to offer loans to business ventures only, not for agricultural purposes. We found out that all these corporations were thriving because of the many petty business people who had difficulty in getting loans elsewhere. This gave us the idea to set up such finance corporations in Wangala where there are also many small businesses in need of loans to meet their running expenses. Six of us got together and each contributed Rs 15,000. We started off with a working capital of Rs 90,000. Our loans to small entrepreneurs range from Rs 2,000 to Rs 25,000 at 23 per cent interest for a maximum period of ten months. We deduct the interest at the time we give the loan. The rest is collected by a man specially engaged to call personally on each of our debtors on a daily basis. He is paid Rs 500 monthly for the job. Our debtors prefer to repay small amounts daily and always do so. The secret of our collector's success lies in his personal contact with our debtors. Unlike the banks we have no loan recovery problem. By now we have altogether advanced about Rs 350,000 and with it have helped small businesses to grow not only in Wangala but also neighbouring villages. The Rs 90,000 working capital with which we originally started our finance corporation has almost doubled during the two years we have been in operation. Our financial success has encouraged some of our fellow

villagers to invest in our venture; this has added another Rs 159,000 for which we pay 16 per cent annual interest to depositors.

Kangowda, one of the founding members, assured us that this also applies to the other corporation in the village and the crowd surrounding us all nodded in agreement.

The success of Wangala's finance corporations made me wonder why none of my enterprising Dalena friends had yet thought of establishing a finance corporation in their village. When I asked them they told me that a few of them are involved in such corporations in Mandya; they felt that the demand in Dalena and neighbouring villages for small business finance was not sufficiently strong to warrant the establishment of a finance corporation in their own village.

The way Wangala finance corporations function has convinced me that they represent ingenious institutions appropriately adapted to the needs of small businesses. The modus operandi of the loan collection is so obviously well suited to debtors' requirements and ensures a high recovery rate. It has the advantage of continuing the personal aspect of creditor–debtor relationships, which used to be the central feature of traditional money-lending arrangements in Wangala; only now loans are set in a new financial environment. The government may therefore be well advised to encourage such finance corporations to take on financing of agricultural activities instead of prohibiting them from doing so. Unlike the government bank branch in Wangala which concentrates on agricultural credit and operates at a loss, these privately organised finance corporations make a handsome profit and lenders as well as debtors are pleased with the way they are run.

NOTE

1. Rakesh Basant and B.L. Kumar, 'Rural Non-Agricultural Employment in India: A Review of Available Evidence', in *Non-Agricultural Employment in India—Trends and Prospects*. Sage Publications, New Delhi, 1994, p. 111.

FOURTEEN

Political Change Factors

WELFARE LEGISLATION

$\mathcal{T}$he myth of the isolated and self-contained Indian village polity has long been exploded. These days villages are increasingly becoming more integrated into the wider society and with it the government plays a more important role in village life. Government legislation affects not only the economic life of villagers but also their political and social relations. Through its macro-policies it impacts on micro-level activities and relationships. In a democracy—which India prides itself to be—citizens are meant to express their views and thereby exert an influence over government decisions by supporting and voting for the policies of one or other of the competing political parties. Whether or not the majority of Dalena and Wangala villagers understand and favour the policies of the political party for which they vote in elections or whether there are also other influences determining their voting is a question which emerged in the course of our recent studies. I tried to explore as much as I could whether and how villagers perceive the policies of the different political parties and how they relate to the MLA elected by them as a member of the State Legislative Assembly (see p. 181)

Ever since independence, India has grappled with what turned out to be objectives that were difficult to reconcile: namely, to ensure both rapid economic growth and a more equitable income distribution. It was soon discovered that the widely-expected 'trickle-down effect' of economic expansion was not taking place; some authorities even claimed that economic growth involved in fact a 'trickle-up effect'. In any case, it appeared very difficult to reconcile the thrust to optimise economic growth with the moral objective of social justice. At the time when India gained independence over 80 per cent of the population still lived in rural areas and followed their traditional caste-dominated socio-economic organisation. The climate of opinion among the majority of Indians was then not ready to accept some of the radical measures the Indian Constitution introduced with its emphatic anti-discrimination clauses. Many of the subsequent attempts to legislate for greater social mobility and change from a society in which status is hereditary into a society in which status depends on individual achievements failed to make much impact. Many earlier pieces of legislation were withdrawn to re-appear worded differently and under different headings to suffer the fate of their predecessors. Governments then realised that what was needed to change social attitudes and practices was a large and integrated education programme. This meant mounting literacy campaigns (see p. 229) for the present adult generation and better provision of primary, secondary and further education for present children and youth and also of course for future generations. The underlying assumption was that a better educated public will be more amenable to a socially more just style of life. It was of course difficult to anticipate with any accuracy how long it would take before *Homo Equalis* would replace *Homo Hierarchicus* in India. However, it was to be expected that it would take about fifty years for education to show results in terms of changing attitudes and social values, particularly in rural areas.

Villagers' Response to Social Legislation Since the prevalence of unemployment and under-employment in rural areas is a contributing factor to the high incidence of poverty, the Government of India has more recently directed its main thrust to alleviate the worst poverty towards the creation of supplementary employment opportunities for the rural poor during the lean agricultural season through various work programmes aimed at giving self-employment and wage employment to the poorer sections of the community. The two wage employment programmes, namely, the National Rural Employment Programme (NREP) and the Rural Landless Employment Guarantee Programme (RLEGP) which were in operation in the country were merged in 1989 into a single rural employment programme known as

Jawahar Rozgar Yojana (JRY)[1] which provides an employment assurance. All those who are in need and seek employment are entitled to paid employment for a hundred days during the lean agricultural season. The scheme was implemented in all those areas in which the revamped public distribution system operated. Its costs are shared between the centre and the states in the ratio of 80 : 20. The JRY programme targets people below the poverty line with special preference given to Scheduled Castes/Scheduled Tribes; 30 per cent of the employment opportunities are reserved for women. The JRY programme encouraged not only the development of productive assets and infrastructure but also the construction of houses for economically weaker sections including Scheduled Castes/Scheduled Tribes. It recommended the adoption of a micro-habitat approach in the construction of such houses to ensure nearness to work place and social communication. In 1994 the cost ceiling for each house constructed under the JRY programme was set at Rs 14, 000 for areas like the Deccan Plateau where Dalena and Wangala are situated. According to this programme house construction must not be undertaken by contractors or government departments but by the beneficiaries themselves. They may engage skilled workmen and contribute family labour. Sanitary latrines are expected to form an integral part of these houses and voluntary agencies are expected to popularise their use. Altogether the JRY programme focuses on alleviating the plight of the most underprivileged rural dwellers by offering them specific support.

In 1955 caste discrimination was still deeply entrenched in Dalena and even more so in Wangala. Peasant elders treated their hereditary Scheduled Caste clients as if they were dependent children; significantly, the term they used for them was *Hale Makkalu*, old children. In those days it did not occur to anyone to consider them as human beings with their own rights. Now that a new generation has taken over village leadership, attitudes have changed considerably with the benefit of education. The majority now openly approve and actively support the measures which offer positive discrimination for the Scheduled Castes. Between 1990 and 1993 the Wangala *grama* panchayat received Rs 217,816 from the government as JRY grant and matched it by contributing Rs 225,000 of council funds. Villagers contributed Rs 50,000 in kind by supplying sand, soil, etc. Altogether in Wangala itself the council spent about 30 per cent of its total expenditure (excepting the amount spent on the panchayat building) between 1990 and 1996 on improving low caste housing. There did not seem to have been any attempt made by the dominant Peasant caste to oppose these housing improvements or to sidetrack the JRY funds for other purposes. When I asked Shangowda, who was born in 1956 and is now a member of the *grama* panchayat and Wangala's 'core group', what further things need to be done in Wangala, he said in this context: 'Our first priority must be to provide houses for all the families, construct drains and tarred roads'. Shangowda represents a new type of political leadership. He obtained a B.A. degree in Mandya in 1980 and even secured a place to study for an M.A. in social sciences.

Unfortunately his father died just then. This necessitated his giving up further study to return home to look after his brothers and the family lands. He is an intelligent and enterprising young man who uses his education not only to further his own interests but also those of his fellow villagers. He owns 6 acres of wet and 5 acres of dry lands and also one cane crusher. Since his marriage in 1987 his wife gave birth to two daughters and then a son. After the birth of his son he decided not to have any more children. Although Shangowda is a much more modern village leader than were his predecessors in 1955, the traditional emphasis on a son still weighs strongly with him. Under T. Thimmegowda's influence he hopes to eliminate intra-village faction opposition and ensure village unity. These two educated Wangala villagers, both committed to improve their village, often meet either in Mandya or Wangala and discuss what strategies will best achieve their objectives. Much of the credit for the development of a more equitable society in Wangala is due to T. Thimmegowda's influence over a group of young and educated political leaders among whom Shangowda is prominent. He refers to them as the 'core group' (see p. 60).

Nevertheless, all is not well yet in Wangala and there are still cases of extreme exploitation. One day as I walked through Wangala's low caste settlement Siddaya, an elderly Scheduled Caste man, approached me. He showed his respect in the usual fashion by touching my feet and his eyes three times. He reminded me and the crowd that had gathered around us of how much I had helped them during my earlier stay in the village. Things that I myself had almost forgotten. He begged my continued help. When I assured him that I would try to help as much as possible he disappeared to return with a big envelope. Before handing it to me he explained that he used to be a *jeeta* servant (bonded labourer) of a Wangala Peasant. The envelope contained lots of legal documents relating to a land dispute in which Siddaya was involved with the wife of his Peasant master. In 1983 the Mandya District Commissioner ruled that the Peasant had wrongfully claimed Siddaya's land and that it must revert to him. In response to my question how it had come about that his land was taken away, he related at length his sad story:

> Many years ago when I was in desperate need of Rs 500 my Peasant master was prepared to lend me the money as long as I pledged my land as security. Later on when I was unable to repay my debt my Peasant master claimed my lands and cultivated them, and I myself became landless. The transaction was conducted under the traditional bonded-labour arrangements. I was therefore overjoyed with the 1983 District Commissioner's ruling, which reflected the abolition of bonded labour in India announced by the Indian Government. Alas, my joy did not last. My Peasant master was not prepared to accept defeat. He hired the services of one of Mandya's most able and expensive lawyers and took the case to the courts. In 1995 the judge declared the District Commissioner's ruling *ultra vires,* and I lost the title to my land once more. I feel very bitter about what I consider a great injustice but now I think that there is nothing more I can do to change it. I am far too poor and too ignorant to appeal against the court ruling.

Siddaya ended with a heartrending plea for my help. I told him that I would try to find out what, if anything, can be done to help him get back the lands to which since the abolition of bonded labour he would seem to have full rights. Subsequently, when I pursued Siddaya's land dispute, I realised that there was very little chance of his reclaiming his lands in the near future. I learned from some senior Karnataka state administrators that it is very difficult and needs a lot of money to get a court's judgement revoked. Siddaya's plight illustrates that there is still a strong element of continuity within Wangala's changing socio-economic caste relationships. Bonded labour has been abolished but its aftermath of injustice still prevails.

As in Wangala, in Dalena too the difference in standards of living between caste and Scheduled Caste villagers has greatly decreased. Because Dalena is part of Yeleyur *grama* panchayat it was not so easy to collect, as in Wangala, the precise details showing how much the village council spends on Scheduled Caste welfare programmes in Dalena. The figures I managed to get show that during the financial year 1995–96 about 11 per cent of the total amount of council funds spent was allocated to improving Scheduled Caste welfare.

Palgowda, the Dalena lawyer (see p. 156), assured me that Scheduled castes in their village now receive much assistance: they have improved houses built under the JRY programme; they have easy access to financial support when they want to purchase bullocks or other agricultural requirements; they are issued with green cards enabling them to buy essential items at subsidised prices, and so on.

There are now more educated Scheduled Castes in Dalena than in Wangala. Five of them have taken advantage of reserved places in the public service and are now employed outside. From Wangala there is as yet not a single Scheduled Caste working as a public servant. On a Sunday in front of a substantial and fairly new Scheduled Caste house in Dalena we spotted a man dressed in trousers, shirt and shoes unlike most other village men who all wear a shirt over a *dhoti* (loincloth). Being employed in Bangalore's forestry department he was just then back in Dalena on his weekly visit to his family. He explained that it was more economical and altogether better for his wife and children to remain in Dalena where they now have a nice home, rather than uproot them to live with him in the city. From the employment card he showed us we discovered that he gets a monthly salary of Rs 3,500. He was obviously proud of his status as public servant and quite satisfied with his salary. He told me that he feels privileged compared with most other Dalena Scheduled Castes who still depend for their livelihood on work as casual labourers.

DEMOCRACY, FACTIONS AND POLITICAL PARTIES

Village Councils

The Mysore Village Panchayat and District Board Act 1952, a revolutionary piece of legislation, introduced universal adult franchise to village government and substituted, at least legally elective for hereditary authority. As I have already discussed (see p. 104) the concepts of majority rule and elected authority were then still so alien to Wangala villagers that they displayed little interest in the election. Although the principle of elected village councils with reserved seats for the underprivileged has remained unchanged, many Acts since 1952 have changed the structure of local government. The 1959 Mysore Village

Panchayats and Local Boards Act decentralised local government administration. It abolished the District Boards and substituted a three-tier local administration consisting of village councils, *taluk* boards and a district development council for each of Mysore's nineteen districts. For instance, the district board for Mandya district, the population of which according to the 1961 Census was 899,210, was replaced by seven *taluk* boards: Mandya *taluk* had a population of 183,403 in 1961. Moreover, each *taluk* was divided into a number of constituencies which elected their representatives on the basis of universal adult franchise. The 1959 Act also raised the minimum size of population for a village panchayat to 1,500 and the maximum to 10,000. This meant that many villages—including Dalena and Wangala—were joined with neighbouring villages under one panchayat. Another Act in 1986, the Karnataka Zilla Parishads, Taluk Panchayat Samithis Mandal Panchayats and Nyaya Panchayats Rules, laid down that 'the *mandal* [group] panchayats shall consist of such number of elected members as may be notified from time to time by the government, at the rate of one member for every 400 population or part there of the *mandal* as ascertained at the last preceding census of which the relevant figures are published' (The Karnataka Zilla Parishads, Taluk Panchayats Rules, 1986). It placed a lot of discretionary powers into the hands of district commissioners by allowing these officials to increase or decrease the area of any *mandal*, alter its name and specify its headquarters. The earlier local government election system of one person one vote was changed by the 1993 Karnataka State Panchayat Raj Act which entitles every voter to cast as many votes as there are members to be elected for the constituency—no voter can give more than one vote to any one candidate. The 1993 Act reinforced the earlier three-tier panchayati raj system and changed the area of a village council to a minimum of 5,000 and a maximum of 7,000 population. The district commissioner is still empowered to declare and change the council headquarters. Membership of *taluk* panchayats was legislated to be a complex mixture of elected local government and state legislative assembly representatives and a rotation of village council chairmen. In many other respects, such as reserved seats for Scheduled Castes/Scheduled Tribes, provisions for 'Backward Castes and Classes' and women remained unchanged. The present chairman of the Wangala *grama* panchayat is a Scheduled Caste from Lokasara, a neighbouring village included in the Wangala council. He is liked and respected by the Peasant council members. There has taken place a considerable change in Peasant political behaviour since 1955. Lokasara then had a majority of Scheduled Castes who in the first democratic village council elections made sure that their numbers were reflected in the composition of the council. The Lokasara Peasants, as the main landowners, were not prepared to accept Scheduled Caste political dominance and called a lockout of their labour. This economic stranglehold put so much pressure on the Lokasara Scheduled Castes that they quickly surrendered their rightful and legal political position to the Peasants. By contrast the new generation of Peasant leaders, most of whom have had the benefit of education, now readily accept the positive discrimination in favour of the Scheduled Castes, which is incorporated in many pieces of legislation. Four of Wangala's seven and three of Dalena's four councillors occupy reserved seats. Significantly, in Wangala and in Dalena one female councillor was elected without the advantage of reservation; two women hold reserved seats in Wangala and one in Dalena.

Council members and staff assured me that there is now no difference in the participation by those with and without reserved seats. In Wangala they all regularly attend council meetings and take part in discussions. Dalena councillors are less actively involved in their *grama* panchayat because the council is less concerned with their village's improvements and secondly, they complain that whenever they request some assistance from the panchayat they only rarely get it. Sharamma, a Dalena Scheduled Caste lady councillor complained that although she has tried for some time to get the council to provide more public water taps and street lighting in Dalena, so far there has been no positive response. She told us that 'the headquarters of our *grama* panchayat are located in Yeleyur, which is a much bigger and more important village than Dalena. Therefore, the panchayat pays much more attention to Yeleyur's development than to Dalena's'.

In terms of the formal village government, democratic elections have certainly replaced hereditary succession. Yet my village friends kept telling me that both in Dalena and in Wangala hereditary Peasant councils still play an active part. They are composed as they have always been of the hereditary elders of the major Peasant lineages in the villages; Dalena's hereditary panchayat is composed of eight such lineage elders and Wangala's of seven. These Peasant panchayats do not meet regularly but only when required. They settle intra-village disputes and discuss arrangements concerning village feasts. Thus even though village government is democratically elected and reserved seats for the underprivileged have been widely accepted, the hereditary Peasant panchayat is still a Peasant prerogative and continues to play a central part in the village polity.

POLITICIANS AND GOVERNMENT RESOURCES

For a democracy to work there must be at least two opposing political parties each pursuing different sets of policies. This gives voters a chance to choose between different policies. In 1955 at the onset of the introduction of democratic village government political parties had not yet entered into panchayat elections. Voters were then expected to elect their representatives only on the basis of the candidates' record. Factions played an important part in the process of village council elections. Opposing factions were composed of lineages and named after the lineage elder. During my earlier studies villagers used the word 'party' to refer to these factions. I often heard them complain *bahala parti* (there is too much factional opposition). There was then no attempt or even pretence to offer voters a choice of policies. Political parties then only got involved with elections for the state assemblies. Even in that context opposing party candidates rarely canvassed by explaining their competing policies; instead they concentrated on rallying round support from large vote banks based on kin and/or caste allegiance by promising them help. A number of electoral studies are available which show how this process worked in detail.

More recently party politics have entered even into intra-village politics. The existence in villages of entrenched factional opposition provided a fertile ground for the major political parties. Dalena's K. Palgowda related this when he traced back the existing village split in political party allegiances to the membership of the two opposing factions which as long ago as 1927 disputed access to the temple they were then planning to build (see p. 157). The tentacles of the two major political parties active in Karnataka—i.e. the Janata Dal and the Congress party—are now well entrenched in village politics. In many villages support for these opposing parties is expressed in violent hostilities.

We asked many villagers in detail why they identify with a particular political party. None of them—not even council members—were aware of any policies pursued by the different parties. Candidates appear to woo the electorate on a personal rather than policy basis. Karegowda, a young Wangala farmer who claims to support the Congress party, said:

> Some years ago my elder brother was introduced by a close friend of his to a leading Congress party politician, who then was a minister in the Karnataka government. This man kept emphasising all he will do to help villagers. He got my brother to agree to ensure that all his lineage members will support the Congress party. Ever since then I have considered myself a Congress party supporter and so have all the others belonging to our lineage.

Before elections candidates usually promise that if they succeed they will channel government support to the electorate. MLAs occupy strategic positions which enable them to honour at least some of their promises and village voters have come to realise this. Government departments are structured in such a way that they in fact strengthen the influence over the allocation of funds which elected MLAs can exert. The distribution of government funds is decentralised. Departments decide at the *taluk* level how much to allocate to the different *grama* panchayats under their jurisdiction. The *taluk* also provides the basis for elections to the legislative assembly. It is thus a very important administrative unit and gives elected MLAs the opportunity to influence the allocation of government funds for individual village development. They occupy strategic positions to exert pressure on *taluk*-based government officials to ensure that they can redeem at least some of their earlier promises. Allocation of government resources meant to promote rural development appears often to be more influenced by political considerations than by need. Villagers know only too well that they have to go through their MLA to get hold of government funds for village improvements. At a session at the headquarters of the Yeleyur *grama* panchayat which includes Dalena, one councillor said, 'Political parties provide the gateway to government goodies and support; we all know this! Politicians are always tempted to offer support in accordance with where they see their best re-election chances, rather than where needs are greatest.'

I was told in Dalena that there are presently government house sites available for which many applications have already been submitted. Councillors complain that the strong competition for these house sites is leading to many intra-village disputes and quarrels. Many applicants are contacting the appropriate politician to increase their own chances. In turn these politicians are busy trying to pull strings to make sure their respective following get most sites.

Wangala seems to be much less subject to political party manipulations than Dalena. Wangala villagers do not have to depend on their MLA to ensure access to government resources. They have their emissary, T. Thimmegowda, strategically placed among the top-ranking administrators in Bangalore, the capital of Karnataka. With his advice and often even through his skilful intervention they succeed in putting their requests directly to the minister concerned. In Wangala the disruptive influence of political parties is counterbalanced by T. Thimmegowda. He thus exerts a unifying influence over Wangala which Dalena lacks. In this chapter I outlined how Wangala and Dalena have changed in outward appearance since 1955 and discussed the various factors responsible for these changes. The next chapter explores how much of the old traditions still persist within the changing village setting.

NOTE

1. For details of the JRY Programme see Government of India, JRY Manual, 1994.

FIFTEEN

New Lives and Old Traditions

Village life in general has changed as a result of the transformation in the outward appearance of rural South India throughout the past few decades. The various change factors already discussed impacted on the economic, political and social lives of villagers. No doubt there have been many changes, but at the same time much has remained the same. The many improvements in levels of living have, however, been accompanied also by some socially undesirable phenomena. All this indicates not only that there is continuity within change but also that there is a social cost of change.

Population Growth and Economic Sustainability

The rapid population growth set within limited availability of land has exerted pressure on villagers to increase crop productivity and/or to seek income from other sources than farming. Between 1955 and 1956 Dalena lands produced staple crops yielding per capita daily 1,295 calories for the 707 individuals then residing in the village; by 1991 the daily per capita subsistence supply of the staple crop had dropped to about 600 calories for a population of 1,566. Some Dalena farmers who own land by the canal use pump irrigation illegally to grow paddy and sugarcane on their village lands. The acreage thus irrigated is limited and its produce therefore does not add much to the total available subsistence food supply. Dalena's population has thus already by far exceeded its land-carrying capacity.

By contrast, Wangala is more fortunate with regard to its subsistence food supplies. The extension of irrigation and cultivated lands together with the use of high yielding varieties of seeds along with double and often even treble cropping per acre year has greatly increased yields. So much so that the daily per capita amount of calories derived from locally grown staple crops has remained almost the same as it was in 1955 for a population of 958 whereas there were almost three times as many people in 1991. Wangala can thus still sustain its growing population.

These per capita totals of course do not imply that each villager consumes that many calories daily; extremes of economic differentiation prevent this. Wangala's larger and wealthier landowners have a higher daily calorie intake and sell their surplus crops, whereas the poorer landless people have to buy their staples and often cannot even meet their basic food requirements; their daily calorie intake is therefore considerably lower.

Wangala's more favourable land-carrying capacity promotes village introversion, whereas the shortfall in Dalena's subsistence food supplies makes villagers increasingly more extroverted. This is the glaring contrast between these two villages, which accounts for much of the difference in the transformation of village life that has taken place in Wangala and Dalena since 1955.

Education as a Determinant of Economic and Social Status

In South Indian villages where farming still constitutes the dominant economic pursuit access to land is one of the determinants of a household's economic status. An additional and increasingly more important factor is education. In the competitive environment in which farmers now have to operate education helps them improve their economic ranking. Economic achievements are usually translated into social status. This does not mean that economic success is the only or even the most important criterion of social status. There are other influences, such as religiosity, ritual office, spirit media etc., which also determine social ranking. For instance, Dalena's Chennu (see T. Scarlett Epstein, *Economic Development and Social Change in South India*, Manchester University Press, 1962, p. 302) and Wangala's Karegowda (see p. 112) do not occupy economically dominant positions in their respective villages, yet both are held in high social esteem just because they are accepted as spirit media (*devaru gudda*), which means literally 'god's hillock'. Such spirit media

> act at certain village festivals or whenever there is a particualr emergency and Peasants wish to consult their deities. Each medium impersonates a particular deity and each village has more than one medium. Sometimes more than one medium represents one deity in a village. Whenever the deities are to be consulted, Untouchable village drummers come to beat the drums, while idols of the particular deity are being worshipped. The ritual and the beating of the drums send the medium into a trance. When the drums suddenly stop and silence reigns, Peasants question him. Most of the questions I recorded on such occasions referred to the chance of survival of a sick member of a family, or to the chance of the wife bearing a son in families without male offspring. Most answers given by the mediums were favourable, but the grant was conditional on the suppliant performing regular offerings to the deity. If the prediction conveyed by the medium turned out to be false, the suppliant never blamed the deity or the medium, but always blamed himself for having failed to perform the offerings. God and mediums are regarded as infallible, while men are fallible (T. Scarlett Epstein, *Economic Development and Social Change in South India*, Manchester University Press, 1962, p. 301).

In theory, the qualification for mediumship should pass from a man to his eldest son. However, this is not always so in practice. Chennu, the retired factory worker of Dalena was the only one who—when the previous monkey-god medium died without a male offspring—survived the final test in the 'transference of mediumship ceremony'; he thus was accepted as *devaru gudda* in Dalena. Karegowda is not the first-born but the younger son of Malla who was one of Wangala's spirit media.

Wangala The Wangala man who is fortunate enough to be an only son of a land-wealthy father is in an excellent position to accumulate considerable wealth. If he has had some education and is reasonably enterprising he uses his money to acquire more land, invest in agricultural processing equipment—such as cane crushers and flour mills—and/or acts as a money lender. In doing so he reinforces his economic position and thereby more often than not also his social status.

Time constraints prevented us from establishing the profitability of the different crops cultivated as we had done in our earlier studies.

We, therefore, tried to get at least an approximation of profits. In the course of several discussion groups we asked farmers how much net yields they estimate they get from one acre of wet land. From this I gathered that two crops of sugarcane can be grown over three years on an acre of wet land, which if jaggery prices are attractive can produce an annual net yield per acre of about Rs 7,000 plus one crop of ragi millets yielding Rs 2,000. Alternatively, two crops of paddy can be cultivated per year on well-irrigated land, which can provide as much as a total net yield of Rs 18,000 per acre. According to this information, which I cross-checked several times by interviewing different groups of informants, the annual net yield per acre of wet land ranges from Rs 9,000 to Rs 18,000. Soaring land prices in Wangala since 1955 indicate the combined effect of rapid inflation, land scarcity and increased productivity. The price of one acre of irrigated Wangala land has increased a great deal. In 1955 such land fetched about Rs 500 per acre. The village land register for 1995–96 records twentyeight sales at an average price of as much as Rs 160,000 which involved two outside buyers. Accordingly, Wangala land prices have multiplied 320 times in the past forty years; during the same period the inflation index has risen from 100 to 1,450. Numerous Wangala households have branched out from farming into activities related to agriculture such as post-harvest processing, but land is still considered *the* most important asset in the village. This means that a man's economic fortune still depends on his access to land.

The South Indian law of inheritance rules that parental property on the death of the household head must be equally divided among all heirs disregarding sex; in practice, land passes mainly down the male line and daughters usually get their share of the parental property in dowry. The size of the parental land holding, the number of heirs and entrepreneurship over successive generations thus determine economic ranking.

Apigowda's case illustrates the experience of a wealthy Wangala villager. He related:

> I am the elder of two sons; my father used to be considered among the richest and most enterprising Wangala men. He owned 12 irrigated acres and one cane crusher. Both he and my mother were illiterate, but they were eager to have their children educated. I attended pre-university training in 1970 when he died. His death meant that I had to give up my studies and instead take over the management of our family property. My brother and I decided to

partition our inheritance. I was left with 6 acres of wet land, one cane crusher and part of the parental two storeyed house.

If my information on per acre yields of irrigated land is correct and I have no reason to believe that it is wrong then Apigowda must have an annual farm income ranging from Rs 66,000 to Rs 108,000 in addition to which he also makes more money from his other business activities. His wealth is reflected in the extent of his productive investment as well as in his impressive lifestyle. He further elaborated:

I added a flour mill and huller to my cane crusher and also operate a fertiliser business. To be mobile I bought a scooter, which makes it easy for me to go to Mandya whenever I have some business to see to there. The money I derive from these various activities helps me to improve my family's life. I recently spent a considerable amount of money on renovating our home. We now have running water and a private latrine.

While listening to Apigowda, who as always was dressed in a spotless white shirt and *dhoti*, we sat on a comfortable settee in his well-furnished front room where there is a large television set and many other amenities which were completely unknown when I first stayed in Wangala. Apigowda does not count among Wangala's biggest magnates as did his father. Yet he appears to be well respected by his fellow villagers and is also a member of Wangala's traditional Peasant panchayat. However, not all heirs of land-wealthy fathers are as successful as Apigowda.

Thimmegowda refers to Malla and Karegowda, the two grandsons of the late Mallegowda, who once was one of the biggest Wangala landowners. Their father was an only son. They, like Apigowda, therefore inherited a considerable area of irrigated lands. Yet they were seemingly unable to manage the property properly. They had to sell some of the land each inherited and now rank only among the middle farmers. The major difference between the two cases appears to be the difference in educational levels. Apigowda has had the benefit of some higher education; by contrast neither Malla nor Karegowda have gone beyond higher primary schooling. Karegowda is still widely respected in Wangala, not for his economic but rather for his spiritual role: he follows his ancestral tradition and acts as spirit medium. The changing fortune of successive Wangala generations of the same family is thus highly volatile.

Population growth has been an important factor in economic volatility, particularly among households with only a small irrigated acreage to pass on to heirs. It meant that many middle farmers were reduced to the status of small or marginal farmers; some have even had to join the ranks of the landless. Only those few men with exceptional enterprising abilities who descended from Middle Farmers have managed to climb the economic ladder of success. Thimmegowda relates the case of Srinivas, a Class IV employee at Mandya Engineering College, who only recently inherited no more than a small irrigated acreage; yet in a few years he managed to become one of the wealthiest Wangala Magnates (see p. 53). Srinivas' case illustrates that it is possible even for a small farmer to raise his economic position, but again one can argue that his success, like Apigowda's, is related to his education. Education constitutes a necessary condition even if it is not a sufficient condition for economic success.

Some of Wangala's small and marginal farmers seek to supplement their meagre farm income by performing other jobs in the village. For instance, Borgowda is employed by the panchayat to look after the village water supply for which he gets a monthly wage of Rs 600 (see p. 67). There are, however, not many other such jobs available in the village. Self-employment in the service industry offers a better chance to earn some money. Nanjegowda with his widowed mother runs a small shop and restaurants as well as a cycle hire shop. In answer to our questions he told us: 'It is not easy to live off the earnings from our different little shops; it varies of course according to demand. I estimate that my monthly net income altogether amounts to no more than Rs 500.'

Hardly any of the poorest Wangala Scheduled Castes have ventured into non-agricultural activities. Most of them still continue their traditional occupation and work as agricultural labourers for Peasant landowners. Those few who are still fortunate enough to own land are likely to dissipate their holdings between numerous heirs before too long. For instance, Kariya related:

I own an acre each of wet and dry land. I have two sons and six daughters. I managed to get five of them already married. To ensure suitable husbands for them I had to spend about Rs 20,000 on each of the five marriages. To do this I of course had to borrow money and therefore I am now heavily indebted.

Kariya's case indicates that although girls rarely get a share of hereditary landed property, a daughter's dowry puts a heavy burden on the family's resources. Inflationary dowry makes it increasingly more difficult for parents to find husbands for their daughters. It is also interesting to note that it never seemed to have occurred either to Kariya himself or to his sons to seek income from other than labouring sources. None of the Scheduled Castes runs a shop or little restaurant. Many of them frequent the Peasant shops and restaurants, where they are still served out of cups and glasses specially reserved for them, clearly illustrating continuity with past practices. Thimmegowda pointed out that the fact that educational levels among the Scheduled Castes are still well below those of other castes could account for their continued focus on farm labour and their acceptance of inferior status.

Our enquiries about the traditional hereditary patron–client relationship between Peasant farmers and their Scheduled Caste agricultural labouring households brought divergent responses: some landowners and some labourers insisted that it has disappeared altogether, while others maintained that it still persists. This I take to indicate that its existence has declined but is still evident in some cases. I could not establish the proportion of cases in which it still exists. What seems certain though is that the general minimum social security that these hereditary relationships offered the Scheduled Caste client households has at least been severely diminished. The government, realising the resulting problem, has attempted to step into the breach by legislating several welfare schemes specifically designed to help both the Scheduled Caste and Scheduled Tribes (see p. 173).

Dalena The Scheduled Castes like many other caste villagers in Dalena have already for many years appreciated the importance of education; in their eyes an educational qualification provides the passport to a public service position. A number of them have achieved their ambition: for example, one works for the forest department in Bangalore and another commutes to Pandavapura, where he is employed as a Food Inspector. The families of both these men reside in impressive-looking urban-style houses in Dalena's Scheduled Caste colony; they each own a few acres of dry land which their womenfolk cultivate.

In Dalena the traditional hereditary labour relationship between Peasant landowners and their hereditary client households had almost disappeared in 1955. Yet it exists to this day between Peasants and some Functionaries. For instance Kala Setty, one of Dalena's Washermen, mentioned:

> Altogether there are now twelve Washermen households in Dalena
> out of which only four continue to wash clothes; the other eight
> have taken up other income-earning activities. I own no land nor
> do I have any other skill besides washing clothes. I am therefore
> glad that I can continue to work as Washerman. I have three sons
> and one daughter who is still at school. We felt we could not cope
> with any more children, so my wife had a tubectomy. My three
> sons assist me in performing my Washerman's duties; they also
> work as casual agricultural labourers if somebody needs their help.
> We weekly collect the dirty clothes from thirtyfive Peasant house-
> holds; we also collect menstrual cloths. We wash everything in the
> canal and return it clean and ironed. Each of the thirtyfive Peasant
> households gives us annually 50 seers of paddy, which at present
> prices is equivalent to about Rs 3,000 and thus yields a monthly
> income of about Rs 250. In addition our Peasant patrons reward us
> also for the services we provide during wedding ceremonies, such as
> carrying the *devaru pettige* (deity box), spreading clean sarees on
> which the wedding procession walks, etc. We do not find it easy to
> make ends meet with what we earn, but at least we can survive. I
> am now worried how I shall manage to arrange the marriage of my
> daughter. I do not have any savings and as the bride's father I am
> expected to spend at least Rs 20,000 on her wedding. How will I be
> able to cope?

Kala Setty was obviously worried about his daughter's future, but
expressed no concern for how his three sons will manage to survive as
Washermen once each will have his own family and will then have no
more than twelve Peasant patrons from whom to expect paddy
rewards. He appears to have too many immediate worries to have
time to think of the predicament his sons will face in future years.
Kala Setty's case sets out the difficulties Dalena men encounter who
still remain dependent for their livelihood on working for some of
their fellow villagers.

   In contrast with Washermen, Dalena's Carpenters realise the need
and appreciate the advantage of seeking customers outside their village.
We met Lingachari, a Carpenter who lives with his wife and two
small sons and one daughter in a house that is situated in the village's
older residential area. He is 35 years old and appears a bright and
enterprising man. What he told us clearly indicates the difference in

attitude between the uneducated local Washerman and the Carpenter who has had the benefit of some education. Lingachari proudly said:

> Having been schooled up to seventh standard and learnt the carpenter craft from my father I now specialise in making doors and windows for houses. With our growing population more houses are being built and therefore there is demand for my skills. I go to wherever I can get work. It takes me about six months to prepare all the doors and windows for a large new house. For this work I usually get about Rs 3,000 and in addition one meal per day. I do not earn an aweful lot of money, but it does enable me to keep my family. My wife and I decided last year that we do not want to have any more children—three is ample!—and so she went to have a tubectomy.

Lingachari, the Carpenter is thus likely to earn annually about twice as much as Kala Setty the Washerman. Lingachari also looks to the future with greater optimism. He plans to put his children through higher education whereas Kala Setty, a man without any schooling, is much more insecure and therefore more worried about how he will manage to get his daughter married.

Mapachari, another of Dalena's Carpenters, also has an interesting story to tell. He is 45 years old and lives with his wife, two sons and one daughter in a house in one of the newer residential areas by the side of a more recently established road that leads to the canal. In 1955 this part of the village was open land without any houses, now it is built up. When we approached him he was busy repairing a plough with the help of his son. Mapachari related:

> About 20 years ago under the government scheme of allocating house sites to homeless people I was given this house site and a Rs 5,000 grant for the construction of a house. This amount was not enough to build a house and I then had no other funds. I decided to work hard and proceeded to save. It took me fifteen years to accumulate enough money. In 1991 I built this house at a cost of Rs 80,000. We now use it not only as residence but also as our workshop. With the help of my sons I try my hands at many different things. We repair ploughs and carts, make doors and windows as well as furniture, such as tables and chairs. We charge Rs 120 for making one window and Rs 200 for one door. We also make new carts with rubber wheels; the rubber wheels including the rod cost

Rs 7,000 and the wooden parts cost another Rs 7,000 inclusive of labour. It takes us about twelve days to complete one cart which we sell for Rs 14,000. Last year we produced about eight carts for customers from neighbouring villages.

While we were sitting and talking with Mapachari on the veranda of his house a truck taking cane from a neighbouring village to one of Dalena's cane crushers stopped and the driver handed over a part of a cart that needed repairing. A little later a Dalena Peasant brought his iron plough for repair. It is evident that Mapachari has established a reputation for his craftsmanship which brings him custom from within and outside his own village. His two sons have learnt their father's skills and expressed their confidence in the future. They apparently feel pretty certain that demand for their services will continue to grow and keep them both busy and provided with a reasonable livelihood.

As we walked back to Dalena's central square we met Chennu, a Peasant now with greying hair, who I remembered as a young man. He greeted us warmly and said:

You can see that I am now an older man. You will remember that when you were first with us in 1955 I was a young man. In reply to your queries I told you all about how I became a *devaru gudda* (spirit medium). Then when you returned in 1970 I had moved with my wife and children to Mandya. You visited us where we lived on the refinery compound. We stayed there until I retired in 1989 when I received a lump sum of Rs 80,000. On retirement I had to vacate the factory house. This made me decide to move back to my native village. I spent quite some time then considering the options of how best to invest the sum I had received on my retirement. My objective was to ensure that it will help to provide not only for my old age, but also for my children. I found constructing a house for renting purposes an attractive proposition. Observing the development of a number of industrial centres in the vicinity of Dalena I expected there will be a demand for rental accommodation from professionals involved in the establishment of new manufacturing enterprises. Weighing up the pros and cons of such a venture I decided to go ahead and build a house on the plot of land situated in the village centre which I had bought already in 1975. My expectations proved correct. No sooner was the house completed when a contractor rented it. He worked on the industrial estate established on Dalena lands. The contractor, having completed his job, moved out only a little while ago. I am now looking for another tenant. To make the house more attractive I wanted to enlarge it with the construction of a basement. But I ran into trouble with the panchayat.

I found Chennu a fascinating personality and explored his background extensively. I considered that his experience illustrated a number of interesting social phenomena I had observed in South Indian villages.

In my 1962 publication I described in detail Chennu's account of how he got himself recognised as *devaru gudda* (deity medium). Usually *devaru guddas* follow in hereditary succession, but none of Chennu's ancestors had been spirit media. He therefore had to struggle to get recognition. By passing the appropriate and severe test he managed to establish his reputation as a medium. Thereby he raised his prestige.

In my 1973 book I used Chennu's case to illustrate how young factory workers who live and work in the town but still own a little land in the village form Share Families to solve the conflicting demands on their lives emanating from their urban employment and their village attachment. When I met him again in 1996 I was thus interested to know whether he is still part of a Share Family and also whether he still acts as spirit medium. He replied:

Since I returned I have taken over from my brother the responsibility of looking after my own lands. Therefore, I no more meet his cash needs. We now live as two separate households. We have dissolved what you had referred to as our Share Family. But I am still a *devaru gudda;* during village festivals I get into a trance for about 20 to 30 minutes when villagers ask questions and the deity replies through me.

In Dalena and many other South Indian villages that have poor soils and depend on irregular rainfall for cultivation, villagers have their eyes on the wider economy and seek employment in secondary manufacturing industries. Educational achievements warrant recognition in Dalena. Villagers proudly relate how many of their men have become doctors, lecturers, lawyers etc.

Education and the Widening of Village Horizons

Expansion of education has triggered off many changes. Though the isolated Indian village has always been a myth, education has opened new vistas for villagers. In 1996 the 17-year-old Wangala

Nanjundaswamy expressed his desire to become a script writer. None of the 17-year-old youths in 1955 ever would have considered such a future. Wangala people admire Thimmegowda for his professional achievement and for the way he still identifies himself as a villager. Another young man who attends Wangala's second year PUC Government Junior College wrote the following poem which encapsulates what Wangala people think of their Thimmegowda:

Great Son of our Village

Born to your parents
Twinkling star of Wangala
A source of justice, morality and religion
Oh, great son of our village
Though you hold high position
You are not selfish
but display concern about your village
You are the pillar of Wangala
An innocent person like a child
Your smile is beautiful
You dream many dreams about Wangala
Those dreams will become true in the near future!
You visit our village many times,
You always enquire about people's problems
By walking round village lanes and meeting
people you help them find solutions for their
problems![1]

A number of other young Wangala students have written similar poems about Thimmegowda and the important role he plays in their society as an educated man who occupies a high public service position, but still identifies himself with his native village.

Continuity within Change

Development in Dalena and Wangala since 1955 has resulted in higher levels of living for most of the population. The expansion of education has shown beneficial changes in most spheres of village life. The benefits are not yet equally shared by all socio-economic strata of rural society, but there are signs that even the poorest are at last beginning to gain. Education has helped many poorer Dalena villagers to secure well-paid employment in the wider economy. Most of these successful men have become so alienated from their rural background that they have completely uprooted themselves from it. A smaller proportion of Dalena emigrants still keep their links with their native village.

Weddings are occasions when kin from far afield are reunited. This emerged clearly when Dalena's Palgowda one day showed me into a house on the village square; it did not look anything out of the ordinary from the outside. Inside, however, it was well furnished; a television set and video player occupied a prominent position. Shushila, a pretty young girl greeted me in English. Though halting it was impressive to hear a young Dalena girl speak English at all. Palgowda explained that she had finished secondary education, which was unusual for a girl. Her wedding took place only the previous month and was a big occasion. She married Kempaya's brother's son— Kempaya was the man who in 1970 I discovered to be extraordinarily enterprising in investing his money in buying strategically placed Mandya land sites. Her two brothers, who both work and live outside Dalena, paid for her wedding; it cost altogether about Rs 200,000.

She sat down next to me on a comfortable settee and showed me the album with her wedding photographs; afterwards while being served milk and bananas I was shown the video taken at her wedding. Though this video demonstrated many of the modern features that have been introduced into Dalena since 1955, when I observed many weddings there, it also illustrated that many of the rituals had remained unchanged e.g., the Washermen still spread out sarees for the wedding procession, which has been the custom at Peasant weddings for generations; a Mandya Brahmin priest conducted the ceremony and many of the rituals I saw on the video seemed familiar to me from the olden days. The wedding feast on the other hand was a lot different from the ones in which I used to partake many years earlier. For Shushila's wedding, tables and chairs were placed on the village square and many hundreds of guests were entertained with a lavish meal which waiters served on stainless steel plates. At the weddings I observed in Dalena in 1955 and 1970 the guests were all seated on the ground and were served a meal on disposable banana leaves. The account and video of Shushila's wedding made me realise how much continuity there still is within a very changed scene.

Youth Association The same thought passed through my mind when I listened to the President of Wangala's Youth Association. He outlined in detail their objectives and their achievements to date. It all seemed very impressive and illustrated that the winds of change were blowing through Wangala. Then when I enquired whether any of the village Scheduled Castes were also members, he shook his head and affirmed that all members were young Peasants. The traditional discrimination Peasants have exercised over many generations against women and lower castes still determine membership of a new institution such as the Youth Association in Wangala.

Village Politics is another arena in which there is continuity within change. The introduction of universal adult franchise and elected village councils has eliminated the previously practised hereditary succession to village offices. There are reserved seats on the formal village councils for women and Scheduled Castes. Yet there still exists both in Dalena and Wangala an informal Peasant panchayat which is composed of hereditary elders of the major Peasant lineages. This panchayat is responsible for a lot of social issues internal to the villages, as for instance the fining of drunkards. It also organises village feasts such as the *Marihabba* (see p. 71) which involves not only Peasants but also Functionaries and Scheduled Castes, but only Peasants take the decisions; no other caste is allowed to participate in the discussions.

Son Preference is another example of cultural continuity; it still largely influences fertility behaviour. Many villagers have become aware of the need to use family planning. They now appreciate that large numbers of children create economic problems for future generations. But most of them still have a strong son preference. They continue procreating until they have at least one son. For example, Wangala's Shangowda had one son after his wife had given birth first to two daughters. He and his wife then decided that three children are enough for them. A large proportion of villagers pursue the same strategy. In this too, old beliefs and customs persist in a changed setting.

Dependency Relationships   I found another example of continuity within change when one day I walked with Thimmegowda round the new Wangala colony, which has a caste-mix. As always when he visits his village crowds of people surround him to put their complaints and requests to him. On that particular occasion many of them complained about cracks in the walls of the houses which had been built for underprivileged villagers under the government housing scheme. Most of the families living in this new colony belong to the Scheduled

Caste. The reduced existence or altogether disappearance of the hereditary patron–client relationship that had existed between Peasant masters and Scheduled Caste households deprived them of the minimum social security they once enjoyed. The numerous schemes with which the government tried to take over the welfare provisions that used to be part of the hereditary relationships between individual Peasant and Scheduled Caste households has meant the latter now regard the government as their patron. They therefore turn to the government for everything they need. It did not occur to any of them that they could easily themselves repair the cracks in the walls about which they were complaining. In other words, their traditional dependency on their Peasant patrons has now been transferred to a dependency on the government.

This made me wonder whether a large extent of government support for them is doing these poor families a lot of good or whether it would not be more beneficial to help them assert their independence...

The Social Cost of Change

Rapid South Indian rural development appears to have been accompanied by serious social problems.

Drinking and Gambling often results in violence. Thimmegowda complains about the decline in moral and ethical standards among villagers. Previously it was taboo for Peasants to touch alcohol and wife-beating was a rare and punishable phenomenon. Now Borgowda, a Wangala Peasant, told us that almost all village men enjoy at least some alcohol in the evening after work. Not everyone drinks excessively, but a considerable number do. These days there is a lot of drunkenness among villagers. The liquor stores which can be found in each village provide ready access to alcoholic beverages. Men seem to be the main offenders in terms of drinking and gambling. When drunk they often become violent and beat their wives and children. If they lose in gambling they are often driven to pledging their wives' jewellery and household possessions. This causes havoc with family relationships. It forces many wives to fend for themselves, to look after their children alone and to keep their families together. I heard many accounts in Dalena and Wangala of such occurrences. In Dalena the drink problem has taken on such proportions that under Palgowda's influence the informal traditional Peasant panchayat introduced a rule according to which any person found drinking or gambling in the village has to pay a fine. The money thus collected is used for development purposes.

Psychological Strain Another regrettable feature I had not encountered in 1955 and which is now prevalent is psychological stress. According to the doctor at Wangala's primary health unit:

> As much as 60 per cent of patients who consult the clinic suffer from psychological stress. Most of them are not severe cases and get better reasonably quickly; all they seem to need is a sympathetic listener to their problems. The more serious cases are transferred to Mandya or if necessary even to Bangalore psychiatric units.

In Dalena and Wangala a growing number of suicides have occurred in recent years. This manifests the existence of stress and strain in these societies. Psychological stress has been on the increase also in Western industrialised society for some time already. It is regrettable that it has now come to bedevil even Indian rural societies that previously were thought to be immune to psychological problems.

HIV/AIDS is another health issue that has been imported into rural areas. The Wangala doctor told us:

> There has already been one case of AIDS in Wangala. It was a young man who when diagnosed was expelled and died three months later. We checked and tested all his village contacts but found them all negative. Now there is another case in Hanuambadi, the neighbouring village; in my judgement the young man will also soon die—there is hardly anything we can do to help HIV/AIDS affected patients.

At the end of my brief return to Dalena and Wangala in 1996, when I came to say my fond farewells to my many village friends, I could not help but wonder whether the various health and social problems villagers now encounter are an unavoidable social cost of change, or whether it may be possible to ensure the advantages of progress without having to suffer the disadvantages?

Note

1. Written in the vernacular by Javaregowda and translated by A.P. Suryanarayana.

SIXTEEN

Predictions: Wrong and Right

*O*n the basis of my 1970 re-study I ventured to forecast by extrapolation what happened since 1955 and how Wangala and Dalena would change over the subsequent thirty years (see pp. 126 and 132). In the preceding chapters I outlined how these villages had in fact changed by 1996. This means that I can now evaluate my own earlier predictions and hope readers will in due course voice their own views in this context.

Wrong Predictions

When I prepared my predictions I did not realise the important role education, technological progress and party politics would play in shaping rural transformation. I have now come to appreciate what I should of course have realised already in 1970—that it takes a long time for the impact of these change factors to take effect. Many Dalena parents already realised in 1955 that education increases their sons' chances of securing public service jobs. They considered a school certificate as a passport to success. However, they did not appear to realise that the adoption of formal schooling would inevitably change the whole societal ethos.

By sending their sons to school parents unknowingly triggered off a radical long-term change in the traditional culture which stressed conformity and punished non-conformity. Schools, with their emphasis on grading students' performances, not only introduced competition but also rewarded non-conformity: the student who performs best gets the highest marks. The education of the young while their elders were still illiterate upset the conventional relationship of respect between sons and their parents. These were the early teething troubles when formal education was first introduced into illiterate village societies. During my earlier studies of Wangala and Dalena many of my village friends and informants complained bitterly about the unsatisfactory relationship with their school-going children: in particular their sons failed to show them the customary respect to which they felt entitled. At the time I discarded their worries as the usual parental discontent with their growing children. I then failed to recognise that their complaints were the beginnings of significant attitudinal and behavioural changes in Wangala and Dalena.

Education   When I returned to my South Indian village friends in 1996 I found to my surprise that many read newspapers regularly and also indulged in reading books. As part of the unforgettable farewell function Wangala villagers organised before my departure they made me put down the foundation stone for a library building they decided to build in my name and stock it with books, journals and newspapers. They wanted to make sure that young and old will have access to a flow of reading matter. Between 1956, when I left India after my first spell of primary studies and my return in 1970, I had no contact with my village friends because only a few young boys were literate in the vernacular, the script of which I never mastered, and none could read and write English. More recently I have been corresponding in English with some of the young village men. Some young students are writing poetry and essays; they have a great variety of interesting job ambitions, such as to become film script writers, lawyers and the like.

Education appears to affect most aspects of life: it has made young couples appreciate the need to have fewer children and to adopt contraceptive devices; it has made farmers learn and adopt more productive agricultural technologies; it has encouraged a concern for health measures, such as safe water supply and drainage. All this throws into relief the important part education plays in broadening villagers' horizons and in promoting fundamental changes in village life.

Technological Progress   In Wangala the adoption of high yielding varieties of seeds and the use of agricultural machinery such as tractors and combine harvesters has not only increased crop yields but also extended the area of cultivable land. This means that Wangala's output can still support an increasing population, though there is of course differential access to food depending on the household's economic status.

In Dalena too at least some farmers have taken advantage of new agricultural technologies. They use power pump sets to irrigate their lands with canal water, which enables them to grow sugarcane and paddy. There are now many power cane crushers and flour mills, both in Wangala and Dalena. Easy access to motorised transport has also changed the village lifestyle. Trucks, buses and scooters facilitate villagers' mobility. They can now go to Mandya and other nearby places on the spur of the moment. This has furthered the urban impact on rural societies and is reflected in many recently built urban-style houses, modern furniture, kitchen equipment etc.

Party Politics I was fortunate in being able to observe the official attempts to introduce democratically elected village councils into Wangala and Dalena while I first stayed there in the 1950s. I found that the convention of hereditary panchayat membership was still an important feature fifteen years later, but elected authority had made some inroads into the practice of status ascription. This made me expect wrongly a slow process of political changes. I failed to consider the growth and strength of political parties and how this would affect village politics. I now know that to secure election to the state legislature candidates have to rally round support from rural areas where the majority of the population still resides. Aspiring politicians of the major national political parties in their electioneering campaigns were quick to realise that existing intra-village factions could provide them with ready block votes. Since faction leaders are usually the elders of the major Peasant lineages, each faction constitutes a vote bank. To secure a faction's political support candidates have to promise its leaders access to some of the resources the government allocates for village development in the expectation that once elected they will be in a position to keep their pledges. This process inevitably accentuates opposition between village factions and, furthered by the ready availability of alcohol in the villages, it often erupts into violence.

All this I failed to include in my 1970 predictions.

Right Predictions

To be honest I must admit that I was pleased to find that at least some of what I had predicted did happen.

Village Introversion and Village Extroversion   In my 1973 book I described Wangala's development as being predominantly village-introverted in contrast to Dalena which displayed village extroversion. I related these different styles of development to the different village environments: Wangala having access to canal irrigation while Dalena's lands remained dry. This led me to predict that the two villages would continue at least for the next thirty years along these different paths of development. This appears to have been the case: Wangala has experienced internal diversification of economic activities; its population take Mandya as their model and aspire for their village to become a growth centre for the surrounding area. Wangala still attracts immigrants. Villagers present a united front vis-à-vis the outside world and resist interference in intra-village matters by the major political parties. This is reflected in a strengthened social identity and cohesion.

As in most other Indian rural societies, in Wangala too there still exist factional opposition and personal animosities and disputes. But Wangala people still show interest in their fellow-villagers' welfare. All of them appreciate the various amenities their village now provides and seem committed to continue along their path of *village introversion*.

Dalena, on the other hand, has lost much of its social identity, as Palgowda so eloquently related (see p. 158). Villagers have become self-centred and are concerned only with their own economic well-being; their village social identity has almost completely disappeared. The low productivity of their dry land forces increasing numbers to seek a livelihood outside their village; many commute while others have already emigrated and cut their ties with their native place. As Dalena is situated near Mandya on the highway connecting Bangalore and Mysore, it has already almost become a suburb of Mandya. Altogether Dalena has pursued the path of *village extroversion* and unless the economic environment of the village changes drastically I expect it will continue to do so at least for the next ten or twenty years.

Population Growth   My demographic forecast for Wangala and Dalena predicted a somewhat higher rate of population growth than has actually materialised. I now realise that I went wrong because I based my calculations on what I saw in 1970: there was then still an almost complete lack of interest in family planning and an absence of awareness of the disadvantages of a large number of offspring. However, what I failed to take into account at the time was the important role education can play in changing behaviour in general and fertility behaviour in particular. Schooling has over the years certainly increased the younger generation's awareness of the advantages of smaller families. Many village women have undergone tubectomies, being pleased to have found an escape from regular childbirth. However, the existing demographic structure of Wangala and Dalena is still so heavily weighted in favour of the below fifteen age group that a considerable rate of population growth is likely to continue for at least another generation.

My forecast for Mandya's population growth has been fairly accurate. By 1991 it had already reached 120,000 and it is therefore pretty certain that by the turn of the century it will reach 150,000, which is what I had expected. It is of course always easier to forecast demographic changes for a town like Mandya, which grows mainly by attracting immigrants from near and far, than it is to predict changes in fertility behaviour for individual smaller societies.

Gender and Caste Discrimination Liberal state legislation has no doubt reduced the degree of gender and caste discrimination that used to exist in Wangala and Dalena, but gender and caste are still important determinants of a villager's socio-economic role and status.

The relationship between male and female villagers has remained far from equal. In fact drinking and gambling among men has resulted in a deterioration of living conditions for women. Many village men these days get drunk and pledge their wives' jewellery in gambling, which often leads to abuse and violence against women. There is as yet no strong women's lobby in these villages to claim their human and constitutional rights. This may emerge with the advent of increasing numbers of educated village women.

Caste has continued to be an important principle of socio-economic organisation. The constitutional privileges awarded to Scheduled Castes and 'Backward Castes' have further reinforced caste identity. In 1955 the difference between the caste and Scheduled Caste residential areas was unmistakably obvious: a gap separated the two areas and most of the caste households lived in larger tiled-roof houses whereas the latter had only small thatched-roof huts. By 1996 the difference was overshadowed by the large expansion of housing sites and the numerous new RCC houses for Scheduled Castes built with government subsidies.

The Wangala and Dalena Scheduled Caste settlement has now become sandwiched between the Peasant caste homes. This does not however mean that closer relations have evolved between Peasants and their Scheduled Caste neighbours. The stigma of 'Untouchability' still persists; e.g., village coffee shops still use special glasses to serve the Scheduled Castes and the poorest village strata is mainly composed of them.

However, as I had expected, there are signs of differentiation along class lines. For instance, though the majority of households in the Wangala settlement for the landless are Scheduled Castes they do live side by side with a number of Functionary households. They reside in the same village section not because of caste identity, which used to be the overriding determinant of the settlement pattern, but because of their landlessness. However, there seem to be only few occasions when a unity among them manifests itself.

Class Differentiation within Caste   I expected the beginnings of class to occur in the two villages. There certainly now exists class differentiation, but it evolved not the way I had expected and certainly not in line with Marxist reasoning. Rather than the relationship to the means of production acting as the overall dividing force between the different socio-economic strata, caste is still the basis for social identity. What has happened is a polarisation between the economic strata within each individual caste. There have been increasing numbers of landless Peasants, a declining proportion of middle class Peasants, and Peasant magnates have become considerably wealthier. A similar process has taken place even among the Scheduled Castes: large proportions among them are landless, some are middle-farmers, and there are now some professional upper class as well; though admittedly the latter are still very small in number. Such a class differentiation is already readily noticeable in Dalena. Those Scheduled Castes who have managed to get educated and secure some of the public service positions reserved for them constitute the elite. They live in new, large and well furnished and equipped houses; their lifestyle obviously differs considerably from other and less fortunate of their community.

In South Indian villages it is in the interest of the poorer strata of the different castes to identify with their caste rather than with like class members of other castes. The Scheduled Caste upper stratum households managed to reach the higher status because by identifying themselves as such they were entitled to take advantage of the preferential treatment the government offers them. Similarly, landless Peasants perceive that their only chance of improving their lot is to stress their Peasant identity; this enables them to take advantage of the privileges offered to 'Backward Castes' of which the Peasants are one. It would not have helped them to follow the Marxist thrust of 'workers of the world unite, you have nothing to lose but your chains!'; they themselves full-well realise this. Dalena's landless Scheduled Castes do not see themselves in a conflict relationship with their own elite, but are in fact proud of their achievement. Liberal state legislation has certainly achieved a decline in caste discrimination but caste has remained the over-riding principle of social organisation in these villages. It looks as if it will continue to be so for the next few decades at least.

I now realise that altogether in my 1970 forecast I must have been too much influenced by the *cultural continuity* I found in Wangala and Dalena after fifteen years of absence. I therefore assumed that it will continue for another thirty years. This made me overlook the impact of change factors, such as education, that take at least one or two generations before they show results. My advice to anybody who embarks on making forecasts for micro-societies on the basis of extrapolating from base-line information is to take into account the impact existing, as well as future, change agents may have.

PART FOUR

The Way Ahead

T. SCARLETT EPSTEIN and T. THIMMEGOWDA

SEVENTEEN

What the Future Holds

$\mathscr{I}$n the preceding chapters we viewed rural development from below. We examined how and why villagers responded to different external influences. We outlined successes and discussed what we perceived as social costs. Undoubtedly tremendous changes in village lifestyles have occurred during the past decades. As was to be expected, these changes have not all been for the better. We base our views on what we learnt from studying Wangala and Dalena over the last forty years. We realise that it is not easy to generalise from a sample of two villages. However, we have found that much of our findings also apply to many other wet and dry land villages in South India.

In this final part we explore the implications of our micro-studies for macro-policies. We explore two-way channels of communication and raise issues that need to receive urgent public attention. We do not pretend to know all the solutions ourselves. All we can do is summarise *what* we consider as the major problem areas and pose questions about *how* developmental activities can become more culturally-sensitive and attuned to rural societies. We discuss seven different problem areas, but stress that these are all mutually interdependent spheres:

- Social awareness: the key to progress
- Population growth and development
- Rural development and growing water shortages
- The role of women in rural development

- Appropriate education
- Political decentralisation and participatory administration
- Democracy, political parties and village factions

Social Awareness: The Key to Progress

In a tradition bound society such as India, the behaviour pattern of an individual is governed by various factors like customs, traditions, socio-religious practices and moral values. Studies have shown that economic factors alone will not bring about the desired kind of social environment and change. Development of scientific knowledge and the fast growing information technology have contributed to the greater awareness among the rural folk. Universalisation of primary education, the dissemination of information and scientific knowledge through mass communication networks and successive democratisation processes over a period of time have accelerated the formation of social awareness among the masses.

Social awareness is the product of various developments in Wangala during the last four decades: advent of irrigation and electricity, introduction of various development programmes and welfare measures by the government, improvement in education, health and civic facilities, improved communication and media exposure to the changing conditions in the wider society have all encouraged Wangala men and women to change their outlook, attitudes and lifestyles. A gradual transformation of villagers' philosophies and beliefs has also been taking place. Our comparative studies over forty years indicate their changing attitudes and behaviour. Traditional beliefs and superstitions have given way to a modern outlook and reasoning. Once upon a time Wangala's men and women believed that a child's birth was God's blessings. Now, they consciously adopt family planning devices to control their fertility. The traditional practice of consulting magic healers to cure their diseases is gradually waning. Most of them now approach doctors for treatment. The practice of animal sacrifices and prayers offered as protection against epidemics is being replaced by appropriate health care measures. Poverty, ignorance, illiteracy and social discrimination are gradually declining. Festivals, marriages and other rituals are being simplified to avoid unnecessary expenditure. All these reforms and improvements are in effect the result of reasoning arising from an improved social awareness among villagers. However, there is still a considerable lack of appreciation of the need to prevent further environmental degradation.

The democratic process of governance and successive elections to village councils, state and central legislatures and other semi-government organisations have increased opportunities for political participation and awareness. This is reflected in the assertiveness among Wangala's progressive educated young men and women. Emergence of an enlightened political leadership and the formation of a Village Development Core Group has been a catalyst for the development and expansion of public facilities in Wangala. Political parties in India through their election manifestos and public contacts have generated an enormous amount of hope and aspiration among people to have their basic needs and demands fulfilled. Consequently, increased pressures are exerted on people's elected representatives and through them on the government. Non-fulfilment of these promises always gets reflected in the anti-establishment trends in successive elections. The debates and discussions on the prospects of candidates and political parties have also contributed to greater social awareness in village societies. Reservations provided under various pieces of social legislation for admission to educational institutions and government jobs are helping to make India's underprivileged sections realise their rights to equal status in society. Wangala Scheduled Caste youths have now begun to organise themselves to fight against social oppression from the upper caste Peasants. Even Vodda migrants demand equal facilities with other castes from government and local bodies.

This is undoubtedly a remarkable development for ensuring social justice and equality. Education and greater social awareness among these communities will help secure their share of benefits in the society. It will not only reduce socio-economic differentiation, but also lead to the integration of various castes and ethnic groups. This trend, if continued with the same vigour, will eliminate professional seclusion and social discrimination and the biases against socially oppressed and depressed castes and classes. As of now the Peasants and upper castes in Wangala are afraid of ill-treating the Scheduled Castes and Voddas for fear of legal action and retaliation. Each section of the communities and castes is trying to unite by forming associations to assert their rights to equality and also to ensure greater participation in the governance of the state and other democratic institutions.

Question: What measures should be taken to speed up the process of increasing social awareness, particularly concerning environmental preservation?

POPULATION GROWTH AND DEVELOPMENT

Awareness of the benefits derived from small families has increased considerably among South Indian villagers since 1955.

Education and Reproductive Health

Our studies of Dalena and Wangala throw into relief the strategic role education can play in bringing about attitudinal changes. Educated young couples now show interest in reproductive health measures. Many young women have already had tubectomies to avoid having more children.

Natural Population Increase will Continue The present demographic structure is such that at least for the next twenty or thirty years population growth is likely to continue at a rapid rate. Unfortunately, we could not compile Wangala's and Dalena's present age structure. We can only glean it from the official statistics for the state of Karnataka. These indicate that more than a third of the total population is still below the age of fourteen years. Only few policymakers appear to realise what this implies. Most policies concerned with population matters focus almost entirely on measures that will reduce fertility. They do not take into account that even if fertility declines the present age structure will result in further population growth for years to come. For instance, even the recent and enlightened Karnataka state agricultural legislation does not refer to the problems increasing numbers pose let alone consider measures necessary to accommodate larger village populations. The sooner relevant policymakers take population growth on board the better it will be all round. Development plans need to cater for the inevitable future population growth. Unless a concerted effort is mounted pretty soon to ease the problem of growing numbers serious economic and social upheavals have to be expected.

As in many other parts of the world in India too an unduly high rate of population growth has jeopardised the sustainability of development. Rural areas have been the worst affected. This has led to more and more villagers migrating to cities. They swell the ranks of the unemployed urban squatters and create many other serious social and economic problems. Something needs to be done pretty urgently to stem the flow of rural-urban migration. Otherwise there will be undesirable repercussions in many parts of India: increasing unemployment, crime and violence, pollution and other serious problems will occur in the overcrowded urban conglomerations and in disintegrated rural societies.

Question: How can rural-urban migration be discouraged?

A *Balanced Population Distribution*

The large majority of Indians still reside in villages. Therefore, the focus has to be on integrated rural development to ensure an overall balance in the distribution of the growing population.

Villages have to be converted into viable economic units and attractive social entities to reduce rural outmigration. Rural development policies and administrative practices need to develop a wholly integrated approach. They must strengthen rural societies. Women's voices must be heard and they must be encouraged to take an active part in the development of their societies. Education must be geared to rural development and social awareness has to be promoted among villagers. Administrators have to change their conventional top-down strategy and adopt two-way channels of communication. Democratic institutions have to be reshaped to stop the political process from re-emphasising intra-village factions. This has been tearing apart many village societies and has led to quarrels and often even violence.

Question: How can villages be transformed into viable socio-economic entities to discourage rural-urban migration?

Rural Development and Growing Water Shortages

External interventions to increase rural incomes have until recently concentrated on improving agricultural productivity. This has succeeded pretty well in South India. Irrigation schemes have relieved farmers from dependence on uncertain and scarce rainfall. Irrigation together with the high yielding varieties of seeds and artificial fertiliser brought about the 'green revolution' which increased the agricultural productivity of irrigated lands manifold. Wangala farmers did well out of the 'green revolution'. So much so that their crop outputs have kept pace with their growing population. This has reinforced their village introversion and strengthened their social unity.

However, irrigated farming practices use up excessive amounts of water, so much so that *water rather than land has now become the scarce resource.* Accordingly, the rural development focus has to change from attempting to optimise agricultural productivity per unit of land to unit of water. This important fact does not appear as yet to be fully recognised either by the authorities or the public at large. The recent temporary closing of the KRS irrigation system in Karnataka for the purpose of re-lining the canals clearly illustrates that the authorities are taking a very narrow view and fail to consider the wider implications of water scarcity.

Question: How can the authorities and the general public be made aware of water scarcity and the need to increase the effectiveness of water usage?

Irrigated versus Dry Land Farming

Irrigation by-passed Dalena; village lands remained dry. Farmers received no advice to help increase the output of their lands. Developers largely ignored lands that could not benefit from irrigation. The Karnataka State Agricultural Policy Statement 1995 openly admits this neglect. It states that areas

> with very low and uncertain rainfall and with low irrigation potential, need to be accorded a high priority in terms of soil and moisture conservation. This is in view of their high geographical coverage, high rate of degradation, widespread poverty and their competition for producing high value crops for exports. The existing programmes of soil and moisture conservation have failed to make an impact because they are inadequately planned on a watershed basis. They have failed to integrate employment generation programmes into their works (The Karnataka State Agricultural Policy Statement, 1995, p. 10).

For many villages like Dalena this recognition may have come too late. Many of their brightest men have already left the village. They could observe their neighbouring areas grow greener and richer, while the yields of their own lands had not increased. A considerable proportion of Dalena men wanted to participate in the economic expansion that they saw happening around them. Since there was no chance of achieving their objective within Dalena, they set about seeking sources of income from the wider economy. In view of the crucial difference irrigation makes to rural societies we discuss agricultural development for dry land and wet land villages separately.

Appropriate Development for Dry Land Villages

Development of dry land cultivation has lagged behind irrigated crop farming. This induced many men in dry land villages to explore income-earning possibilities outside agriculture.

Economic Diversification and Village Extroversion Many dry land villages such as Dalena are now situated within a regional economy, which has been expanding because of canal irrigation. This has created higher aspirations even among dry land farmers while their own farm economy stagnated. Their land yields remained low and subject to uncertain weather conditions. Increasing population made life even more difficult for them.

Even dry land farmers living in remote areas far from any economic expansion these days know and want more affluent lifestyles. Ready access to modern media raises their aspirations. Compared with their relatively well-to-do counterparts in irrigated villages they understandably consider themselves deprived.

Many men are eager to rise to the challenge. They seek to find a niche for themselves in the wider economy. They turn to education and diversification of their economic activities. Thereby they meet demands arising outside their own village economy. This leads them to pursue a path of village extroversion. Undoubtedly it brings them economic benefits. However, these economic benefits must be weighed against the social costs involved. All the brightest Dalena men with professional training have found jobs outside their natal village and almost all of them have left the village. Those with vocational skills secured industrial employment in the vicinity and commute. Only the less fortunate men stay behind. These semi-educated unemployed tend to regard farming below their dignity and fail to secure any other source of income. In their frustration many take to drink and make a social nuisance of themselves. They become an economic and social burden to their families. Dalena men associate success with life outside rather than within their village. This alienated them from their natal society.

A number of interacting factors are responsible for the disintegration of their society. The productivity of their village lands has not increased; their village economy stagnated. There was no demand for processing dry land crops. Some cane crushers and flour mills were established in Dalena to process paddy and cane grown in other villages. After the first honeymoon period with crop processing

Dalena entrepreneurs began to face difficulties in competing with cane crushers located in irrigated villages; transport costs posed a problem. There are no other small scale enterprises in Dalena to provide income and employment for men within their village. Education did not equip Dalena men with skills they could utilise in their own village. To reap the benefit of their education men had to leave the village and compete in the wider economy. Industrial development concentrated in urban areas and/or industrial estates sucked them out of their village. Dalena men cling to village extroversion to keep their heads above water.

Several Dalena men enquired already years ago about the possibility of establishing industrial enterprises in their own village. As an example they mentioned the production of match boxes. Official response was negative; nothing happened along those lines. Villagers themselves did not possess the necessary expertise to put their ideas into practice; no external help was forthcoming. A few years ago some of Dalena's acreage was designated as an industrial estate. At the time nobody thought of advising villagers how to start small manufacturing ventures. The sites were bought by urban entrepreneurs. As a result those Dalena men who owned the land of the industrial estate made a windfall profit by selling it at inflated prices. It did not result in a flow of further income, which is what the villagers want.

With hindsight it seems a pity that nobody advised villagers at the time how to establish small labour-intensive industrial enterprises. Had this been done it may well have prevented Dalena's social anomie. As it was, many Dalena men succumbed to economic pressures and joined the flood of rural-urban migrants. This had a devastating effect both on the villagers left behind and on the growing urban conglomerations. Villages denuded of their brightest and ablest men lack in social awareness and are therefore likely to lose their social identity to the detriment of the nation at large. This is what has been happening in Dalena. To halt and reverse this process of rural alienation is thus a matter of great urgency.

Question: How can dry land villagers diversify their village economy without destroying their social unity?

Access to Irrigation Canal irrigation created a dividing line in Mandya district between those villages that could access canal water and those that could not do so. Villagers whose lands remained dry felt embittered. Dalena farmers claim that authorities discriminate against them. The canal encroached on their lands while the law prohibits them from diverting canal water to their dry fields.

Already in 1970 some of those who owned lands adjoining the canal displayed entrepreneurship: they invested in irrigation pump sets to extract water from the canal. Immediately, legal constraints stopped them accessing canal water. By 1997 a considerable number of Dalena farmers who own land near the canal were prepared to break the law. There are now as many as thirtysix power operated irrigation pumps on Dalena lands. Palgowda, himself a lawyer, showed me what he was doing. He used the opportunity of the re-lining of the canals to lower by 5 feet the pipe that extracts canal water for pumping to his lands. This means that in future he will be able to divert water even when the canal water level will be no more than a foot high. He assured me that he was not worried in the least about breaking the law and said:

> I am convinced that farmers with land above canal level have an equal right to benefit from irrigation as those with lands below that level. As long as it is illegal for Dalena farmers to irrigate their lands we of course do not pay any water tax. All of us are prepared to pay the tax the moment our use of canal water is recognised as legal.

From his point of view his argument seems to make a lot of sense. I discussed it with some relevant senior government officials, none of whom appeared aware of the global water scarcity. All they said was that to allow such uncontrolled access to canal water would prevent correct estimates of the water flow required to meet irrigation commitments.

Question: How can dry land villages bordering irrigation schemes best be involved in the growing regional economy?

Appropriate Development for Irrigated Villages

Wangala and many other villages have benefited from irrigation schemes. They have experienced considerable increase in incomes. Though Wangala's population has grown almost threefold over the past four decades the extension and intensity of farming has so far managed to keep pace with increasing numbers. However, this can hardly be expected to continue for many more years. Only further revolutionary agricultural technologies can save the situation. Such new technologies do not seem likely in the near future. Therefore, even irrigated lands will soon cease to yield sufficient output to carry the total village population.

If crop cultivation can no more sustain the village population, alternative income generation becomes necessary. In wet villages with large areas under cash crops there always exists an internal market. Therefore, economic diversification usually begins with the development of tertiary services, such as coffee shops, retail stores that sell consumer goods, farm inputs and other products. Crop processing ventures also show promise. There are now numerous cane crushers and flour mills in Wangala. Such vertical integration could be further pursued. For example, the jaggery processed in village cane crushers might be processed into sweets and/or used together with locally grown fruit to produce fruit juices. These proposals are already in the pipeline. The 1995 Karnataka State Agricultural Policy proposes an integrated approach to rural development. It combines agriculture, horticulture, sericulture, fisheries and animal husbandry under a single entity. Moreover, in tune with the present world-wide emphasis on joint public and private sector ventures the new agricultural policy encourages private investment—even foreign capital—particularly in agro-processing and rural economic and social infrastructure.

These are innovative and laudable policy changes. However, the departmental boundaries that separate different governmental activities still prevent rural development from becoming a fully integrated process. There does not seem any good reason why certain industrial processes should not be located in rural areas. For example, agricultural tools and equipment might profitably be manufactured in villages. There is, however, a separate department of industry which does not consider industrial development in rural areas within its sphere of responsibility.

Some enterprising Wangala men have questioned me about the possibility of manufacturing ploughs and other agricultural equipment in their village. This seems a feasible proposition. However, as it is, their know-how is still too limited to organise such manufacturing businesses. They need help and advice before they can expect to succeed in industrialising their village economy.

Question: Should an industrial extension service be established to advise on appropriate manufacturing ventures located in rural areas?

THE ROLE OF WOMEN IN RURAL INDIA

India's liberal legislation aimed at integrating women into the socio-political system of villages. According to law there are reserved seats for women in village councils. When this reservation was first introduced it was implemented only to satisfy legal requirements. It did not lead to women exercising any political power. Men usually nominated female councillors and made sure that they were elected. Women's councillorship was no more than a window-dressing exercise. Over the years this has changed. Female councillors now consider themselves to represent their constituents' interests. They still do not however see themselves as representing more specifically the interests of village women. Only in a few South Indian villages have women developed a strong female identity and organised themselves into pressure groups. There are of course good reasons for the lack of a female consciousness.

Men Still Decide Women's Economic Roles

Traditionally village women have been involved in crop cultivation. They worked as paid and unpaid farm labourers under the direction of male farmers. They usually performed the most labour-intensive operations: they weeded and transplanted. There existed an overall gender-specific division of labour. When irrigation increased agricultural productivity farmers began to prefer their wives to stay away from the land. According to customary prestige criteria a woman doing farm work marks her family as ranking among the poor. It thus became a matter of prestige for men to claim that their womenfolk no more had to help with cultivation. As long ago as 1955 some Wangala farmers claimed that their womenfolk were ladies of leisure while I could see them still performing farm labour.

On the other hand, dry land villages such as Dalena, where crop yields remained low, have become more dependent on female support in crop cultivation. Even the wives of some of the richest Dalena men still work on the land. Men explained that they actually needed the continued help of their womenfolk. They themselves must be free to seek chances elsewhere, sure in the knowledge that their lands are being tended in their absence. Therefore most female labour in Dalena is still unpaid. There is less demand for female paid farm labour in dry land than in wet land villages, because dry land farming does not involve transplanting or the same amount of weeding as do wet crops. Dalena's Scheduled Caste women provide the pool of paid labour and only a few caste women actually work as 'coolies'. All this clearly indicates that in both dry and wet land villages, to suit their own interests men have decided what role women are to play in their societies.

There have been very few cases in South Indian villages where women themselves voiced their own demands. The social setting in general and the residence pattern in particular militated against the development of women's pressure groups. In line with tradition a girl was expected to marry outside her natal village and move to her husband's place. This meant that peer groups of girls dispersed on marriage. In any one village resident young women originated from many different villages. Moving into a new environment these young women had to accommodate to men and women—in particular their mothers-in-law—who were strange to them and often even hostile. This helps to explain why young village women lack a unifying factor and fail to form pressure groups.

In recent years marriage customs have changed. Increasing numbers of Wangala girls have married and settled within their village. This provides a more fertile basis for women to present a united front and voice their demands.

Question: How can rural women be encouraged and helped to become equal partners with their male counterparts to take their rightful place in village societies?

APPROPRIATE EDUCATION

Over the past few decades education has undoubtedly been one of the most important keys to rural development in South India. However, the evidence from Dalena and Wangala also indicates some negative effects: for instance, massive rural outmigration and large numbers of frustrated educated/semi-educated unemployed young villagers.

Now that the large majority of young South Indians have access to schooling it is time to ensure that the existing educational structure and the content of education become tuned to changing conditions.

Educational Structure

Until recently, most training institutions for advanced learning in India were located in a few large cities. This has resulted in the brightest rural youngsters having to move often far away from their village homes for the years of their study. During these years they understandably became urbanised and alienated from their rural background. This is precisely what happened to many Dalena men. The low dry land productivity induced Dalena men to seek income outside their village economy. To do so they needed to be educated. Some of them have become professionals, such as doctors, surgeons, and lawyers in towns and cities, dissociating themselves from their native villages. Others have acquired technical skills and now work in factories outside their village. Those who have been less fortunate in securing employment in the wider society constitute an economic and social burden not only to their respective families but also to the whole of Dalena. Their aspirations by far exceed their finances which makes them disgruntled. In trying to escape from reality many of them take to alcohol which often results in quarrels and fights.

The education of which Dalena men have taken advantage has alienated them from their natal societies. Most of the brightest villagers emigrated: those with specialised skills have secured industrial employment in the vicinity of Dalena and commute daily. The less successful are left behind as angry young men. As a result Dalena's social fabric is being torn apart; intra-village reciprocal relationships that held the society together are rapidly disappearing. If Dalena continues along its path of change it is doomed to lose its social identity altogether and become a suburb of Mandya with all the problems that accompany urban life in India these days.

Question: What educational changes should be made to avoid village societies losing their social identity?

Decentralised Education and Social Identity   Wangala has been much more fortunate in this respect. Canal irrigation made lands more productive; villagers, therefore, continued to concentrate on farming and did not feel the need to reach outside Wangala for additional sources of income. Wet land cultivation needed more labour. Farmers, therefore, at first wanted to maximise the use of subsistence labour. In 1955 they were not keen to send their sons to school. Even those boys who did go to school were expected to help with farming.

For Wangala farmers education was not an important asset. This accounts for their much more recent display of interest in education as compared with their Dalena counterparts. When in the late 1960s some of their young people were ready to start tertiary studies, fortunately for them educational facilities had already expanded in Mandya to a considerable extent. This enabled Wangala students to commute between their village and Mandya. They thus retained much of their village identity. This is reflected in continued commitment to their natal village. Only a few aspire to become urbanites. Most of the educated devote their training and efforts to the development of their own village. Wangala has taken the decentralisation of education one step further: there is now even a Pre-University College (PUC) in the village. It enables young students to stay in Wangala until they begin their undergraduate training and commute to Mandya. They thus remain firmly rooted in their village.

No doubt Wangala's social fabric has also changed over the last few decades. However, there is still a strong and visible village unity. People still care for each other and most are ready to help a fellow villager in need. This is not meant to imply that Wangala villagers are all angels without a selfish streak. However, on the whole they display much more societal concern than is noticeable in Dalena, where education has promoted individualism and social anomie.

The decentralised educational facilities from which Wangala benefited have promoted social awareness and village identity rather than a yearning for the city lights, which is what happened in Dalena. As it is obviously undesirable for most of the educated villagers to move to urban areas, educational facilities need to be decentralised. This will certainly not be possible without compromising excellence for convenience. On the other hand, there is no good reason to believe that the existing education structure is the only one or even the best. Surely different socio-economic conditions require different educational arrangements. In Western countries too educational facilities have been changing in tune with changes in lifestyles.

Question: How can villagers be given access to appropriate further education without alienating them from their rural environment?

Open University   Britain pioneered the Open University system to meet the demand for tertiary education by the growing proportion of the population unable to take up conventional full- or part-time study. Many parts of the Third World have tried to emulate this example without paying sufficient attention to the different socio-economic conditions that prevail in their respective countries. The Indira Gandhi National Open University (IGNOU) represents an example of trying to transplant a British-rooted educational innovation without apparently much attempt to adapt it to the Indian setting. It has so far succeeded in reaching only a relatively small number of mainly urban students. It has failed to reach rural areas, where the majority of the population resides, and where further educational needs are greatest.

Question: How can an open university education reach rural areas?

Cultural Heritage

To avoid the total disappearance of the rich folk culture it is important to ensure it is transmitted to future generations. It will not be much longer before all the wise but illiterate village elders, who are versed in folk culture, will have passed away. After their death it will be very difficult if not impossible to revive the folk culture.

It seems a great pity that the opportunity is missed to familiarise village children with their local history. Local geography is another subject that might be more closely linked with the immediate school environment.

Question: How can the rich South Indian folk culture be recorded to make it available for posterity?

Competition versus Conformity

Undoubtedly South Indian villagers need to take their rightful place in the world society of tomorrow. To do so they not only have to absorb knowledge but also develop an enquiring frame of mind and learn to compete. However, competition conflicts with dominant conventional village norms that stress conformity and discourage competition. By contrast modern Western cultures invariably emphasise competition.

The present Indian educational system, introduced under British rule, relies on students competing for grades in the context of examinations and thus emphasises competition. Such conflicting cultural norms pose a dilemma for young students faced with a choice.

Question: How can education preserve India's folk culture without disabling villagers from competing in the global economy?

Education and Village Identity

An increased emphasis on social awareness is a pre-condition of strengthening the village identity of future generations. Presently, many villages do not have a single individual committed and able to ensure village improvements. Dalena has its Palgowda and Wangala has Thimmegowda. Both these men try to act as social catalysts for their villages. Thimmegowda has had more success in promoting Wangala's village unity than has Palgowda in Dalena, although the former resides in the capital of Karnataka, while the latter lives in Dalena itself.

One of the most difficult tasks of formal education is to promote strong social awareness and commitment to further development among future generations. Against the emphasis on rooting education much more in the immediate school environment it can be argued that this will lead to village isolationism. This is certainly a danger that must be borne in mind when designing educational changes.

Question: How can rural school curricula become more village oriented without creating societies dominated by 'villagism' or 'isolationism'?

Formal, Informal and Non-formal Education

Educational success can never be fully achieved by concentrating on formal schooling only. It can be achieved only if it is in harmony with informal socialisation that takes place during early childhood. Furthermore, it must also be accompanied by appropriate non-formal training.

Before formal education was introduced in rural areas, knowledgeable village elders used to pass on local cultural heritage from generation to generation by word of mouth. Hardly any of their tales ever appeared in print. The spread of literacy among school children has made them prefer the written to the spoken word and it becomes obvious that many of the educated young villagers resent showing their illiterate elders and oral tradition any respect. The young of today grow up knowing very little about their own local history and folklore. Serious conflicts have already occurred over this issue between fathers and sons in many Wangala and Dalena families.

Question: How can formal, non-formal and informal education be harmonised to ensure education meets social needs?

Education and Gender Inequalities

Schooling is widely considered more important for boys than for girls. The proportion of female students decreases rapidly after primary education. Yet there is already plenty evidence available that indicates that appropriately educated women constitute a valuable social asset. Today's girls are the mothers of tomorrow. Educated mothers ensure improved lifestyles for future generations.

Formal schooling is seen by many villagers as a passport to a public service career. There is thus hardly any recognition of and the role education has to play in preparing youngsters for rural life. Village parents want their sons to enjoy the security of a public service position. They do not have such aspirations for their daughters.

Question: How can parents be made to appreciate the importance of sending not only their sons but also their daughters for further education?

Question: How can education preserve India's folk culture without disabling villagers from competing in the global economy?

School Curricula

Present and future rural generations must be made aware of the environmental problems imminently facing the world in general and their own societies in particular, and how they should take this into account in their daily activities.

Question: How can schools teach the practical aspects of environmental preservation?

Agriculture and all that this involves is another subject that is presently sadly neglected in school curricula. Hardly any village school includes 'farming' among the subjects taught. Yet in most villages agriculture still constitutes the major source of income. Since children do not have to pass an examination in 'farming' and their parents often consider education as a passport to public service employment, farm work is awarded only low prestige. This is reflected in the way many unemployed educated/semi-educated villagers refuse to help with their families' farm work. As we have seen in Dalena these young men often become a burden rather than a support for their parents.

Question: How should farming be taught in village schools?

Other Vocational Subjects

Skill training, such as carpentry, tailoring and the like, when offered as optional subjects in village schools would sponsor the development of craft skills based on aptitude rather than on hereditary caste occupation. This might have a welcome by-product by providing a more effective solvent of caste differentiation than many of the existing pieces of liberal legislation have proved to be.

Question: How can different vocational subjects be taught in village schools and who should teach them?

POLITICAL DECENTRALISATION AND PARTICIPATORY ADMINISTRATION

Mahatma Gandhi, architect of Indian independence, advocated 'Swaraj' or self-rule, which implies the rule of the people. This concept forms the basis for democratic decentralisation and the establishment of panchayati raj (people's council) institutions in India. The objective is to strengthen the institutions of self-government at the village, *taluk* and district levels. It is built upon the premise that, all 'power' in a democracy rightfully belongs to the 'people'. Thus, the essence of democracy lies in empowering people to govern their affairs themselves within their jurisdiction. The emerging trends in recent years is the decentralisation and devolution of powers to the local self-institutions constituted at various levels. Most of the Indian states have adopted a three-tier panchayati raj system and empowered each level with appropriate legislative enactments. Wangala's village panchayat came into existence under the Mysore Village Panchayat and District Boards Act of 1952 and subsequent amendments to the Act in 1985 and 1991. It has successfully replaced the hereditary system by a democratic process of elections to the village council. Reservations for Scheduled Castes/Scheduled Tribes, women and other Backward Classes have opened avenues for better participation of underprivileged sections of society in the processes of self-governance. All this enables greater participation of people in the day-to-day administration with the objective of improving public welfare. It obviously implies active involvement and sharing of responsibility by the people or their representatives in the implementation of government programmes. In Wangala, for instance, the conscious involvement of the village community under the leadership of the 'core group' has helped in securing several public facilities in recent years. The erstwhile political leaders depended fully on the government for establishing public facilities which failed to materialise due to lack of collective village participation.

T. Thimmegowda recounts his own experience:

As a villager who is now an IAS officer, I undoubtedly helped Wangala but I was only a catalyst. The young and educated village panchayat members themselves have more recently helped in mobilising people's support for realising these benefits. Today, Wangala has many of the facilities to which villagers aspire, made possible mainly by the villagers' involvement in mobilising monetary contributions and public support. The villagers have already collected substantial public contributions and deposited them with the government for securing a maternity unit and World Bank assisted village sanitation programme. Wangala's experiment is worthy of emulation, if only the citizens of other villagers are also prepared to attempt improving their villages.

However, it would be difficult to expect collective support in all the villages in the country, as many villagers are divided according to different political and ethnic allegiances. In a multi-party democratic process, the leaders and their followers have polarised themselves into separate groups or factions to mobilise and strengthen their support base. As a result, the villages and families are divided into several factions working at cross purposes. It has thus become difficult to enlist collective support and participation of people to achieve the objective of public welfare. Here lies the challenge for political leaders; administrators and bureaucrats have to create an environment for mobilising public support and their active participation. The prevailing apathy among the general public towards the implementation of government programmes and maintenance of public utilities and beneficiary-oriented assets causes great concern. Programmes such as the construction and maintenance of school buildings, hospitals, drinking water supply, street lights, village hygienic conditions and protective health care measures need effective public involvement. Similarly, beneficiary-oriented schemes such as the construction of houses for the poor, the distribution of remunerative assets and grants of old age pensions need effective vigilance and monitoring to ensure proper utilisation of these benefits.

The recent trends of privatisation, liberalisation and globalisation have thrown open several issues regarding government intervention in public affairs. One of these issues relates to the minimal intervention of government in public activities to allow private organisations and initiative to provide more effective services. Therefore, one would expect greater initiative and participation by the people in the activities concerning public affairs. In India, the real issue is how far and to what level these initiatives could be encouraged to accelerate the pace of development. Here comes the role of private enterprise, voluntary organisations and local initiatives in lending their support to realise the objectives of a welfare state. However, the role of the bureaucracy must not be undermined; their initiative, conscious effort and committed involvement is still a necessity.

It is not an exercise in self-praise if I narrate my personal Civil Service experiences in this context. As an IAS officer hailing from a rural background, I have undertaken several initiatives to establish close contact with rural people to help them in solving their many problems and grievances. In my career as Deputy Commissioner of the districts of Kolar and Chickmagalur, I have formulated certain guidelines for officers working under my jurisdiction to develop close contact with the people to understand and appreciate their problems and grievances and to help them in solving them at their own door steps. This programme is known as *grama sandarshana* (village contact programme). Many poor villagers often found difficulty in approaching public offices and government functionaries to get redress for their grievances. In order to avoid harassment and hardship for such villagers, a periodical village visit programme was organised to improve the public delivery system at the cutting edge level of bureaucracy. Several benefits like old age pensions, land grant certificates, updating of land records and the benefits under various development and welfare programmes were distributed on the spot in the presence of the villagers during the village contact programmes. This ensured at least to some extent a bureaucratic transparency and quick delivery of benefits and services by minimising red-tape and bureaucratic hurdles.

Villagers always responded positively to these mass contact programmes. I utilised these opportunities to make villagers aware of their role in the acquisition and maintenance of public assets and services as well as the need for public vigilance in monitoring the utilisation of benefits. The results of these mass contact programmes were encouraging, so much so that this type of programme has been conducted also by other officers in different districts with the participation of ministers and representatives of local self-government institutions.

During my tenure as Deputy Commissioner and District Magistrate of Kolar and Chickmagalur districts in Karnataka, efforts were made with the co-operation of other officers to mobilise substantial public contributions for the completion of long pending district auditoriums and stadiums. The success of this was due to the effective participation of the people and their committed involvement in the completion of these government sponsored projects.

The total literacy campaign is yet another programme which envisages campaign mode implementation and people's participation. The emphasis was on voluntary participation of people and environment building. This approach to enlist people's participation has achieved great success in many parts of the country. In my career as a civil servant, I always had the co-operation and goodwill of the public. My approach was to involve people and work with them in executing development works and public projects. My prime goal is people's welfare for which both civil servant and public representatives should work together to achieve results.

Political decentralisation and public participation in administrative matters eventually leads to improved transparency in the delivery mechanism and ensures public accountability. This also helps to minimise public criticism of the administration and government. The responsibility of proper implementation becomes a venture shared jointly by the government and citizens. Recently, signs have appeared of a growing tendency among citizens to organise themselves into vigilance committees, consumer forums, citizens' committees, etc., in important towns and cities. The government is also encouraging people's participation in better management of public utilities by constituting advisory councils, boards of visitors and consultative committees in schools, hospitals, boards and corporations. In Bangalore, the citizens' forums have undertaken to share the responsibilities of certain civic functions like garbage disposal, water supply management, distribution of essential commodities etc. The growing awareness among citizens due to better education and media exposure of the omissions and commissions of government and public organisations is creating a better environment for increased public participation in administration.

Question: How can increasing people's participation in administrative matters be encouraged and institutionalised not only in urban but also rural areas?

DEMOCRACY, POLITICAL PARTIES AND VILLAGE FACTIONS

Democracy is an outgrowth of Western society. It therefore has a built-in Western cultural bias. It is based on the assumptions that voters act as individuals and that as such they examine policies of opposing political parties to decide who to support. The emphasis on individual decision-making reflects Western reality fairly accurately but it deviates from most developing country rural cultures.

Individual, Majority and Unanimous Decisions

In South Indian villages decisions are rarely made by individuals; larger groups, such as the extended family, a kin group, a faction, a caste or even the whole population of a village jointly make decisions. What is at stake determines which group becomes activated in the decision-making process. According to custom, decisions have to be unanimous. Sometimes traditional village council discussions have to go on for several days and nights before the different hereditary members finally reach a consensus. When there were diverse views it was obviously difficult to reach unanimity; yet it had to be reached. The concept that an individual or the majority has the right to decide is alien to South Indian village cultures.

Question: How can the democratic system be culturally-adapted to accommodate traditional political practices?

Village Factions and their Role as Vote Banks

Political parties in India use the customary emphasis on group unanimity as a stepping stone to achieving political power. They realise that almost all Indian villages are divided into factions composed of lineages. These factions constitute ready-made vote banks for politicians. Our Dalena friends told us that candidates for political office hardly ever try to enlighten them about the political manifesto of the party they represent. They pursue a different strategy that turns out to be more effective. They establish contact with the leader of one of the village factions and then woo him by promising substantial help after election success. They know full well that if they get the leader's support not only he but also all those in his faction will follow suit. Villagers realise that politicians occupy powerful positions and may secure or deny villagers access to government support. According to the administrative structure that presently exists in South India, allocation of government help to individual villages takes place at the sub-district level. The sub-district is also the unit that elects MLAs. An MLA is thus in a powerful and strategic position to exert influence over the distribution of government resources.

Politicians understandably have a vested interest in strengthening intra-village factions and aligning a village faction to the party they represent. The names by which villagers now refer to their factions clearly indicates the merging of party with faction interests. Years ago Dalena's two opposing factions were known by the name of their respective leaders; now they are referred to by the name of the party to which each has become aligned. This has heightened the hostility between village factions and often erupts into violent disputes. In Wangala the political parties have not had quite the same divisive impact as in Dalena. Wangala's 'core group', composed of young educated men who realise the importance of village unity, has managed to tone down the influence of opposing factions. Therefore, prospective MLAs use Wangala Peasant lineages as vote banks rather than factions. The existence of more than two such lineages obviously blurs the lines between opposing parties. In Wangala they say: 'Political parties are important only immediately before the day of election; as soon as ballot boxes are closed they cease to matter!'

Question: How can the political process be changed to eliminate or at least reduce the divisive influence political parties exert on rural societies?

The issues we discussed and the questions we raised here need urgent attention. We have tried to outline why and how the lack of cultural sensitivity results in considerable and yet unnecessary social costs of rural development. We suggest that if future development becomes more culturally-sensitive this will avoid many of the pitfalls.

We conclude in the hope that this book will contribute at least a little to increase public awareness of the successes and failures of South India's rural transformation since independence and that this will lead to minimising the social costs of future rural development.

Appendix 1: Note on Documentary Film

This film, titled 'Village Voices: Forty Years of Rural Transformation in South India', offers a unique opportunity to view the different paths of development that a large canal irrigation scheme triggered off in Wangala, an irrigated village, and Dalena, a dry land village, both situated in the same culture area of Mandya sub-district in South India.

The study on which the film is based was begun by Dr T.S. Epstein in 1954 and has continued up to the present day. It is the only study in the whole of India in which the same researcher covers a period as long as fortythree years.

The film not only presents how the villagers themselves see the changes that have taken place, but also how one of them, T. Thimmegowda, now a senior administrative official, perceives the development and how the expatriate researcher analyses it.

The film focuses on the problem of rural development. It indicates the importance of culturally-sensitive development strategies. Wangala, the irrigated village, is on the way to becoming a model growth centre; increased per acre productivity and extension of irrigated acreages has facilitated the land-carrying capacity to accommodate increasing numbers. Wangala continues to be a village introverted; villagers continue to have a strong social identity and feel proud of their village achievements. By contrast, Dalena has become more and more village extroverted, so much so that social anomie has set in and the village will soon disappear altogether and become absorbed as a suburb of the nearby expanding town of Mandya.

In order to participate in the growing regional economy Dalena people had to go outside their villages; many now are professionals, such as doctors, lecturers, teachers who have left Dalena altogether; others commute and work in manufacturing establishments as mechanics, electricians, clerks, etc.

The film poses a challenge not only to developers but also to a wide public concerned with rural development. It concludes by posing searching questions to which answers need to be found.

The official film team of Dr Beate Engelbrecht and Manfred Krüger from the German Institut für den Wissenschaftlichen Film has made this into an informative as well as artistic film, not only interesting but also a pleasure to view.

The video will be accompanied by the publication of *Village Voices— Forty Years of Rural Transformation in South India* by T.S. Epstein, A.P. Suryanarayana and T. Thimmegowda, Sage Publications (India), 1998.

Director	Beate Engelbrecht
Camera	Manfred Krüger
Anthropology	Scarlett Epstein
Editing	Abbas Yousefpour
Technical Data	VHS, Colour, ca. 60 min
Commentary and Subtitles	English, German
Production	1997
Publication	July 1998
Film Nr.	
Price VHS/Pal	

Production/Distribution	Institut für den	
	Wissenschaftlichen Film	Nonnenstieg 72
	gem. GmbH, Göttingen	D-37075 Göttingen
Phone	0551/5024-0	Postfach 2351
Fax	0551/5024-400	D-37013 Göttingen

Appendix 2: Poems

A Sample of Poems
written by Wangala Students in Honour of
T. Thimmegowda and T. Scarlett Epstein

As already outlined in the text, I was overwhelmed by the welcome we received on our return to Wangala, but what pleased me most and somewhat surprised me was the enthusiastic reception we were given by the village youth too. After all, I was a complete stranger to them—many of them had never seen me before—yet they too, like their elders seemed to want to reach out to me and embrace me in their society. A few of the young students were inspired even to write poems about T. Thimmegowda and myself. Included here are two of the several poems presented to us: the first is about T. Thimmegowda and demonstrates the important part his continuing identification with his native village occupies in their lives and how proud they are of his achievements; the second indicates what Wangala people think and feel about their expatriate researcher. These young poets show great promise and I hope and expect that their talents will bring them and their society wide acclaim in the future.

T. Scarlett Epstein

T. THIMMEGOWDA — A HEART'S DESIRE

Please come to your home village!
Without forgetting the place!
Oh! Hero of our village
Do not forget your home village!
Oh! you made Heroism heroic
Please help your native place and
Always be kind to our village
Please console the sufferer

Oh! Good Samaritan!
Help the distressed person!
Do not give tit for tat
even to enemies;
This is my heart's desire
This is my sincere blessing!

T. Javaregowda
Wangala, 1997

YOUR BLESSINGS BE WITH US

Kempamma, you came to our place without fear
Our village chieftains honoured you
Our school children were surprised to see you
        Your blessings be with us!

Your heart is big
You symbolise the word 'love'
You are a visible goddess for us!
You have appeared before us thrice!

Our beloved Kempamma
Listen to my music
Where are you? Our village knows you
May you live for hundred years—please visit us again!
        Your blessings be with us!

Where are you? Where are you?
Please do not go on leaving us!
Please go on writing about our village
I shall never, never forget you........
        Your blessings be with us!

Where do you come from?
There is no other woman like you!
You lead a good life—You are our mother
You are our village goddess
Please come soon again to our village!
Listen: here are my best wishes for you!
        Your blessings be with us!

D. Nanjundaswamy
Wangala, 1997

Appendix 3: Questionnaire

*D*ear Reader,

We hope that you have found our book informative and that it will encourage you not only to learn more about the various aspects of Third World rural transformation but also to continue the dialogue about the pros and cons of development.

We take the unconventional step to include a questionnaire, which we shall be pleased if you will answer and return to us c/o

> SAGE PUBLICATIONS (INDIA) PRIVATE LTD.
> PO Box 4215, NEW DELHI 110048,
> INDIA

We hope in this way to establish a network of people concerned with rural development.

Is this the first village study book you have read?	Yes	No
If no, do you find ours	less	more
	interesting?	interesting?
Do you work for a voluntary organisation?	Yes	No
Do you support a voluntary organisation?	Yes	No
Do you have any answers to our questions in Chapter 17?	Yes	No

If yes, what are they?

_____

_____

_____

Do you think there are other relevant important questions?	Yes	No

If yes, what are they?

_____

_____

_____

Do you want to be kept on the mailing list of further village study publications?

Name:

Address:

Glossary

Adi Karnataka	:	Scheduled Caste in South Indian villages
Arathi Tatti	:	decorated plate used in holy ritual
bahala parti	:	too much factional politics
bandi	:	cart parade
Bangarasanna	:	variety of paddy
beedis	:	country cigarettes
chappals	:	sandals
Dalit	:	oppressed castes
devaru gudda	:	spirit/deity medium
devaru pettige	:	deity box
dhoti	:	loin cloth
Divali	:	festival of lights
Gandahalli Palu	:	male group
grama panchayat	:	village council
Gram Sandarshana	:	village contact programme
gram sevak	:	trained village level worker
Gowdara Vatara	:	a major Peasant lineage in Wangala
Hale Makkalu	:	'old children' a term used for the hereditary Scheduled Caste clients of Peasant caste households
Hennahalli Palu	:	female group
hotelu	:	village coffee shop
Huchamma habba	:	a South Indian village festival
Jatka	:	horse-drawn cart
Jeeta	:	bonded labourer
karaga	:	pots
Kuduvali	:	the union of a divorced man or woman with his or her new spouse
Mahalaya	:	a festival revolving around Goddess Durga

Mahalaya Pitrupaksha	:	an auspicious period during the festival
maharani	:	queen
mandal panchayat	:	group panchayat
Marichowdi	:	a South Indian village deity
Meerasu	:	privileged Peasants
Muyyi	:	voluntary reciprocal goodwill gift
nyaya panchayat	:	hereditary Peasant caste council/traditional village council
panchayat	:	council
panchayati raj	:	policy of grassroots democracy
Patel	:	village headman
pooja	:	worship
pucca	:	solidly built
rangoli	:	a traditional Hindu form of decorative patterns on floors or doorsteps using rice flour or coloured powder
Rathnachudi	:	variety of paddy
Sankranti	:	annual festival celebrated on 14 or 15 January
sandy	:	fair
Shanbhogue	:	village accountant
Shramadaan	:	voluntary labour
taluk	:	sub-district
Thoti	:	low-ranking village servant
Thoti Inam	:	land gifted by the government
vataras	:	hereditary lineages
veelya	:	a formal presentation of areca nuts and betel leaves to every village household before a young bride departs to join her husband
Vodda	:	a Tamilian Stonecutter caste whose trade became redundant and who migrated as the poorest of the poor in search of work

About the Authors

T. Scarlett Epstein is currently a Director of four organisations—SESAC (Social Assessment Consultancy), Hove, UK; C.E.P. Environment Co. Ltd, Windsor, UK; Intervention (Policy Consultants) Pvt. Ltd, Bangalore, India; and Somra Ltd, Dhaka, Bangladesh. She has previously been research Professor at the University of Sussex and a Visiting Professor at the universities of Minnesota and.California and the Ben Gurion University of the Nagev, Israel. In addition, Professor Epstein has served as a consultant to several national and international organisations including the World Bank, the OECD, UNICEF, the FAO, ESCAP and the European Union.

A prolific writer, Professor Epstein has previously published twelve books including *Economic Development and Social Change in South India* (1962); *Capitalism, Primitive and Modern* (1968); *South India: Yesterday, Today and Tomorrow* (1973); *Women, Work and Family* (1986); and *Improving NGO Development Programs* (1995). She has also written more than fifty articles and is the editor of a series entitled *Women in Development*; of the *Newsletter for Small Rural Enterprises in Africa*; and of *Rural Development in Practice*.

A.P. Suryanarayana retired from government service as Deputy Director of the Project Formulation Division, Planning Department, Government of Karnataka (1982–89). Having studied statistics at the University of Mysore, he started his career as a Research Assistant to T. Scarlett Epstein and thereafter joined the Government of Karnataka, where he served variously as Assistant Director of the Research and Statistical Unit, Department of Social Welfare (1975–88); Senior Statistical Assistant in the Office of the District Statistical Officer, Kolar; in the Directorate of Economics and Statistics (1967–75); and as Progress Assistant in Community Development Blocks and as Computer in the Area Nut Survey (1958–67). His parent department was Directorate of Economics and Statistics.

T. Thimmegowda belongs to the Indian Administrative Service (IAS) and is currently Housing Commissioner, Karnataka Housing Board, Bangalore. His previous assignments include Director of Survey, Settlements and Land Records, Bangalore; Deputy Commissioner and District Magistrate of Chickmagalur District and Kolar District; Secretary, Bangalore Development Authority, Bangalore; and Special Deputy Commissioner and Additional District Magistrate, Bangalore District.

Originating from one of the villages discussed in this book, he excelled himself by being awarded a first in his M.A. economics at Bangalore University. He was subsequently a Lecturer at P.E.S. College of Science, Mandya, Karnataka, before joining the IAS. Mr Thimmegowda has retained a strong commitment to his native place and has played a strategic role in the promotion of rural development, and ranks among the pioneers of participatory administration.